CW01667905

The Reader's Digest Good Health Cookbooks

Vegetables, Pasta and Rice

The Reader's Digest Good Health Cookbooks

VEGETABLES, PASTA AND RICE

PUBLISHED BY THE READER'S DIGEST ASSOCIATION LIMITED LONDON SYDNEY CAPE TOWN

VEGETABLES, PASTA AND RICE
was edited and designed by
The Reader's Digest Association,
and is based on The Cookery Year,
Copyright © 1973 The Reader's Digest
Association Limited, London.

First Edition
Copyright © 1985
The Reader's Digest Association Limited
25 Berkeley Square
London W1X 6AB

Copyright © 1985
Reader's Digest Association
Far East Limited

Philippines Copyright 1985
Reader's Digest Association
Far East Limited

All rights reserved.
No part of this book may be reproduced,
stored in a retrieval system,
or transmitted in any form
or by any means, electronic,
electrostatic, magnetic tape, mechanical,
photocopying, recording or otherwise,
without permission in writing
from the publishers

® READER'S DIGEST
is a registered trademark of
The Reader's Digest Association, Inc.
of Pleasantville, New York, U.S.A.

Printed in Great Britain

Contents

How to use

The Good Health Cookbooks

Dieting need not be dreary. Whatever diet you may follow, you can still enjoy the classic dishes. Often, all you need are alternative ingredients that suit the recipe and suit the requirements of your diet. This book gives you the recipes for those classic dishes from *The Cookery Year*. It also gives you those vital alternatives. It has, in fact, several features unique in cookery books. In the special "Alternatives" column on each page, we identify how high each recipe is in salt, sugar, fat, cholesterol and fibre. We also give the calorie count. We check if it is gluten-free and wholefood. Then we suggest how you could adapt the recipe to any diet you, your family, or your guests might want to follow.

We do not lay down what diet you should follow. That is your decision. The book assumes that you yourself know what you want to do and tries to help you to do it by making suggestions (not commands), some or all of which you may want to follow. Perhaps you have been told to cut down drastically on salt; perhaps you have been thinking for some time that you should eat a little less sugar; perhaps you have a friend coming to a meal who cannot eat gluten or who is avoiding food high in cholesterol. You do not have to buy a new cookbook for each diet. You do not have to produce alternative meals for every guest. With these books, you can simply adapt the existing recipes to suit your needs.

You will find that we make use of a few conventions. This is mainly in order to avoid constant repetition. **The asterisk** (*) is used as follows:

1) Salt* indicates that this item may be omitted for those on a low-salt diet; the salt level of the recipe as given in the "Alternatives" column is calculated on the assumption that this salt has been omitted and that any ingredients that sometimes contain salt and sometimes don't (e.g. tinned tomatoes) have been bought in their salt-free version.

2) Gluten-free* indicates that the recipe is free of gluten so long as gluten-free flour (or bread or breadcrumbs) is used where appropriate.

3) Wholefood* indicates that the recipe is wholefood if wholemeal flour (or bread or breadcrumbs), brown rice and unrefined sugar are used where appropriate.

The levels of salt, **sugar**, **fat**, **cholesterol** and **fibre** for each recipe are denoted by symbols in the "Alternatives" column:

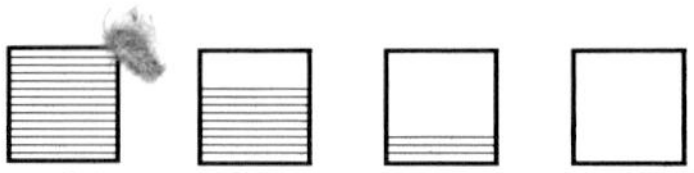

HIGH MEDIUM LOW NEGLIGIBLE

For definitions of what constitutes a high threshold level of any one of these, see under the appropriate diet on the following pages. Less than half this threshold level is considered low.

Calorie counts are given, firstly for the recipe as a whole and secondly as an indication of how many calories may be avoided as a result of following particular alternative suggestions.
Calories are automatically lost when either sugar or fat is significantly reduced. The calculations for calorie-

loss can be no more than approximate, and occasionally are omitted, as so many factors can vary: the fat level of fish and meat at different times of the year, the exact amount of fat trimmed off a cut of meat, or the amount of sugar that will make a dish acceptably sweet to a particular palate.
To convert calories to kilojoules, multiply the figure for calories by 4·18.

Cooking hints on when it is appropriate or helpful to use a pressure cooker, slow cooker, food processor, freezer or microwave are indicated by a tick, together with any further information required. With a microwave it is always essential that you also consult the manufacturer's instructions, as cooking times vary from cooker to cooker.

Measurements are expressed in both imperial and metric units. The figures are rounded up or down as necessary. As this is an international publication, we have borne in mind that teaspoons and tablespoons vary in capacity from country to country, but in any recipe where we have used these measurements, the dish should not be affected by such variations. For a check on the comparative values of these measures, consult the tables on the inside of the book's covers.

With practice you should find that the technique and alternatives recommended in this book will work with recipes from other books. In this way it becomes simple to adapt recipes so that they are both healthy and delicious. That is how it ought to be.

The Diets

Low-salt diet

Sodium is acknowledged to be a contributory factor in hypertension (high blood pressure) and thus in coronary heart disease and strokes; it can also be involved in some kidney disorders.

By far the most concentrated source of sodium is common salt (sodium chloride), and many processed foods contain a lot of added salt.

Diets which are very severely restricted in sodium are on occasion prescribed, but we are not concerned with them here. A certain minimum of both sodium and chloride is essential to good health, and the majority of salt-conscious people will simply want to cut out excessive consumption.

While setting an exact figure is very difficult, as the total level of salt in a meal depends on the combination of foods eaten, a target of 5 grams a day (generally considered to be not excessive) can usually be reached by cutting down on cooking or table salt as well as on monosodium glutamate. Foods such as salted or cured pork products and most cheeses should be eaten only in small quantities. Then the sodium occurring naturally in meat and fish, even in sodium-rich shellfish, need not be avoided.

It is important to check the labels on tins. Some tomatoes, for instance, are canned with added salt, others not. Egg whites and dried fruit are also relatively high in sodium and should not be overindulged in.

Salt substitutes are available but we do not specify them: they do not taste like salt and anyone suffering from heart or kidney disease should not take them without medical approval.

Many of those wishing to cut down on salt will also want to combine this with cutting down on fat. Therefore, for example, although double cream contains much less sodium than single cream or milk does, we do not advocate replacing milk with double cream.

Salt is used to to mean both common salt (sodium chloride) and sodium in general. Where the level of salt in the recipe is given, this takes into account sodium occurring naturally in the ingredients; in the list of ingredients, salt refers, as usual, to the sodium chloride commonly used for seasoning.

The salt content of a recipe is taken to be high if it contains the equivalent of more than 2 egg whites or ½ pint (300 ml) of milk per person.

Low-sugar diet

Sugar is "empty calories": it provides no nutrients, but concentrated calories for a very little weight of food.

Sugar is the first thing to go if you are on a calorie-controlled diet. It is also known to encourage tooth decay; and high consumption, especially of refined sugar, has been correlated with certain diseases.

Refined sugar is pure sucrose, the form of sugar which is the least desirable. Sugar occurs naturally in other forms – for example, fructose in fruit, lactose in milk, dextrose (glucose) and maltose. These do not always have the same harmful effect on the body as sucrose, and are not eaten in anything like the same sort of quantity.

A low-sugar diet, therefore, usually aims at cutting out as much refined sugar as possible. This can be done simply by using less of it and deliberately cultivating a less sweet tooth, or by replacing it to some extent with other forms of sugar. Honey, for instance (which is mainly fructose and glucose, with little sucrose) is sweeter than sugar so less of it is needed. In this way you can cut down on both sucrose and the total quantity of sugar. Molasses, although a form of sucrose, has a very strong taste and again a teaspoon of it can sometimes be used instead of a tablespoon or more of sugar.

In this book, when the level of sugar in a recipe is indicated, it takes into account both the general level of sugar, including all its various forms – sucrose, fructose, glucose etc. – as well as any added sugar specified in the recipe. In the list of ingredients, sugar refers to the added sugar which is virtually pure sucrose. The suggestions for decreasing the sugar content of a recipe almost always refer to sucrose.

We are not concerned here with sugar substitutes nor with special diabetic sweeteners and jams. We do not aim to preserve an ultra-sweet taste. What we aim to do is to cut down the amount of refined sugar and to make more use of fruit and of small quantities of honey and molasses. The results will be definitely less sweet but still delicious.

The sugar content of a recipe is taken to be high if it contains the equivalent of more than 1 tablespoon of sugar per person.

Low-fat and low-cholesterol diets

One of the most common reasons for eating less fat and cholesterol is that there appears to be an undisputed link between the presence of cholesterol in the blood and liability to heart attacks.

Populations who eat less fat have lower levels of heart disease, although their consumption of oil may be high, as in many Mediterranean countries. The exact link has not yet been established, and it appears that other foods, for example garlic, onions and polyunsaturated fat, as well as fibre, have the ability to lower blood cholesterol. However, more and more people are coming to the conclusion that cutting down on fats, especially saturated fats, cannot do them any harm. Certainly it will help calorie control: fat contains twice as many calories per ounce as protein or carbohydrate.

Whether you want to lose weight or reduce the risk of a heart attack, low-fat and low-cholesterol diets are similar in many ways. Both encourage cutting down on the saturated fats which contain cholesterol.

Saturated fats are usually of animal origin but not always: coconuts, for example, have a saturated fat content of 83%. Unsaturated fats are mainly of vegetable origin and are further divided into monounsaturated and polyunsaturated fats. (These terms refer to the way in which their molecules are chemically bonded.) They are generally liquid at room temperature.

Monounsaturated fats (the most usual example is olive oil, which is 73% monounsaturated fat) have no effect on the level of cholesterol in the blood. Polyunsaturated fats can in fact, as stated above, actually lower the blood cholesterol level. There are a few foods which are very high in cholesterol relative to their fat content, notably shellfish, fish roes, and organ meats such as liver, kidney, brains and sweetbreads.

Those on a low-fat diet will want to cut down on all fats and oils. Those aiming at a low-cholesterol intake will want to eliminate as far as possible all saturated fats and will be cautious about eating shellfish and offal. This book shows you how to do either or both of these.

However the book does not purport to give a diet which actually lowers blood cholesterol. For instance, in the recipes olive oil is often specified. Those on such a diet will replace olive oil with safflower, soya or sunflower oils. Nor does this book attempt to give a fat-free diet. Such a diet should only be attempted under medical supervision, and even then it is bound to have a minimal fat content. Some fat is necessary in our diet, particularly linoleic acid, an essential fatty acid, which cannot be manufactured by the body: it is found in vegetable oils, particularly safflower oil.

Some particular foods that will be found useful in both low-fat and low-cholesterol diets are:

- skimmed milk, both liquid and dried
- low-fat cheese, particularly cottage cheese and low-fat curd cheese, such as quark or fromage blanc
- smetana (5–10% fat as opposed to 18% in sour cream)

For low-cholesterol diets:

- safflower, soya, sunflower and walnut oils
- (for frying over high heat): corn or peanut oils. It is, however, better to avoid frying over high heat as far as possible, since this changes the composition of the oils into something resembling saturated fat
- soft margarines with a high percentage of polyunsaturated oils (all margarines labelled "all vegetable" are virtually cholesterol-free)

The fat and cholesterol content of eggs is found only in the yolks, but in many cases yolks can be decreased or omitted, sometimes with a proportionate increase in the number of whites used.

The fat content of a recipe is taken to be high if it contains the equivalent of more than any 2 of the following per person:

$\frac{1}{2}$oz (1 tablespoon) double cream or oil
$\frac{1}{4}$oz (7 grams) butter, lard, suet or margarine
1 egg yolk
$\frac{1}{2}$oz (10–15 grams) ham, bacon, pork or cheese

The above applies also to the cholesterol content of a recipe, except that unsaturated oils are freely allowed, and over $\frac{1}{2}$ an egg yolk is considered to be high.

Fibre

The importance of fibre in the diet is now widely recognised, and many people pursue a high-fibre diet.

Since one of the best and easiest ways of increasing fibre intake is to eat a slice or two of wholemeal bread with your meal, the recipes themselves have not (except in one or two cases) been modified to include more fibre. The original versions of the recipes are always based on fresh ingredients, including vegetables, fruit and nuts (most of which are high in fibre), and wholefood adaptations are available for almost all the recipes, thus helping to increase the fibre level.

Gluten-free diet

As coeliac sufferers are being identified more and more frequently, so the need for a gluten-free diet for them and for other gluten-sensitive patients is becoming widely recognised.

A gluten-free diet involves complete exclusion of gluten (a protein, found mainly in wheat but also, in a different form and to a lesser extent, in rye, barley and oats). Commercial gluten-free flour is available and can be used successfully for bread, and some pastry and cakes; if it is difficult to find or expensive to buy just for one recipe, there are other flours, many of which are familiar to those on wholefood diets, which are gluten-free. Chick pea flour, brown rice flour, cornflour, potato flour and soya flour are perhaps the best known.

All labels on tins and jars must be carefully read, as wheat flour is a common ingredient not just in the obvious breads, biscuits, cakes, pastries and many cereals, but in packet soups, baking powder, sausages, stock cubes, bottled sauces and baked beans as well as in some brands of mustard, ground white pepper, curry powder and cheap chocolate.

Gluten-free grains include rice, maize, millet and buckwheat. Cornflour, chick pea flour and split pea flour are all suitable for making white sauces. For soufflés, cornflour and potato flour (the latter is denser than wheat flour and half the amount given in the recipe is usually enough) can be used. Any of these will do for coating food which is to be fried. Millet flakes make a good gluten-free alternative to a breadcrumb coating.

As a gluten-free diet is often low in fibre, it is advisable to eat plenty of brown rice, other whole grains and potatoes. Pectin (available dried from specialist suppliers) can be used as a binding agent in doughs and batters; grated fresh apple can also sometimes be used.

Intolerance of gluten is often associated with an inability to digest fats, so that a low-fat diet may also need to be followed.

Wholefood diet

Since the recipes in this book are based firmly on fresh seasonal produce, they need little alteration to be acceptable to lovers of wholefood.

The main items to avoid are refined flour and sugar. Wholemeal flour and bread, and brown rice or sugar; can be used instead as desired. When buying brown sugar, look for the name of the country of origin on the packet. If this is not given, the sugar may be white sugar that has been coloured brown with caramel.

In the case of sugar, it may also be necessary to follow any suggestion given for reducing the total amount. A high level of even the comparatively unrefined brown sugar is not usually considered wholefood. Anything other than this will be covered in the Alternatives column. Where quantities or proportions are affected, as for instance in baking, this will also be covered.

Vegetarian diet

Many of the recipes in this book are suitable as they stand for vegetarians. It has been thought worthwhile to suggest adaptations for the remaining recipes so that they too can be cooked for vegetarians.

CHILLED CARROT SOUP

It is well worth trying this soup of Mexican origin. It can be served hot, but the subtle flavour is more pronounced if the soup is chilled.

PREPARATION TIME: *20 min*
COOKING TIME: *45 min*
CHILLING TIME: *1 hour*
INGREDIENTS *(for 6):*
$1\frac{1}{4}$ lb (550 g) carrots
1 onion
3–4 cloves garlic
1 potato
1 oz (25 g) butter
2 pints (1·2 litres) beef stock
Salt and black pepper*
GARNISH:
Finely chopped parsley

Peel and thinly slice the onion; peel and crush the garlic. Melt the butter in a heavy-based pan, and cook the onion and garlic gently over low heat. Keep the pan covered with a lid until the onion is soft and transparent but not coloured. Meanwhile, top, tail and scrape the carrots, and then chop them roughly; peel and chop the potato. Add these to the onion and continue cooking, covered, for about 8 minutes. Bring the beef stock to the boil and pour it over the vegetables. Bring the contents of the pan to simmering point and maintain this over lowest possible heat for about 30 minutes.

Remove the soup from the heat and allow to cool slightly before liquidising it until smooth. Alternatively, rub the soup through a fine sieve into a bowl. Chill the soup in the refrigerator for at least 1 hour.

Serve the soup in individual bowls, sprinkled with the finely chopped parsley.

LEBANESE CUCUMBER SOUP

There are many variations of this popular Middle Eastern soup. It can only be served cold, but is refreshing in hot weather and looks tempting with a few pink shrimps floating on top.

PREPARATION TIME: *15 min*
CHILLING TIME: *about 1 hour*
INGREDIENTS *(for 4–6):*
1 large or 2 small cucumbers
$\frac{1}{2}$ pint (300 ml) single cream
5 fluid oz (150 ml) natural yogurt
1 clove garlic
2 tablespoons tarragon vinegar
Salt and black pepper*
2 level tablespoons finely chopped mint
GARNISH:
1 tablespoon finely chopped cocktail gherkins
Sprigs of mint
18 shrimps (optional)

Wash and dry the cucumber. Do not peel it, but grate it coarsely into a bowl. Stir in the cream and the yogurt. Peel and crush the garlic, and add to the cucumber, together with the vinegar. Season to taste with salt and freshly ground pepper. Stir in the chopped mint. Chill the soup in a refrigerator for at least 1 hour.

Serve the pale green soup in individual bowls.

For a summery look, garnish each bowl with chopped gherkins or a sprig of fresh mint. On special occasions, float a few shelled shrimps on top of the soup instead of the green garnish.

CRÈME VICHYSSOISE

Despite its French name, this soup was created by the chef of a New York hotel in 1910 and has since become universally famous. It is always served chilled.

PREPARATION TIME: *30 min*
COOKING TIME: *35–40 min*
CHILLING TIME: *3 hours*
INGREDIENTS *(for 6):*
2 lb (900 g) leeks
1 lb (450 g) potatoes
2 oz (50 g) butter
1 stick celery
1 pint (570 ml) chicken stock
1 pint (570 ml) milk
Salt and black pepper*
Freshly grated nutmeg
$\frac{1}{2}$ pint (300 ml) double cream
GARNISH:
Grated carrot

Trim the roots and coarse outer leaves from the leeks and wash them thoroughly in cold water. Slice the leeks diagonally into $\frac{1}{4}$ in ($\frac{1}{2}$ cm) pieces. Peel and coarsely dice the potatoes. Melt the butter in a large sauté pan and add the leeks and potatoes. Cook the vegetables over moderate heat for 7 minutes, stirring continuously. Add the scrubbed and coarsely chopped celery to the pan. Pour over the stock and milk, and bring the soup to the boil. Season with salt, freshly ground pepper and nutmeg. Simmer the soup for 25 minutes or until the vegetables are tender.

Allow the soup to cool slightly before liquidising it or rubbing it through a sieve. Correct seasoning and stir in the cream.

Chill the soup in the refrigerator for 2–3 hours. Serve in individual bowls.

CHILLED CARROT SOUP

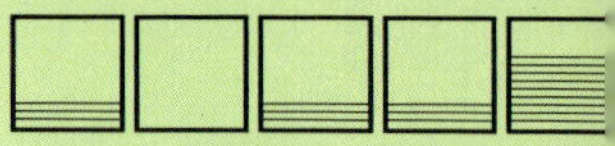

GLUTEN-FREE WHOLEFOOD
TOTAL CALORIES: ABOUT 425

This is a very healthy soup, using potato rather than cream as a thickening agent. The **fat** can be reduced even further by using only half the amount of butter, and the **cholesterol** eliminated by using oil instead (Calories lost: up to 93.)
For a **vegetarian** soup, replace the beef stock with vegetable stock, mixed if you like with a little milk (skim milk can be used). (Calories lost: up to 25.)

Pressure cooker: [✓]
Freezing: [✓] up to 2 months.
Microwave: [✓]

LEBANESE CUCUMBER SOUP

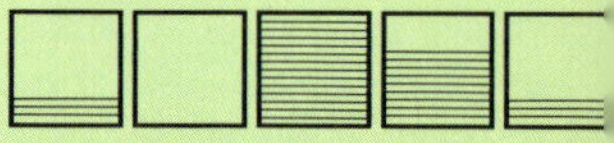

GLUTEN-FREE WHOLEFOOD
TOTAL CALORIES: ABOUT 840

To reduce the **fat** level to low, replace the cream completely with more yogurt: this would be traditional in Lebanon. For very low **cholesterol** use yogur as above instead of cream, and omit the shrimps. (Calories lost: up to 539.)
For a **vegetarian** soup, omit th shrimps and garnish with extra mint (or coriander).

Food processor: [✓] to grate the cucumber.

:RÈME VICHYSSOISE

SALT SUGAR FAT CHOL FIBRE

LUTEN-FREE WHOLEFOOD
OTAL CALORIES: ABOUT 2795

'o reduce the **fat** and **holesterol** levels to low, eplace the butter with 1 ablespoon oil, the cream with alf the quantity of low-fat ogurt or buttermilk, and the nilk with skim milk. (Calories ost: up to 1680.)
'his soup is **vegetarian** if water r vegetable stock is used nstead of chicken stock.

'ressure cooker: √
'reezing: √ up to 2 months.
Aicrowave: √

;AZPACHO ANDALUZ

SALT SUGAR FAT CHOL FIBRE

LUTEN-FREE* WHOLEFOOD* VEGETARIAN
OTAL CALORIES: ABOUT 2090

'o reduce the **salt** content to ow, look for unsalted tomato uice, and use unsalted bread. 'heck the tinned peppers are nsalted, or use fresh. Use only few black olives, or avoid hem entirely if you are aiming or a very low salt intake.
'he **fat** level can be reduced to ow simply by using half the mount of oil, omitting the nayonnaise and using toast nstead of croûtons. (Calories ost: up to 890.)
'ooked brown rice could be sed instead of **gluten-free** read, as the soup is liquidised.

'ood processor: √ to chop he tomatoes.

GAZPACHO ANDALUZ

On a hot summer day, a chilled soup is particularly welcome. This Andalusian salad soup is also decorative, served with several crisp, colourful garnishes. In Spain, ice cubes are added to each soup bowl before serving.

PREPARATION TIME: *35 min*
CHILLING TIME: *1–2 hours*
INGREDIENTS *(for 6):*
$1\frac{1}{2}$ lb (700 g) tomatoes
4 large, $\frac{1}{2}$ in (1 cm) thick slices stale bread
2 large cloves garlic
4 teaspoons herb or red wine vinegar
3–4 tablespoons olive oil
$\frac{3}{4}$ pint (425 ml) tinned tomato juice
2 tinned sweet red peppers
1 large Spanish onion
1 small cucumber
Salt and black pepper*
2 tablespoons mayonnaise (optional)
$\frac{3}{4}$ pint (425 ml) iced water
GARNISH:
1 small cucumber
2 small peppers
4 large tomatoes
Bread croûtons (page 83)
Black olives
Raw onion rings, sliced hardboiled eggs (optional)

Skin the tomatoes (page 92), remove the seeds and chop the flesh finely. Cut the crusts off the bread and crumble it into a large bowl. Peel and crush the garlic into the bowl. Stir in the vinegar and gradually add as much olive oil as the crumbs will absorb. Stir in the tomato flesh and juice and mix thoroughly. Chop the red peppers finely; peel and grate the onion and cucumber and stir all three into the tomato mixture. Season to taste with salt and freshly ground pepper. Put the mixture into a liquidiser until smooth, or rub it through a fine sieve.

The soup should be perfectly smooth – it can be made more creamy by adding mayonnaise (page 85). Dilute the soup with iced water until it has the consistency of thin cream. Adjust seasoning. Chill the soup in the refrigerator.

The garnishes are traditionally served in separate small bowls, and the contents stirred into the soup until it is nearly solid. Peel and dice the cucumber, chop the prepared peppers and the skinned tomatoes. Fry the bread croûtons, and peel and thinly slice the onion. Small stoned black olives can also be served.

CHILLED WATERCRESS SOUP

Watercress is most often used as a garnish or in salads. It also makes a good basis for a smooth-textured chilled soup.

PREPARATION TIME: *20 min*
COOKING TIME: *45 min*
CHILLING TIME: *2 hours*
INGREDIENTS *(for 6–8):*
2 bunches watercress
¾ lb (350 g) potatoes
1 onion
2 pints (1·2 litres) brown stock or bouillon
1½ oz (40 g) butter
1 bay leaf
1 clove garlic (optional)
Salt and black pepper*
3 tablespoons double cream
GARNISH:
Grated nutmeg (optional)

Wash the watercress thoroughly in cold water and discard any tough stalks and yellow leaves. Peel and thickly slice the potatoes and the onion. Put the potatoes, onion, watercress, stock, butter, bay leaf and peeled garlic (if used) in a large saucepan. Season with salt and pepper.

Bring the soup to the boil, cover the pan with a lid and simmer until the potatoes and onion are quite soft. Remove the bay leaf and rub the soup through a coarse sieve. Alternatively, let the soup cool a little before liquidising it.

Return the smooth soup to the pan, stir in the cream and heat the soup through without boiling. Pour into individual bowls and leave to cool before chilling.

Just before serving, sprinkle a little freshly grated nutmeg over the soup.

Serve with toast.

FARMHOUSE SOUP

This French vegetable soup makes a substantial meal on its own. Select vegetables according to availability and choice – the quantities in the recipe are merely a guide. Peas, green beans and watercress may be added when the soup comes to the boil.

PREPARATION TIME: *30 min*
COOKING TIME: *1 hour*
INGREDIENTS *(for 6):*
2–3 carrots
1–2 turnips
2–3 parsnips
1–2 leeks
½ small head of celery
1 large onion
2 oz (50 g) mushrooms
2 rashers streaky bacon
½ lb (225 g) tomatoes
2 oz (50 g) butter
1½–2 tablespoons plain flour
¼ pint (150 ml) milk
1½ pint (900 ml) white stock
Salt and black pepper*
Lemon juice
Mixed herbs
GARNISH:
1 tablespoon chopped mint or parsley
Bread croûtons (page 83)

Wash and peel the carrots, turnips and parsnips; dice them finely. Remove the roots and outer coarse leaves from the leeks, wash them thoroughly under cold running water and chop roughly. Scrub the celery and slice the sticks finely; peel and roughly chop the onion. Trim and slice the mushrooms finely. Remove the rind from the bacon and dice the rashers. Skin and roughly chop the tomatoes (page 92).

Melt the butter in a large

CHILLED WATERCRESS SOUP

SALT SUGAR FAT CHOL FIBRE

GLUTEN-FREE WHOLEFOOD
TOTAL CALORIES: ABOUT 895

To reduce **fat** and **cholesterol** levels to low, replace the butter with vegetable margarine or simply reduce it to ¾ oz (20 g). Replace the cream with low-fat yogurt or cultured buttermilk. (Calories lost: up to 326.)
This soup is **vegetarian** if vegetable stock is used.

Pressure cooker: ✓
Freezing: ✓ up to 2 months.
Microwave: ✓

FARMHOUSE SOUP

SALT SUGAR FAT CHOL FIBRE

GLUTEN-FREE* WHOLEFOOD*
TOTAL CALORIES: ABOUT 1485

If the bacon is halved the level of salt will be low, assuming unsalted butter is used.
To reduce the **fat** and **cholesterol** levels to low, omit the bacon and soften the vegetables in 1 tablespoon of oil, adding a little stock and covering tightly. Use skim milk, and toast or cubes of firm tofu instead of croûtons. (Calories lost: up to 695.)
This soup is **vegetarian** if the bacon is omitted and water or vegetable stock used.

Pressure cooker: ✓
Freezing: ✓ up to 2 months.
Microwave: ✓

'RENCH TURNIP SOUP

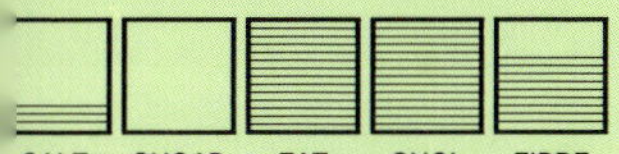

.LUTEN-
'REE* WHOLEFOOD* VEGETARIAN
'OTAL CALORIES: ABOUT 1500

'o reduce the **fat** and
:**holesterol** levels to low, soften
he vegetables in 1 tablespoon
il, omitting the butter. To
hicken the soup, instead of
:ombining egg yolks and
louble cream, add 1–2
ablespoons split red lentils
vhile simmering. (Calories lost:
p to 715.)
)mitting the flour and adding
entils will add **fibre** as well as
eing automatically **gluten-free**
nd **wholefood**.

'ressure cooker: ✓ up to the
tage of adding the eggs.

Microwave: ✓

:REAMED PEA SOUP

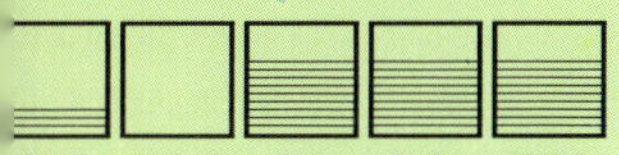

;LUTEN-FREE* WHOLEFOOD*
'OTAL CALORIES: ABOUT 995

'o reduce the **fat** and
:**holesterol** levels to low,
eplace the cream with
metana, quark or low-fat
'ogurt and the croûtons with
lmonds, walnuts or tofu dice.
Calories lost: up to 480.)
tablespoon of potato flour
nakes a good **gluten-free**
lternative to wheat flour;
eplace the croûtons as above.
'hese alterations also make the
oup **wholefood**.

'reezing: ✓ up to 2 months.

Microwave: ✓

heavy-based pan and fry the bacon, onion, celery and mushrooms over moderate heat until soft, but not browned. Add the prepared carrots, turnips, parsnips and leeks and fry them lightly. Remove the pan from the heat and stir in enough flour to absorb the remaining fat. Gradually blend in the milk. Return the pan to the heat, stir in the hot stock and bring the soup to the boil, stirring continuously. Add the tomatoes, stir well and bring the soup to simmering point.

If necessary, thin the soup with water or more milk. Season to taste with salt, freshly ground pepper, lemon juice and a pinch of mixed herbs. Cover the pan with a lid and simmer the soup over very low heat, until the root vegetables are tender, after about 45 minutes.

Serve the soup hot, garnished with mint or parsley and crisp bread croûtons. Garlic bread or a separate bowl of grated cheese would make the soup even more substantial.

Any left-over soup can be sieved or liquidised and thinned to taste with milk or tomato juice. Before serving, stir a little cream into each bowl and garnish as before.

FRENCH TURNIP SOUP

The first white turnips of the season appear in spring. The French frequently use these tasty, inexpensive root vegetables for a creamy soup.

PREPARATION TIME: *20 min*
COOKING TIME: *45 min*
INGREDIENTS *(for 6–8):*
¾ lb (350 g) turnips
½ lb (225 g) potatoes
1 leek
1 onion
2 oz (50 g) butter
1 oz (25 g) plain flour
3–4 pints (about 2 litres) vegetable stock
Salt and black pepper*
2 large egg yolks
3 tablespoons double cream
GARNISH:
Bread croûtons (page 83)

Peel and dice the turnips and potatoes and rinse them in cold water. Remove the roots and coarse outer leaves from the leek, cut in half and rinse thoroughly under cold running water to remove all traces of dirt. Chop the leek coarsely. Peel and roughly chop the onion.

Melt the butter in a large pan and add the vegetables; cover the pan with a lid and cook the vegetables over low heat for about 10 minutes, without browning them. Add the flour and cook for a few minutes, stirring continuously. Gradually blend in the stock and season to taste with salt and freshly ground pepper. Simmer the soup over low heat for about 30 minutes, or until the vegetables are cooked.

Let the soup cool a little before putting it in the liquidiser or rubbing it through a fine sieve. Re-heat the soup over low heat.

Beat the egg yolks with the cream in a small bowl, blend in a little of the hot soup and then stir it all back into the soup. Stir over low heat for a few minutes, without allowing the soup to boil. Correct seasoning if necessary.

Serve at once, with a separate bowl of bread croûtons.

CREAMED PEA SOUP

It is well worth using fresh young peas for this, even though it entails the effort of shelling them. The taste really does come through; frozen peas are not at all the same.

PREPARATION TIME: *10 min*
COOKING TIME: *20 min*
INGREDIENTS *(for 4):*
10 oz (275 g) shelled green peas
1 oz (25 g) unsalted butter
2 level tablespoons plain flour
2 pints (1·2 litres) strained stock
2 tablespoons double cream
*Salt**
Bread croûtons (page 83)

Cook the shelled peas gently in salted water for 10–15 minutes or until tender. Some people like to add a teaspoon of sugar and a squeeze of lemon juice to keep the bright colour. Drain them as soon as they are cooked and rub them through a fine sieve or purée them in a liquidiser.

Make a smooth roux (page 84) from the butter and flour, and blend in the stock. Bring the mixture to the boil, add the pea purée and simmer for 10 minutes.

Strain this soup, add the cream and season with salt. Heat the soup through and serve it garnished with bread croûtons.

MINESTRONE

This soup, of Italian origin and with numerous regional variations, is substantial enough to serve as a meal on its own. For the first course of a meal, increase the amount of stock or use less vegetables.

PREPARATION TIME: *15 min*
COOKING TIME: *30–35 min*
INGREDIENTS *(for 4):*
1–2 carrots
1–2 sticks celery
1 onion
1 small turnip
1 potato
1 oz (25 g) unsalted butter or 2 tablespoons olive oil
1 clove garlic
1½ pints (900 ml) ham or beef stock
2 large tomatoes
1 small leek
1 teacup shredded green cabbage or Brussels sprouts
1 oz (25 g) rice, spaghetti or quick-cooking macaroni
Salt and black pepper*
GARNISH:
2–3 oz (50–75 g) Parmesan cheese

Peel or scrape the carrot, wash the celery and chop both finely. Peel and finely chop the onion, turnip and potato. Heat the butter or oil in a large, heavy-based pan and add the prepared vegetables, together with the peeled and crushed garlic. Sauté the vegetables for a few minutes until they begin to soften, then add the hot stock (from a boiled bacon joint or beef stock made up from a stock cube). Cover the pan with a lid and simmer the soup over low heat for 15 minutes or until the vegetables are almost tender.

Skin the tomatoes (page 92); cut them in half, remove all seeds and chop up the tomato flesh. Trim the roots and coarse outer leaves from the leek, wash thoroughly under cold running water, then shred it finely. Add the tomatoes, the leek and washed shredded cabbage or sprouts to the pan; bring the soup back to the boil. Add the rice or spaghetti, breaking it into small pieces, or the macaroni.

Simmer the soup over low heat – without the lid – for a further 10–15 minutes. Season the soup to taste with salt and freshly ground pepper and serve a bowl of grated Parmesan cheese separately.

BORSHCH

There are numerous variations of this famous Russian soup, but beetroot and soured cream are traditional in every borshch, whether it is served hot or cold.

PREPARATION TIME: *25 min*
COOKING TIME: *1 hour 20 min*
INGREDIENTS *(for 6):*
1 lb (450 g) uncooked beetroot
1 onion
1 leek
1 carrot
1 turnip
1 large potato
1 stick celery
2 pints (1·2 litres) strong beef, chicken or duck stock
1 bay leaf
1 tablespoon chopped parsley
Salt and black pepper*
1 level tablespoon tomato purée
1 level teaspoon caster sugar
1 tablespoon lemon juice
5 fluid oz (150 ml) soured cream
GARNISH:
3 level tablespoons chopped mint or chives

Peel the beetroot, set aside 4 oz (100 g) and dice the remainder finely. Peel and thinly slice the onion; trim the roots and coarse outer leaves from the leek, wash it thoroughly under cold running water and chop it finely. Wash and peel the carrot and turnip, and shred into very thin strips. Wash, peel and dice the potato. Scrub the celery and chop it finely.

Put the prepared vegetables in a large pan with the stock, bay leaf, parsley, and a good seasoning of salt and freshly ground pepper. Cover the pan with a lid and simmer the soup for 30 minutes. Mix together the tomato purée, sugar and lemon juice in a small bowl and add to the soup. Continue cooking the soup over low heat for a further 30 minutes or until the root vegetables are tender.

Ten minutes before serving, grate the reserved beetroot and add it to the soup. Thin with a little more stock if necessary. Stir 4 or 5 tablespoons of the soup into the soured cream and gradually stir this mixture back into the soup. Heat the soup through without boiling and serve at once, sprinkled with chopped mint or chives.

To serve the borshch cold – borshch givrée – chill the soup (it can be puréed if preferred) thoroughly before adding the soured cream. Before serving, add a little more lemon juice. Pour the soup into individual bowls, each containing an ice cube, and top with a swirl of soured cream. Finely chopped spring onion, hard-boiled egg and grated cucumber can also be sprinkled on the top as a garnish, to give a decorative and appetising effect.

MINESTRONE

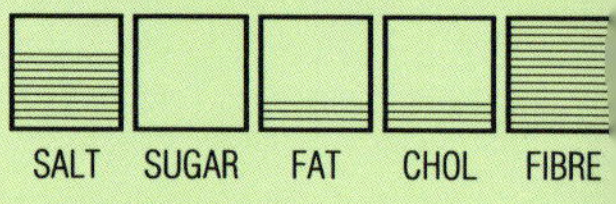

WHOLEFOOD*
TOTAL CALORIES: ABOUT 800

For a low **salt** level, use unsalted beef stock and not ham stock (avoid stock cubes), and only 2–3 tablespoons Parmesan. (Calories lost: up to 216.)
The **fibre** level will depend on the size of vegetables chosen. It will be higher if wholewheat pasta is used.
For a **wholefood** soup, use either wholewheat pasta or brown rice; rice is traditional in minestrone.
For a **gluten-free** soup, replace the pasta with haricot beans which have been cooked in the stock. These are also traditional in minestrone.
For a **vegetarian** soup replace the meat stock with water or vegetable stock.

Freezing: ✓ up to 2 months.
Microwave: ✓

BORSHCH

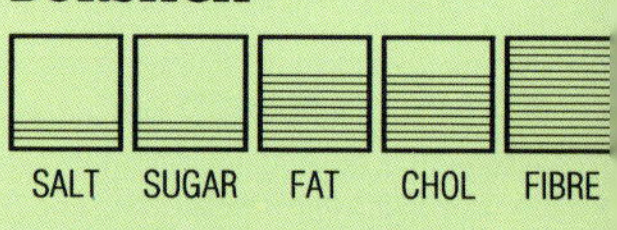

GLUTEN-FREE WHOLEFOOD*
TOTAL CALORIES: ABOUT 755

The low **salt** level assumes the stock is unsalted.
The **fat** and **cholesterol** levels can be reduced by replacing the sour cream with the same amount of quark, thick low-fat yogurt or smetana, smetana being the most traditional in the dish. Make sure the stock is not fatty. (Calories lost: up to 243.)

Jse vegetable stock for a **vegetarian** soup.

Freezing: ☑ up to 2 months.

Microwave: ☑

FRENCH ONION SOUP

SALT SUGAR FAT CHOL FIBRE

GLUTEN-FREE* WHOLEFOOD*
TOTAL CALORIES: ABOUT 1365

The **salt** level can be reduced to ow by halving the amount of cheese used, and making sure he stock is unsalted. For very ow salt, use unsalted bread. The **fat** and **cholesterol** levels can be reduced to low by cooking the onions in 2 easpoons butter and 2 easpoons oil, instead of the butter given, and again by using less cheese, say half, or substituting cottage cheese. (Calories lost: up to 600.) Use water or vegetable stock for a **vegetarian** version.

Pressure cooker: ☑ (without he topping).

Freezing: ☑ up to 3 months without the topping.

Microwave: ☑

FRENCH ONION SOUP

Although Les Halles in Paris no longer exists, onion soup is permanently associated with that famous market. The porters kept out the cold by drinking vast mugs of this traditional soup.

PREPARATION TIME: *20 min*
COOKING TIME: *1 hour*
INGREDIENTS *(for 4):*
1 lb (450 g) onions
2–3 oz (50–75 g) unsalted butter
2 pints (1·2 litres) chicken or beef stock
*½ level teaspoon salt**
1 oz (25 g) plain flour
4 slices French bread, ½ in (1 cm) thick
4 oz (100 g) Gruyère cheese

Peel and thinly slice the onions. Melt 1 oz (25 g) of the butter in a large saucepan and add the onions. Cover with a lid and cook over low heat for about 15 minutes, until the onions are soft and transparent. Remove the lid and continue frying the onions, stirring occasionally, until they are golden brown. Stir in the stock and salt. Replace the lid and simmer the soup for 30 minutes. In a small basin, mix the flour with ¼ pint (150 ml) of water until thoroughly blended. Add to the soup and stir until it comes back to the boil. Simmer for 2–3 minutes until the soup has thickened, then draw the pan off the heat.

Meanwhile, butter both sides of each slice of French bread; grate the cheese and sprinkle half over the bread. Bake the bread, on a baking tray, in a pre-heated oven, at 350°F (180°C, mark 4) until the bread is crisp and the cheese has melted. Arrange the bread in individual bowls and pour over the hot onion soup.

Serve the remaining grated cheese in a separate bowl.

LETTUCE SOUP

A surplus of home-grown lettuce, or those not quite crisp enough for a salad, can be used for an economical soup. The pale green, light-textured soup is ideal on a chilly summer or autumnal day.

PREPARATION TIME: *10 min*
COOKING TIME: *15 min*
INGREDIENTS *(for 4–6):*
8 oz (225 g) lettuce leaves
*Salt**
1 small onion
1½ oz (40 g) butter
¾ pint (425 ml) chicken stock
Black pepper, caster sugar, grated nutmeg
¾ pint (425 ml) milk
1–2 egg yolks
2 tablespoons single cream
GARNISH:
Bread croûtons (page 83)

Wash the lettuce leaves thoroughly and blanch them for 5 minutes in boiling salted water. Drain and rinse under cold running water. Chop the leaves; peel and finely chop the onion.

Melt the butter in a saucepan and fry the onion it it for 5 minutes, until soft. Add the lettuce shreds, setting a few aside. Pour the stock over the onions and lettuce and bring the soup to the boil. Season to taste with salt, freshly ground pepper, sugar and nutmeg.

Allow the soup to cool slightly before liquidising it or rubbing it through a sieve. Add the milk to the soup and reheat gently; simmer for 5 minutes.

Lightly beat together the egg yolks and cream. Spoon a little of the hot, but not boiling, soup into this and blend thoroughly. Pour the egg mixture into the soup and simmer gently until the soup thickens. On no account should it reach boiling point, or the eggs will curdle.

Just before serving, add the rest of the lettuce shreds. Ladle the soup into plates and serve with a bowl of crisp bread croûtons, or toast.

ELIZA ACTON'S APPLE SOUP

In 1845, Eliza Acton published her *Modern Cookery*, the first important English cookery book. It included this recipe for a tart apple soup. Miss Acton gives Burgundy as the place of origin, but a similar soup was known in medieval Britain.

PREPARATION TIME: *10 min*
COOKING TIME: *30 min*
INGREDIENTS *(for 6):*
¾ lb (350 g) cooking apples
2 pints (1·2 litres) beef or mutton stock
½ level teaspoon ground ginger
Salt and black pepper*
4 rounded tablespoons long grain rice

Remove all fat from the surface of the prepared cool stock (page 81). Wash the apples and chop them roughly, without removing peel or core. Bring the stock to the boil in a large pan, add the apples and cover the pan with a lid. Simmer the soup over low heat until the apples are tender.

Pour the soup through a sieve, rubbing through as much of the fruit pulp as possible. Stir in the ginger and season with salt and ground pepper. Re-heat the soup and remove any scum.

While the soup is cooking, boil the rice in plenty of salted water. Drain thoroughly through a sieve and keep the rice warm.

Spoon the soup into bowls, and serve the rice separately.

LETTUCE SOUP

SALT SUGAR FAT CHOL FIBRE

GLUTEN-FREE* WHOLEFOOD*
TOTAL CALORIES: ABOUT 1165

To reduce the **fat** and **cholesterol** levels to low, softe the onion and lettuce in 2 teaspoons oil, omitting the remaining butter. Use skim milk, and to keep the cholesterol level to low, replace the yolks with 1 whole egg beaten into smetana or quark. (Calories lost: up to 571.) Using almond flakes instead of croûtons will make the soup **gluten-free**. Substitute vegetable stock for the chicken stock to make it **vegetarian**.

Freezing: ✓ up to 2 months.
Microwave: ✓

ELIZA ACTON'S APPLE SOUP

SALT SUGAR FAT CHOL FIBRE

GLUTEN-FREE WHOLEFOOD*
TOTAL CALORIES: ABOUT 470

This recipe needs no changes t make it fit healthy eating guidelines, provided the stock is well skimmed of fat. To raise the **fibre** level a little and make the soup **wholefood**, use brow rice, cooked for 45 minutes in 2¼ times its volume of water. You can use vegetable stock for a **vegetarian** soup.

Freezing: ✓ up to 2 months (without the rice).
Microwave: ✓

TOMATO SOUP

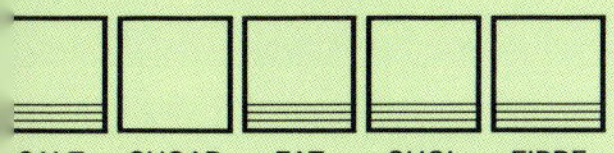

SALT SUGAR FAT CHOL FIBRE

LUTEN-FREE WHOLEFOOD*
OTAL CALORIES: ABOUT 590

This soup needs no changes to uit healthy eating guidelines.

reezing: ✓ up to 2 months.
Microwave: ✓

MEXICAN HOT POT SOUP

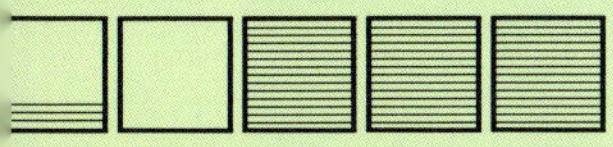

SALT SUGAR FAT CHOL FIBRE

LUTEN-FREE WHOLEFOOD
OTAL CALORIES: ABOUT 1420

The **salt** level is low assuming hat unsalted butter is used, nd the tomatoes, kidney beans nd chick peas bought are nsalted, or fresh tomatoes and ried pulses are used.
The **fat** and **cholesterol** levels an be reduced to low by using tablespoon of oil, in place of acon fat or butter, to soften he onion, or by preparing this tage the other way round: even ery lean minced beef will rovide enough fat to brown tself, if heated gently in a eavy-based pan, to which the nion can then be added.
nstead of garlic bread, include arlic in the dish, and serve vith unbuttered rolls. (Calories ost: up to 235.)

reezing: ✓ up to 2 weeks.
Microwave: ✓

TOMATO SOUP

This is a very simple, basic method of making soup, and one which brings out to the full the true taste of the tomatoes. Try to find really ripe and sweet ones, preferably the kind known as beef tomatoes, which have far more taste than the ubiquitous Moneymaker.

Short grain (or round grain) rice, such as the Italian Arborio rice, is probably the best for this kind of soup, but if there is none to hand, long grain rice can quite well be used.

PREPARATION TIME: *25 min*
COOKING TIME: *30 min*
INGREDIENTS *(for 6):*
1 lb (450 g) ripe tomatoes
1 onion
1 oz (25 g) butter
Salt and black pepper*
3 oz (75 g) long grain rice
2 pints (1·2 litres) white stock
Bouquet garni (page 99)

Peel and finely chop the onion. Skin the tomatoes (page 82), cut them in half and remove the seeds with a teaspoon. Chop the tomato flesh roughly. Melt the butter in a large heavy-based pan and cook the onion over low heat until transparent. Add the tomato flesh, and season with salt and pepper. Blend in the rice and stock, and add the bouquet garni. Bring the soup to boiling point and cover the pan with a lid. Reduce the heat and simmer the soup for 15–20 minutes, or until the rice is tender. Remove the bouquet garni.

Rub the purée through a sieve – a liquidiser will not get rid of any remaining tomato pips. Re-heat the soup and adjust seasoning.

MEXICAN HOT POT SOUP

This is the kind of winter soup which is a meal in itself. The ingredients include red kidney beans and chick peas. Dried beans should be soaked overnight.

PREPARATION TIME: *10 min*
COOKING TIME: *45 min*
INGREDIENTS *(for 4):*
1 large onion
1 green or red pepper
2 oz (50 g) bacon fat or butter
½ lb (225 g) minced beef
14 or 16 oz (400 or 450 g) tinned tomatoes
14 oz (400 g) tinned or 4 oz (100 g) dried red kidney beans
8 oz (225 g) tinned or 2 oz (50 g) dried chick peas
¾ pint (425 ml) stock or bouillon
½ level teaspoon chili powder
*Salt**
GARNISH:
Lettuce

Peel and finely chop the onion, cut off the stalk base of the pepper, remove the seeds and chop the pepper finely. Melt the fat in a large heavy-based pan, and fry the onion until it begins to colour. Add the meat and continue frying over medium heat until it is well browned.

Add the tomatoes with their juice, the drained or soaked beans, chick peas and chopped pepper. Stir in the stock or bouillon, mixing thoroughly. Season to taste with chili powder and a little salt. Cover the pan, and simmer the soup for 30 minutes. Allow to cool; put through a liquidiser or rub it through a sieve.

Re-heat the thick soup before serving. Garnish with finely shredded lettuce and serve with hot garlic bread: cut a crusty loaf into thick slices and spread each with garlic butter. Put the slices back to the original loaf form, wrap it in foil and heat in the oven for about 10 minutes, at 350°F (180°C, mark 4).

APPLE AND NUT SALAD

Soured cream is a refreshing, less fatty dressing than mayonnaise. It is here combined with fruits, nuts and vegetables in a crisp salad to serve with cold meat.

PREPARATION TIME: *30 min*
INGREDIENTS *(for 4–5):*
4 crisp dessert apples
3 teaspoons lemon juice
3 oz (75 g) shelled walnuts
¼ pint (150 ml) soured cream
3 oz (75 g) white cabbage
3 sticks celery
12 large radishes
2 oz (50 g) stoned raisins
Salt and black pepper*

Wash and core the apples and chop them into rough chunks. Put them in a bowl and sprinkle the lemon juice over them to prevent the apples going brown. Chop the walnuts roughly and set aside one-third for garnish. Pour the soured cream into a bowl and stir in the apples and walnuts.

Remove any damaged and coarse outer leaves from the cabbage, wash it and cut out the thick centre stalk. Shred it finely, first one way then the other. Scrub and thinly slice the celery. Remove leaves and roots from the radishes and slice them evenly. Wash the raisins and cut them in half.

Stir all these ingredients into the soured cream and season to taste with salt and freshly ground pepper. Spoon the salad into a serving dish and garnish with the remaining walnuts.

SALADE NIÇOISE

There are numerous versions of this Provençal hors-d'oeuvre, but all have in common the basic ingredients of lettuce, eggs, anchovy fillets, black olives and tomatoes.

PREPARATION TIME: *25 min*
INGREDIENTS *(for 6):*
2 eggs
½ lb (225 g) French beans
¾ lb (350 g) firm tomatoes
½ onion
1 lettuce heart
½ green pepper
¼ pint (150 ml) garlic-flavoured French dressing (page 85)
4 oz (100 g) tin of tuna fish
Small tin anchovy fillets
2 oz (50 g) small black olives

Hardboil the eggs for 8–10 minutes, then plunge them into cold water. Shell and quarter them, and set aside to cool. Top and tail the French beans, wash them and cook in boiling salted water for 5–8 minutes; drain and set aside to cool.

Skin the tomatoes (page 92) and cut into quarters. Peel and thinly slice the onion, break it into individual rings. Wash and dry the lettuce. Clean the pepper, cut out the core and seeds, and slice it thinly.

Put half the French dressing in a shallow bowl and toss the shredded lettuce and beans in it. Drain and flake the tuna fish and arrange it, with the drained anchovy fillets, olives, green pepper and onion rings, on top of the lettuce and beans. Surround with the quartered tomatoes and hardboiled eggs. Sprinkle over the remaining dressing and serve the salad immediately.

ARTICHOKES WITH MUSHROOMS

Artichoke bottoms with garlic dressing make an unusual side salad for cold meats and poultry. Alternatively, serve the artichokes as a first course.

PREPARATION TIME: *25 min*
COOKING TIME: *45–60 min*
INGREDIENTS *(for 6):*
6 large globe artichokes
12 large mushrooms
6 tablespoons olive oil
6 tablespoons white wine vinegar
1 clove garlic
Salt and black pepper*

Trim off the stems and rinse the artichokes thoroughly under cold running water. Put them in a large saucepan of boiling water, cover with a lid and boil until a leaf pulls away easily. Remove the artichokes, then drain them upside-down and leave to cool completely.

Wash and trim the mushrooms; cut them into slices, discarding the stalks. Pour the oil into a small bowl, add the vinegar and peeled and crushed garlic; season to taste with salt and freshly ground pepper.

Pull off and discard all the leaves and the fine filaments round the base of the artichokes. Set the artichoke bottoms on individual serving plates, and arrange the mushroom slices on top; pour over garlic dressing.

APPLE AND NUT SALAD

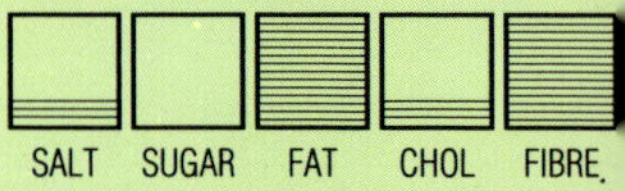

GLUTEN-FREE WHOLEFOOD VEGETARIAN
TOTAL CALORIES: ABOUT 1045

Walnuts are roughly half oil; to limit the **fat** content of the salad to low, use only 2 oz (50 g), and replace the soured cream with low-fat yogurt. This will give a very low **cholesterol** content too. (Calories lost: up to 374.)

Food processor: ☑ for chopping.

SALADE NIÇOISE

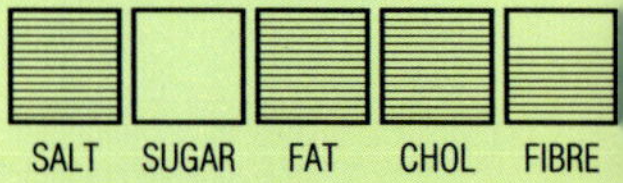

GLUTEN-FREE WHOLEFOOD
TOTAL CALORIES: ABOUT 2255

Tuna fish, anchovies and olives are all very high in **salt** when preserved. To limit this amount, replace the anchovies with cubes of boiled potato, and use only 1 oz (25 g) olives. However, the level will still be fairly high unless you substitute fresh fish for the canned tuna, lightly poaching or steaming it. To reduce the **fat** level, choose tuna canned in brine rather than oil (or again, use fresh fish), and olives kept in brine rather than in oil. Make a French dressing with only 2 tablespoons oil, using a well-flavoured olive or walnut oil to give the small amount maximum impact. For a low **cholesterol** dish, use only 1 egg. (Calories lost: up to 1555.)

ARTICHOKES WITH MUSHROOMS

SALT	SUGAR	FAT	CHOL	FIBRE

GLUTEN-FREE WHOLEFOOD VEGETARIAN
TOTAL CALORIES: ABOUT 930

To reduce the **fat** level to low, use only 3–4 tablespoons oil and the same of vinegar or lemon juice. This simply means the dish has less dressing. If wished, a dollop of quark or smetana can be placed on top of each portion. An alternative dressing can be made using tahini (sesame seed paste). Mix 3 tablespoons with the same amount of water until smooth. Blend in 3 tablespoons oil and add lemon juice, garlic and seasonings to taste. (Calories lost: up to 270.)

FRESH ASPARAGUS

The asparagus season lasts only a few weeks. It has such a good, subtle flavour that the best way to serve it is the simplest, as here.

PREPARATION TIME: *10 min*
COOKING TIME: *20–30 min*
INGREDIENTS *(for 4):*
2 lb (1 kilo) asparagus
6–8 oz (175–225 g) butter or 6 tablespoons olive oil and 2 tablespoons white wine vinegar
Salt and black pepper*

Wash the asparagus carefully and lightly scrape the lower parts of the stems, away from the delicate tips. Young fresh asparagus needs no further preparation, but if the stems are woody towards the base, trim off the wood, keeping the stems at a uniform length.

Tie the asparagus in bundles of 10–12, using soft tape so as not to damage the stems. Bring a large pan of lightly salted water to the boil. Place the bundles of asparagus upright in it, with the tips above the water. Time of cooking varies according to the age, size and length of the asparagus, but as a general rule asparagus is cooked when the tips are soft to the touch.

Untie the asparagus and drain carefully without breaking the tips. Serve the asparagus on individual plates, either warm with melted butter or cold with a French dressing (page 85), served separately. Asparagus is traditionally eaten with the fingers. Dip the tips in the butter or dressing and leave any woody parts of the stems. Finger bowls, with luke-warm water and a slice of lemon, are required.

FRESH ASPARAGUS

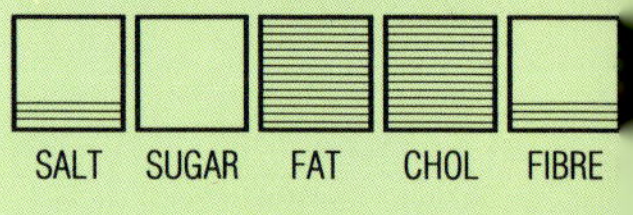

GLUTEN-FREE WHOLEFOOD VEGETARIAN
TOTAL CALORIES: ABOUT 1745

The high **fat** and **cholesterol** levels assume that butter is used. If French dressing is used instead, the fat content is only half that of butter. The amount can be reduced to medium or low by mixing 1 tablespoon olive oil with 4 tablespoons of smetana. Or less oil can be used, reducing the vinegar in proportion. If oil and vinegar are used, the cholesterol is nil. (Calories lost: up to 1369.)

Freezing: ☑ up to 1 year.

AVOCADO, PEAR AND NUT SALAD

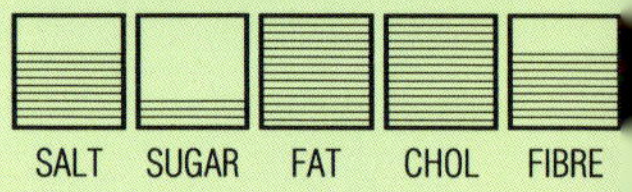

GLUTEN-FREE WHOLEFOOD* VEGETARIAN
TOTAL CALORIES: ABOUT 1580

The **salt** content can be reduced to low by using mustard rather than Worcestershire sauce, and unsalted nuts.
Avocadoes have a very high oil level. However, their rich texture makes it simple to replace the cream with low-fat yogurt or quark, so the **fat** level can be cut to medium, and the **cholesterol** to very low. The nuts also have a high oil level, about 50%; so use half the amount, toasting before chopping as this gives a more pervasive flavour. (Calories lost: up to 452.)
This is **gluten-free** if the mustard used contains no gluten. Check the label.

AVOCADO AND CITRUS SALAD

SALT SUGAR FAT CHOL FIBRE

GLUTEN-FREE WHOLEFOOD* VEGETARIAN
TOTAL CALORIES: ABOUT 1000

The high **fat** level comes from the oil in the avocado, and cannot be avoided except by reducing the proportion of avocado to other ingredients. This can be done without making the salad too citrus-dominated by adding about 6 oz (175 g) cubed melon or ripe pear to the mixture, in place of each avocado you choose to omit. (Calories lost: up to 241.)

GUACAMOLE

SALT SUGAR FAT CHOL FIBRE

GLUTEN-FREE WHOLEFOOD VEGETARIAN
TOTAL CALORIES: ABOUT 980

Avocados are naturally about 20% oil on average, although the amount can vary between 11% and 39% according to season. This means that 3 oz (75 g) avocado provides about ½ oz (about 15 g) oil, making a high **fat** dish. The only way to reduce the amount, apart from serving smaller portions, is to omit the added oil and replace up to half the avocado with sieved cottage cheese or ricotta. (Calories lost: up to 457.) One way of serving smaller helpings is to use the dip to stuff a jacket potato.

Food processor: ✓

Freezing: ✓ up to 2 months.

AVOCADO, PEAR AND NUT SALAD

Avocado and dessert pears discolour quickly when peeled. For this salad it is essential to mix the dressing first and sprinkle the diced pears generously with lemon juice before blending them quickly into the dressing.

PREPARATION TIME: *15 min*
CHILLING TIME: *1 hour*
INGREDIENTS *(for 6)*:
3 avocados
7½ fluid oz (200 ml) soured cream
2 teaspoons tarragon vinegar
Salt and black pepper*
French mustard or Worcestershire sauce
Caster sugar
Juice of a lemon
1 large or 2 small dessert pears
3 tablespoons salted almonds or peanuts
GARNISH:
Chopped chives

Put the soured cream in a mixing bowl and stir in the vinegar. Season to taste with salt, freshly ground pepper, mustard or Worcestershire sauce and a little sugar. Mix thoroughly.

Cut the avocados in half, remove the stones and carefully scoop out the flesh. Leave a narrow inner lining of flesh on the avocado shells and set them aside. Cut the flesh into dice and put them in a bowl. Sprinkle with lemon juice. Peel, core and dice the dessert pear, add to the avocado and sprinkle with the remaining lemon juice.

Chop the salted almonds roughly and set a little aside for garnishing. Mix the remainder with the avocado and pears. Pour over the dressing and blend thoroughly. Pile the salad into the avocado shells and wrap each half in foil. Chill for 1 hour.

Just before serving, unwrap the avocado shells, arrange them on small plates and garnish with the chopped almonds and chives.

AVOCADO AND CITRUS SALAD

Slightly overripe avocados mixed with citrus fruit provide a tangy starter. Alternatively, serve the salad with cold ham, chicken or shellfish.

PREPARATION TIME: *30 min*
INGREDIENTS *(for 4–6)*:
3 large avocados
Juice of a small lemon
1 large grapefruit
1 large orange
Caster sugar (optional)
GARNISH:
Orange segments
Mint

Peel the avocados. Cut them into quarters and remove the stones; cut the flesh into thin sections and pour the lemon juice over them. Cut a slice from top and bottom of the grapefruit and orange so that they stand flat on a board. Cut downwards, in narrow strips, through peel and pith and remove. With a sharp knife, cut between the flesh and segment skins; put the flesh into a large bowl and squeeze the segment skins over the fruit so that no juice is wasted.

Carefully blend the avocado and lemon juice with the citrus fruits; sweeten to taste if necessary. Spoon the mixture into individual serving dishes and garnish with skinned orange segments and sprigs of mint.

GUACAMOLE

This is a Mexican hors-d'oeuvre or dip of avocados. Very ripe avocados, suitable for mashing, are often sold cheaply.

PREPARATION TIME: *10 min*
CHILLING TIME: *30 min*
INGREDIENTS *(for 6)*:
3 ripe avocados
½ small grated onion
2 crushed cloves garlic
1 tablespoon lemon juice
1 tablespoon olive oil
Salt and black pepper*
Cayenne pepper
¼ teaspoon Worcestershire sauce
Tabasco sauce

Cut the avocados in half and remove the stones. Mash the avocado flesh with the onion and garlic until smooth. Blend in the lemon juice and oil; season to taste with salt, freshly ground pepper, cayenne and the sauces. Chill for 30 minutes.

Serve on individual plates on lettuce leaves, or in serving glasses. Mixed raw vegetables, such as celery sticks, or slices of carrot, green pepper and radish, could be used for the dip.

TOMATO ICE

The Italians invented the water ice or sorbet, which is an iced and sweetened juice or extract. This adaptation of a sorbet makes a refreshing starter.

PREPARATION TIME: *10 min*
COOKING TIME: *25 min*
FREEZING TIME: *4 hours*
INGREDIENTS *(for 6):*
3 lb ($1\frac{1}{2}$ kg) ripe tomatoes
1 small onion
2 level teaspoons marjoram
1 level tablespoon tomato purée
Juice of a lemon
Caster sugar to taste
GARNISH:
Mint, lemon or cucumber

Wash, wipe and roughly chop the tomatoes. Peel and roughly chop the onion. Put the tomatoes, onion and marjoram in a large saucepan. Bring to the boil, cover with a lid and simmer over low heat for 25 minutes or until the tomatoes are soft. Stir occasionally to prevent the tomatoes sticking to the pan. Rub the mixture through a sieve into a large bowl, and stir in the tomato purée, lemon juice and caster sugar. Leave the mixture to cool. Spoon it into a plastic freezer container, cover with a lid and freeze for at least 4 hours or overnight.

Turn the mixture out when frozen solid, crush with a rolling pin and pile the tomato crystals into individual serving glasses. Garnish with sprigs of mint, lemon or cucumber slices.

TOMATOES WITH HORSERADISH MAYONNAISE

For this dish choose large firm tomatoes of even size. Serve them on their own, chilled, as a starter. They also make a good picnic dish, and can be served as a side dish with cold meat or grilled steaks and chops.

PREPARATION TIME: *20 min*
CHILLING TIME: *2 hours*
INGREDIENTS *(for 4–6):*
8 firm tomatoes
$\frac{1}{4}$ pint (150 ml) mayonnaise (page 85)
*Salt**
$\frac{1}{4}$ pint (150 ml) double cream
Lemon juice
2 rounded tablespoons fresh grated horseradish
GARNISH:
Chopped chives, chervil, basil or parsley

First prepare the mayonnaise and set it aside. Skin the tomatoes (page 92), and slice off the tops with a serrated knife. Carefully scoop out the seeds and juice with a teaspoon, without breaking the flesh. Sprinkle the inside of the tomato cups with salt, stand them upside down on a plate to drain, and chill them in the coldest part of the refrigerator for 2 hours.

Lightly whip the cream and mix it into the mayonnaise; add lemon juice to taste and stir in the grated horseradish (the tomato caps may also be chopped and stirred into the mayonnaise). Chill on the bottom shelf of the refrigerator for about 1 hour.

Just before serving, spoon the horseradish mayonnaise evenly into tomato cups and sprinkle with chopped herbs.

TOMATO ICE

SALT SUGAR FAT CHOL FIBRE

GLUTEN-FREE WHOLEFOOD* VEGETARIA
TOTAL CALORIES: ABOUT 240

This recipe needs no changes to fit healthy eating guidelines, apart from limiting the **sugar** used to flavour, and if possible, using unsalted tomato purée.

Food processor: √

Freezing: √ up to 6 months.

Microwave: √ for the tomatoes.

TOMATOES WITH HORSERADISH MAYONNAISE

SALT SUGAR FAT CHOL FIBRE

GLUTEN-FREE WHOLEFOOD VEGETARIAN
TOTAL CALORIES: ABOUT 2170

The high **fat** level can be reduced to low by replacing the mayonnaise with a low-fat style of dressing, now easy to buy, and the cream with smetana, low-fat yogurt or cultured buttermilk, giving an even lower **cholesterol** count as well. A mixture of sieved cottage cheese (or ricotta) and smetana could replace the mayonnaise and cream altogether. (Calories lost: up to 1562.)

HONEYDEW CUPS

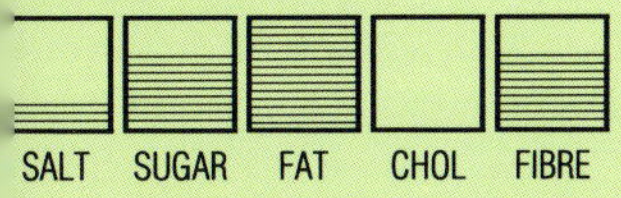

GLUTEN-FREE WHOLEFOOD* VEGETARIAN
TOTAL CALORIES: ABOUT 1170

To reduce the **fat** level to low, use only 2 tablespoons oil, and one of lemon juice or vinegar. Make up the volume of dressing with quark, low-fat yogurt, or 2 tablespoons tahini (sesame paste) blended to a smooth purée with 2 tablespoons water. (Calories lost: up to 520.)

MELON AND HAM GONDOLAS

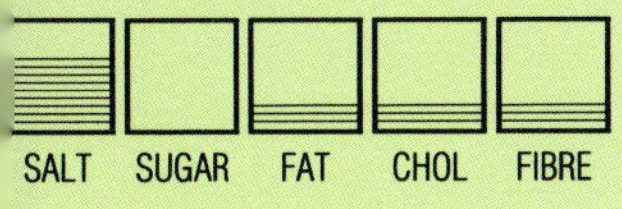

GLUTEN-FREE WHOLEFORD
TOTAL CALORIES: ABOUT 200

This kind of ham is extremely salty: even a small slice will provide around 200 mg sodium, or 500 mg salt, about 10% of a desirable daily maximum. The **fat** and **cholesterol** levels are low simply because the portions of ham are small, say under ½ oz (10–15 g) a slice. However, this assumes that the fatty edge of the ham is not eaten.
A leaner alternative and one which keeps to the Italian theme, is thin slices of *bresaola*, from the mountains of Northern Italy. This is beef cured by being air-dried, rather in the same way as Parma ham. It also goes well with melon, either honeydew or Charentais. (Calories lost: up to 30.)

HONEYDEW CUPS

A well-chilled melon salad is a good choice before a rich main course. Honeydew or cantaloupe melons are the least expensive, but for a special occasion, choose three small Ogen or Charentais melons.

PREPARATION TIME: *40 min*
CHILLING TIME: *1 hour*
INGREDIENTS *(for 6):*
1 honeydew or cantaloupe melon
1 cucumber
Salt and black pepper*
6 tomatoes
DRESSING:
1–2 level tablespoons caster sugar
3 tablespoons lemon juice or tarragon vinegar
6 tablespoons salad oil
GARNISH:
2 teaspoons each, chopped mint, chives, and chervil or parsley

Peel the cucumber and cut it into ½ in (1 cm) dice; sprinkle with salt and leave to stand for 30 minutes. Cut the melon in half across and remove the seeds. Carefully scoop out the flesh in small balls, or cut it into small wedges. Skin the tomatoes (page 92), cut them in half and remove cores and seeds. Chop the tomato flesh roughly.

Mix the ingredients for the dressing, adding the oil last of all. Rinse the cucumber in cold water and pat dry on absorbent kitchen paper.

Put the melon, tomato and cucumber in a large bowl, pour over the dressing and mix well. Chill the salad in the refrigerator for 1 hour, stirring occasionally.

Serve the salad in individual glass bowls and sprinkle with the mixed chopped herbs.

MELON AND HAM GONDOLAS

Sweet ripe melon combines perfectly with raw ham, such as Parma ham, or with the Westphalian variety from Germany. This dish is traditional in Italy, but is now popular also throughout the world.

PREPARATION TIME: *12 min*
INGREDIENTS *(for 6):*
½ large ripe honeydew melon
6 wafer-thin slices raw ham
Juice of a lemon
Black pepper
GARNISH:
Lemon wedges

Chill the melon thoroughly. Cut it into six long slices, scoop out the seeds and cut the skin away. Put one piece of melon on each slice of ham and wrap the ham neatly over the melon. Sprinkle with lemon juice and freshly ground pepper.

Serve the melon gondolas garnished with wedges of lemon.

LEEKS VINAIGRETTE

In place of the inevitable green salad of lettuce and cucumber try this cold leek salad as a side dish with any type of meat.

PREPARATION TIME: *15 min*
COOKING TIME: *30 min*
INGREDIENTS *(for 4):*
8 small leeks
1 bay leaf
Salt and black pepper*
1 level teaspoon caster sugar
2 tablespoons wine vinegar
¼ level teaspoon made French mustard
3–4 tablespoons olive oil
1 level tablespoon freshly chopped parsley
GARNISH:
2 hardboiled eggs

Remove the coarse outer leaves from the leeks; trim off the roots and cut away the green tops, leaving about 4 in (10 cm) of white stem on each leek. Slice the leeks in half lengthways, open them carefully and wash well under cold running water to remove all traces of grit.

Tie the halved leeks in four bundles, put them in a pan of boiling salted water and add the bay leaf. Bring back to the boil, then lower the heat to simmering point. Cover the pan with a lid and cook the leeks for 30 minutes or until tender. Lift them carefully from the water and leave to drain and cool.

Arrange the cold leeks in a serving dish and prepare the dressing: put salt and freshly ground pepper in a mixing bowl, add the sugar, vinegar and mustard. Blend thoroughly before adding the oil, mixing well. Taste for sharpness, adding more vinegar if necessary. Stir in the chopped parsley, and spoon the dressing over the leeks. Leave to marinate until ready to serve.

Garnish the leeks with slices of hardboiled eggs.

FRIED LEEKS

This dish is an excellent starter and is probably best served lukewarm. It can also be served hot with any grilled or roast meat, or as a side dish or salad with cold ham and chicken.

PREPARATION TIME: *10 min*
COOKING TIME: *25 min*
INGREDIENTS *(for 4–6):*
2 lb (900 g) leeks
4 tomatoes
6 tablespoons olive oil
2 cloves garlic
1 bay leaf
*Salt**
Juice of ½ lemon
Black pepper

Cut away the roots and any damaged green leaves from the leeks, slice them in half lengthways and wash under cold running water to remove all traces of grit. Cut into 1 in (2½ cm) slices. Skin the tomatoes (page 92). Heat half the oil in a large frying pan and add the leeks. Peel the garlic and crush over the leeks, then add the bay leaf. Season to taste with salt and freshly ground pepper.

Cover the pan with a lid and cook over low heat for 20 minutes. Chop the tomatoes, add them to the pan with the rest of the oil and cook for a further 5 minutes. Remove the bay leaf.

Spoon the leeks into a serving dish and sprinkle the lemon juice over.

LEEKS À LA NIÇOISE

French vegetable dishes or salads prepared *à la niçoise* imply the addition of tomatoes and usually a garlic flavouring. This dish can be served hot with grilled fish, meat or chicken or cold as an hors-d'oeuvre.

PREPARATION TIME: *15 min*
COOKING TIME: *20 min*
INGREDIENTS *(for 4):*
2 lb (900 g) young leeks
½ lb (225 g) tomatoes
3–4 tablespoons olive oil
*Salt**
1 large clove garlic
1 tablespoon fresh chopped parsley
Lemon juice
Black pepper

Cut the roots and most of the green tops off the leeks, so they are of even length. Rinse them thoroughly under cold running water and dry them on absorbent paper.

Skin the tomatoes (page 92) and chop them roughly.

Heat the oil in a flameproof casserole over medium heat and put in the leeks side by side. Fry until lightly coloured underneath, then turn them over and season with salt and freshly ground pepper. Cover the casserole with a lid, and cook the leeks over gentle heat for 10 minutes or until the thick white part is tender. Lift out the leeks and keep them warm.

Add the tomatoes, crushed garlic and parsley to the casserole and cook briskly for 2 or 3 minutes, stirring continuously. Adjust seasoning and sharpen to taste with lemon juice. Put the leeks back into the sauce and serve hot or cold.

LEEKS VINAIGRETTE

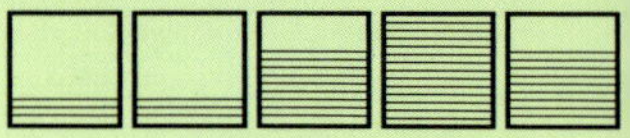

SALT SUGAR FAT CHOL FIBRE

GLUTEN-FREE WHOLEFOOD VEGETARIAN
TOTAL CALORIES: ABOUT 925

To give a low **fat** and **cholesterol** content, use only 2 tablespoons best quality oil, plus 3 tablespoons thick low-fat yogurt. Replace the egg garnish with thin slices of red pepper, ground coriander seed or some coarsely grated carrot. (Calories lost: up to 410.)

Microwave: √ for the leeks.

FRIED LEEKS

SALT SUGAR FAT CHOL FIBRE

GLUTEN-FREE WHOLEFOOD VEGETARIAN
TOTAL CALORIES: ABOUT 1120

To reduce the high **fat** level, use only 1 tablespoon of oil in the leek pan, and add a few tablespoons of stock before covering and cooking. This method of half-frying, half-steaming gives a delicious result. The mushrooms can be added without any extra oil. (Calories lost: up to 675.)
The fibre level assumes that you use most of the leeks: the green parts, provided they are not damaged, need not be discarded.

Freezing: √ up to 3 months. Once frozen it is best reheated and eaten hot rather than served as a salad.

Microwave: √ for the leeks.

LEEKS À LA NIÇOISE

SALT SUGAR FAT CHOL FIBRE

GLUTEN-FREE WHOLEFOOD VEGETARIAN
TOTAL CALORIES: ABOUT 855

To reduce the amount of **fat** to low, use only 1 tablespoon of oil, with 2–3 tablespoons of stock; cook the leeks by a mixture of frying and steaming, as in the notes on the previous recipe. (Calories lost: up to 405.)
To make sure that the green parts do not get over-cooked while waiting for the thicker white parts to become tender, cut deep slits from the base 2 in (5 cm) up the leek in a cross, allowing the cooking heat to penetrate the base of the leek more easily.

Freezing: √ up to 3 months. Once frozen it is best reheated and served hot rather than as a salad.
Microwave: √ for the leeks.

ONIONS À LA GRECQUE

SALT SUGAR FAT CHOL FIBRE

GLUTEN-FREE WHOLEFOOD* VEGETARIAN
TOTAL CALORIES: ABOUT 1455

The low **salt** level assumes that the tomato paste is unsalted, leaving only a small amount from the wine.
The amount of **sugar** added is generous; many people will be satisfied with only ½ oz (10 g). (Calories lost: up to 157.)
To reduce the level of **fat** to low, use only 2 tablespoons best quality oil, preferably cold-pressed, which will give maximum flavour for quantity. (Calories lost: up to 405.)

ONIONS À LA GRECQUE

This French classic hors-d'oeuvre of baby onions provides an unusual first course. The baby onions should be served chilled.

PREPARATION TIME: *1 hour*
COOKING TIME: *40 min*
CHILLING TIME: *2 hours*
INGREDIENTS *(for 6):*
1½ lb (700 g) small onions
SAUCE:
1 pint (570 ml) dry white wine
2 oz (50 g) caster sugar
5 tablespoons olive oil
8 juniper berries
Juice of a lemon
1 bay leaf
2¼ oz (65 g) tin of tomato paste
6 sprigs parsley
¼ teaspoon basil
*Salt**
Black pepper
GARNISH:
3 tablespoons chopped parsley

Bring a large saucepan, holding at least 3 pints (1¾ litres) of water, to the boil.

Cut the tops and bottoms from the onions and drop them into the boiling water for 1 minute. Drain the onions in a colander; cool slightly before peeling the onions.

Put all the sauce ingredients, with ½ pint (300 ml) of water, into a heavy-based pan; season this sauce to taste with salt and freshly ground pepper before adding the peeled onions.

Bring to the boil and simmer over low heat for 20 minutes or until the onions are tender, but not disintegrating. Remove the onions; mark the level of the sauce and boil briskly for about 15 minutes or until it has reduced to three-quarters.

Strain the sauce through a sieve over the onions; leave to cool and chill for a few hours in the refrigerator.

Serve the onions, in the sauce, in soup plates and garnish the dish with the finely chopped parsley.

FRENCH BEANS MIMOSA

A green salad need not be composed of the ubiquitous lettuce and cucumber – crisp cooked beans make a refreshing change.

PREPARATION TIME: *10 min*
COOKING TIME: *3–4 min*
INGREDIENTS *(for 4–6)*:
1 lb (450 g) young French beans
*Salt**
6 tablespoons olive oil
2 tablespoons lemon juice
GARNISH:
1 large hardboiled egg

Top, tail and wash the beans, leaving them whole. Cook them in salted water for 3–4 minutes – they should stay crisp. Drain the beans and arrange them in a round shallow serving dish, radiating from the centre.

Pour the olive oil, mixed with the lemon juice, over the still-warm beans. Add more salt if necessary, and set the beans aside to cool.

Separate the white and yolk of the hardboiled egg. Chop the white finely and rub the yolk through a coarse sieve.

Before serving, decorate the beans. Arrange the egg white in the centre of the dish and scatter the yolk among the beans to resemble mimosa.

ONION FLAN

The recipe for this rich creamy flan comes from Alsace in France. Serve it hot or cold, cut into wedges, as a first course. It can also be served with a green salad as a main course for a light lunch.

PREPARATION TIME: *45 min*
COOKING TIME: *40 min*
INGREDIENTS *(for 4–6)*:
1 lb (450 g) onions
2 oz (50 g) unsalted butter
1 bay leaf
Salt and pepper*
6 oz (175 g) shortcrust pastry (page 98)
2 large eggs
Grated nutmeg
$\frac{1}{4}$ pint (150 ml) double cream
$\frac{1}{4}$ pint (150 ml) milk

Peel the onions and slice them thinly. Melt the butter in a frying pan and add the onions and bay leaf. Season with salt and pepper and cover the onions closely with a piece of buttered greaseproof paper. Cover the pan with a tight-fitting lid and cook the onions over low heat for 30 minutes or until they are soft and golden. Shake the pan occasionally to prevent them sticking.

Prepare the shortcrust pastry and roll it out, $\frac{1}{4}$ in ($\frac{1}{2}$ cm) thick, on a lightly floured surface. Line an 8–9 in (20–23 cm) wide flan ring, standing on a baking tray, with the pastry. Trim the edge and prick the pastry base with a fork. Beat the eggs lightly in a large bowl and season with salt, pepper and nutmeg. Stir in the cream and milk. Drain the onions in a colander, remove the bay leaf and spread the onions over the pastry case. Strain the egg mixture through a sieve over the onions.

FRENCH BEANS MIMOSA

SALT SUGAR FAT CHOL FIBRE

GLUTEN-FREE WHOLEFOOD VEGETARIAN
TOTAL CALORIES: ABOUT 935

To reduce the **fat** level to low, use only 2 tablespoons best quality oil, to give maximum flavour, and add 4 tablespoons low-fat yogurt or quark to the mixture. This will change the appearance of the dish, giving a thicker, less transparent coating to the beans, but is attractive in its own way. If preferred, put the dressing in the centre of the beans, covering with the egg white, and only toss together when serving. (Calories lost: up to 575.)

ONION FLAN

SALT SUGAR FAT CHOL FIBRE

GLUTEN-FREE* WHOLEFOOD* VEGETARIAN
TOTAL CALORIES: ABOUT 2625

To reduce the **fat** level, use a different pastry base, such as yeast dough or a scone dough made with 8 oz (226 g) self-raising flour, 2 oz (50 g) butter and $\frac{1}{4}$ pint (150 ml) skim milk. Cook the onions in only $\frac{1}{2}$ oz (10 g) butter, or replace this with soft margarine or oil, adding a few spoonfuls of stock to prevent them drying out. For the filling, make a thick white sauce by pouring $\frac{1}{2}$ pint (300 ml) very hot skim milk onto a tablespoon of cornflour that has been mixed to a paste with a very little milk. Return this mixture to the saucepan and stir over gentle heat until it boils. Remove the pan from the heat and stir in one whole

eaten egg. Season to taste and ontinue with the recipe. These hanges give a low fat and **holesterol** content. (Calories ost: up to 1018.)
This dish can be cooked vithout pastry in a casserole, nd served with a decorative dge of mashed piped potato to nake it **gluten-free.**

reezing: [√] up to 3 months.

ORN ON THE COB

SALT SUGAR FAT CHOL FIBRE

LUTEN-FREE WHOLEFOOD VEGETARIAN
OTAL CALORIES: ABOUT 1950

Reducing the **fat** and **holesterol** means finding a atisfactory replacement for the utter dressing. You can simply rush the cobs with melted utter, using about 1 teaspooon er cob, then sprinkle enerously with pepper (giving ow fat and cholesterol), or lace the cooked cobs on a hot rill for a minute on either side o bring out the flavour, then erve without any dressing. Calories lost: up to 1155.)

BEETROOT WITH ORANGE

SALT SUGAR FAT CHOL FIBRE

LUTEN-FREE WHOLEFOOD VEGETARIAN
OTAL CALORIES: ABOUT 480

This recipe needs no changes to uit healthy eating guidelines. For an even more acceptably **wholefood** dish, use the no-dded-sugar marmalade vailable from health food tores.

Bake the flan in the centre of an oven pre-heated to 400°F (200°C, mark 6) for 40 minutes. When cooked, the pastry should be golden and the filling set; it will sink slightly as the flan cools.

CORN ON THE COB

Sweet corn is a favourite vegetable in America and is gaining popularity in Europe. Corn on the cob should be creamy in colour and with soft tender kernels. Serve the cobs as a separate vegetable course.

PREPARATION TIME: *10 min*
CHILLING TIME: *1 hour*
COOKING TIME: *5 min*
INGREDIENTS *(for 4):*
4 corn cobs
4–6 oz (100–175 g) butter
Salt and black pepper*
2 level teaspoons caster sugar

Pepper butter, to be served with the cobs, should be made well in advance so that it can be chilled. Stir the butter until smooth and season highly with freshly ground pepper and extra salt to taste. Shape the butter into an oblong roll and wrap it in foil or greaseproof paper. Chill in the refrigerator.

Remove the leaves and silky tassels from the cobs and put them, with the sugar, in a shallow pan holding just enough boiling water to cover them. Keep the water on the boil and cook the cobs for just 5 minutes. Drain.

Serve the cobs at once, with the butter cut into $\frac{1}{4}$ in ($\frac{1}{2}$ cm) thick slices on a separate plate. Insert special cob holders, small skewers or strong toothpicks at either end of each cob by which to hold it, and provide finger bowls.

BEETROOT WITH ORANGE

In this salad, cooked beetroot is combined with orange marmalade, fine-shred or sweet. The two flavours blend surprisingly well and suit any strong game, goose or duck.

PREPARATION TIME: *5 min*
COOKING TIME: *10 min*
INGREDIENTS *(for 4):*
1 lb (450 g) cooked beetroot
1 oz (25 g) unsalted butter
1 heaped tablespoon marmalade
Juice of half orange
GARNISH:
Slice of orange

Skin and cut the cooked beetroot into dice. Measure the butter, marmalade and orange juice into a saucepan, heat until the butter melts, then add the beetroot. Simmer gently, stirring occasionally, for about 10 minutes, until the liquid has evaporated and the beetroot is evenly glazed.

Spoon the beetroot into a hot serving dish. Cut towards the centre of a thin orange slice, twist the two halves in opposite directions and place it on the beetroot as a garnish.

RATATOUILLE

This Provençal dish, in which all the vegetables complement each other, can be served as soon as cooked but is even better if left overnight for the flavours to develop. It makes an excellent starter and is good both hot and cold.

PREPARATION TIME: *30 min*
COOKING TIME: *50 min*
INGREDIENTS *(for 6–8):*
2 large courgettes
2 large aubergines
5 large tomatoes
1 large green pepper
1 small red pepper
1 large onion
2 cloves garlic
6 tablespoons olive oil
Salt and black pepper*

Cut the stalks off the courgettes and aubergines. Wash well and cut them crossways into $\frac{1}{4}$in ($\frac{1}{2}$cm) thick slices. Put them in a colander, cover with a plate and weight this down; leave for 1 hour to press out excessive moisture. Skin the tomatoes (page 92) and chop them roughly. Wash the peppers, remove the white inner ribs and all seeds, and dice the flesh. Peel and coarsely chop the onion and garlic.

Heat the oil in a large frying pan and fry the onion and garlic for 5 minutes over low heat until transparent. Add the peppers, cook for a further 10 minutes, then add the remaining ingredients and season to taste with salt and freshly ground pepper. Cover the pan with a lid and cook the mixture over low heat for 35 minutes, stirring from time to time. Correct seasoning.

ENDIVE AND ORANGE SALAD

A slightly sharp, refreshing salad which goes well with most kinds of game, cold meats or stuffed joints. Either endive or chicory can be used: both have the slightly bitter taste that combines well with orange. The red chicory of Treviso, *radicchio rosso*, makes a vivid colour contrast with the orange. Grapefruit can also be used: the pink variety is very sweet and adds yet another touch of colour.

PREPARATION TIME: *20 min*
INGREDIENTS *(for 6):*
1 head of endive (flat or curled) or 4 heads of chicory
3 oranges
French dressing (page 85)

Remove any brown outer leaves from the endive or chicory and the root ends from the chicory. Wash and drain thoroughly, then cut the endive or chicory into thin slices, crossways. Peel the oranges with a sharp knife, removing all the white pith with the peel. Slice the oranges thinly in cross-section and remove the pips. If the oranges are large, cut each slice in two.

Mix the endive or chicory and the orange slices in a serving bowl, and pour over the French dressing (made with orange juice instead of vinegar). Toss and serve.

CUCUMBER IN SOURED CREAM

This unusual salad, in a refreshing summery dressing, goes well with both hot and cold meats. It is especially suitable with roast beef, veal or chicken.

PREPARATION TIME: *15–20 min*
CHILLING TIME: *2 hours*
INGREDIENTS *(for 4–6):*
1 large or 2 small cucumbers
$1\frac{1}{2}$ level tablespoons plain flour
$\frac{1}{2}$ level teaspoon each of salt, caster sugar and dry mustard*
2 tablespoons tarragon or white wine vinegar
2 egg yolks
4 tablespoons olive oil
5 fluid oz (150 ml) soured cream
2 tablespoons finely chopped chives

Put the flour, salt, sugar and mustard in a small, heavy-based pan with 1 tablespoon of water. Cook over low heat, stirring until the ingredients are thoroughly blended. Gradually add the vinegar and 2 tablespoons of water. Continue cooking until the mixture has thickened to a smooth sauce. Bring this quickly to the boil, then simmer for 2–3 minutes.

Remove the pan from the heat and beat the egg yolks into the sauce, one at a time. Add the oil, a few drops at a time. Chill in the refrigerator.

About an hour before serving, stir the soured cream and the chopped chives into the sauce. Return it to the refrigerator.

Wash and peel the cucumber (remove the seeds if necessary) and cut it into $\frac{1}{2}$in (1 cm) cubes. Just before serving, stir the cucumber into the soured cream.

RATATOUILLE

SALT SUGAR FAT CHOL FIBRE

GLUTEN-FREE WHOLEFOOD VEGETARIAN
TOTAL CALORIES: ABOUT 985

To give a low **fat** level, use only 2 tablespoons olive oil, of best quality, to soften the onions and garlic, adding a few tablespoons of stock and covering the pan with a lid to prevent the vegetables becoming dry. (Calories lost: up to 540.)

Freezing: ✓ up to 9 months.
Microwave: ✓

ENDIVE AND ORANGE SALAD

SALT SUGAR FAT CHOL FIBRE

GLUTEN-FREE WHOLEFOOD VEGETARIAN
TOTAL CALORIES: ABOUT 1245

To reduce the **fat** level to low, use only 3 tablespoons of French dressing (i.e. 2 of oil and 1 of orange juice), replacing the remaining oil with low-fat yogurt, or, for a slightly higher fat content, smetana. (Calories lost: up to 774.)

CUCUMBER IN SOURED CREAM

SALT SUGAR FAT CHOL FIBRE

GLUTEN-FREE* WHOLEFOOD* VEGETARIAN
TOTAL CALORIES: ABOUT 1140

To reduce the **fat** and **cholesterol** levels to low, replace the dressing as follows.

⁄lix 2 heaped tablespoons ›owdered skimmed milk with ½ ›int (300 ml) water. Put in a .quidiser with 1 tablespoon oil, small egg and 2 tablespoons ırragon or white wine vinegar. ‌lend slowly. Gradually add 1 ablespoon flour, and 1 easpoon mustard and season to aste with salt, pepper, and ugar. Continue blending until uite smooth. Pour into a aucepan and bring to boiling oint, stirring continuously. immer gently for 3–4 minutes. eave to cool and stir in ¼ pint 150 ml) smetana or low-fat ogurt 1 hour before serving. Calories lost: up to 731.)

ETTUCE, CHEESE AND RUIT PLATTER

SALT SUGAR FAT CHOL FIBRE

LUTEN-FREE WHOLEFOOD VEGETARIAN
OTAL CALORIES: ABOUT 1775

t is assumed that you have ısed fresh pineapple or rings inned in juice with no added **ugar**.
f only 2 tablespoons of French ressing are used, the dish will e low **fat** (apart from the valnuts, which could be halved n amount), and free from **holesterol**.
lternatively, a dressing of low-at yogurt mixed half and half vith lemon juice and apple uice is very good. (Calories ost: up to 1054.)

LETTUCE, CHEESE AND FRUIT PLATTER

A salad of cheese and fruit makes a light and nourishing lunch on its own. Choose seasonal fruit such as oranges and pineapple, or sliced bananas, first tossed in lemon juice

PREPARATION TIME: *10 min*
INGREDIENTS *(for 4)*:
1 small head of lettuce
Bunch watercress
2 oranges
4 pineapple rings
8 oz (225 g) plain cottage cheese
French dressing or mayonnaise (page 85)
GARNISH:
2 oz (50 g) shelled walnuts

Separate the leaves of the lettuce and cut off any coarse stems and damaged leaves; wash the leaves and dry them thoroughly on a clean cloth. Remove the lower coarse stems of the watercress, and wash the leaves. Cut a slice from the top and base of each orange before removing peel and all white pith; slice the oranges thinly across.

Arrange the lettuce in the centre of a platter with the orange slices and pineapple rings around the edge. Arrange the cottage cheese on the fruit and garnish with sprigs of watercress.

Chop the walnuts coarsely and sprinkle them over the cheese. Mayonnaise or a good French dressing may be served separately, with crusty bread and/or crispbread and butter.

SAVOURY CUCUMBER

Cucumber rarely appears cooked, but in this French recipe, stuffed cucumbers are served hot as a savoury snack.

PREPARATION TIME: *10 min*
COOKING TIME: *50 min*
INGREDIENTS *(for 6):*
3 cucumbers
6 oz (175 g) long grain rice
1 large onion
$4\frac{1}{2}$ oz (125 g) butter
8 oz (225 g) mushrooms
4 rashers lean smoked bacon
Salt and black pepper*
3 eggs
GARNISH:
Chopped parsley

Wash, but do not peel, the cucumbers. Cut each in half crossways, then cut each half in two lengthways. Scrape out the seeds with the point of a teaspoon and discard. Cook the cucumbers for 10 minutes in boiling, lightly salted water; drain through a colander and keep warm.

Cook the rice in a large pan of boiling salted water for 25–30 minutes. While the rice is cooking, peel and chop the onion, and cook over gentle heat in 2 oz (50 g) of the butter until translucent, but not brown.

Trim and thinly slice the mushrooms; add to the onions. Remove the rind and cut the bacon into narrow strips; add to the mixture in the pan and season with salt and freshly ground pepper. When the rice is cooked, drain in a sieve and rinse under cold running water. Stir it into the onion mixture, adding 2 oz (50 g) of butter. Cook over low heat, stirring occasionally, for 5–10 minutes.

Lightly beat the eggs and season with salt and pepper. Cook two or three small omelettes in the remaining butter. Roll the omelettes up and cut them into strips about $\frac{1}{2}$ in (1 cm) wide. Add these to the rice mixture.

To serve, arrange the cucumber 'boats' on a hot dish and spoon the rice mixture over them. Sprinkle with chopped parsley.

CUCUMBER WITH PRAWNS AND MUSHROOMS

Cucumber is usually served raw in salads or sandwiches, but it loses nothing of its flavour or freshness by being cooked. This quick little hors-d'oeuvre has something of the delicate taste of Chinese food.

PREPARATION TIME: *15 min*
COOKING TIME: *15 min*
INGREDIENTS *(for 4):*
1 large or 2 small cucumbers
Salt and black pepper*
4 oz (100 g) button mushrooms
$1\frac{1}{2}$ oz (40 g) butter
1 rounded teaspoon plain flour
$2\frac{1}{2}$ fluid oz (75 ml) chicken stock
$2\frac{1}{2}$ fluid oz (75 ml) single cream
Soya sauce (optional)
4 oz (100 g) shelled prawns
GARNISH:
Finely chopped chives, basil or dill
Cucumber twists

Wash the cucumber, but do not peel it. Cut it into $\frac{1}{2}$ in (1 cm) dice and cook for 3–4 minutes in boiling, lightly salted water. Rinse the cucumber in cold water and drain thoroughly in a colander. Trim the mushrooms and cut them into $\frac{1}{4}$ in ($\frac{1}{2}$ cm) thick slices.

Melt the butter in a small pan and cook the mushrooms for 2–3 minutes or until lightly browned. Add the diced cucumber and simmer, covered with a lid, for 2–3 minutes over low heat. Sprinkle in the flour and blend thoroughly; gradually add the stock and cream, stirring the mixture until smooth. Bring gently to the boil and season to taste with salt, freshly ground pepper and a few

SAVOURY CUCUMBER

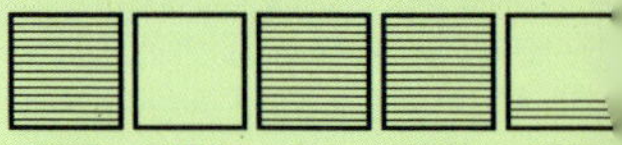

GLUTEN-FREE WHOLEFOOD*
TOTAL CALORIES: ABOUT 2490

The high **salt** level comes mainly from the bacon, if the butter used is unsalted. It can be reduced to low by replacing the bacon with diced peppers. This will make the dish **vegetarian** and also reduce the **fat** and **cholesterol**, while maintaining the colour of the dish. For low fat, instead of cooking the vegetables in butter, use 1 tablespoon of oil. Mushrooms produce liquid of their own. For a low cholesterol count, use only 1 egg. For more fibre, use brown rice, cooking in $2\frac{1}{4}$ times its volume of water so the water is all absorbed after 40–50 minutes of simmering: this retains in the rice vitamins and minerals that, using the other method, are transferred to the water and thrown away. (Calories lost: up to 970.)

Microwave: ✓

CUCUMBER WITH PRAWNS AND MUSHROOMS

GLUTEN-FREE* WHOLEFOOD*
TOTAL CALORIES: ABOUT 670

Do not use more than the few drops of soya sauce specified or the **salt** level will be high. Prawns are naturally fairly high in salt, although not compared to foods such as smoked fish. If wished, reduce the amount

sed, possibly replacing some
ʼith monkfish cubes, as this
sh has a scampi-like texture. It
lso has much less **cholesterol**
ıan prawns have.
ʼhe **fat** can be reduced to low
y cooking the mushrooms in a
an lightly brushed with oil,
mitting the butter, and
eplacing the cream with
metana or creamy milk. If this
 done, and monkfish now
sed instead of half the prawns,
ıe cholesterol will also be low.
Calories lost: up to 276.)

EARS IN TARRAGON
REAM

SALT SUGAR FAT CHOL FIBRE

LUTEN-FREE WHOLEFOOD* VEGETARIAN
TAL CALORIES: ABOUT 1570

or a low **fat** and **cholesterol**
vel, replace the cream with
uark or smetana. (Calories
ost: up to 1020.)

VALDORF SALAD

SALT SUGAR FAT CHOL FIBRE

LUTEN-FREE WHOLEFOOD* VEGETARIAN
TAL CALORIES: ABOUT 1880

Valnuts are roughly half oil,
ʼith a particularly high level of
noleic acid – an essential
utrient. However, if wished,
alve the amount used. This
ill give a low **fat** dish if you
so replace the mayonnaise
ʼith a mixture of quark with
easoning as suggested; low fat
ogurt could also be used half
nd half with smetana.
Calories lost: up to 1436.)

drops of soya sauce. Simmer for another 2–3 minutes, then stir in the prawns and heat through.

Spoon into a warmed serving dish or individual deep scallop shells. Sprinkle with the herbs and decorate with thin twists of cucumber. Serve the cucumber mixture immediately, with thinly sliced brown bread and butter, or crisp toast fingers.

PEARS IN TARRAGON CREAM

For this simple first course, choose firm, but ripe, squat pears. They are served with a classic French tarragon cream.

PREPARATION TIME: *10 min*
CHILLING TIME: *1 hour*
INGREDIENTS *(for 6):*
6 dessert pears
½ pint (300 ml) double cream
2 tablespoons tarragon vinegar
Caster sugar
Salt and black pepper*

Chill the pears in the refrigerator. Beat the cream and vinegar together until thick, but not too stiff. Season to taste with sugar, salt and freshly ground pepper. Peel and halve the pears and scoop out the centre cores with a teaspoon.

Serve the pears, rounded side up, on individual small plates and with the tarragon cream spooned over them.

WALDORF SALAD

This salad was created at the Waldorf-Astoria Hotel in New York. The tart combination of apple and celery is an excellent counter-balance to rich meats.

PREPARATION TIME: *20 min*
STANDING TIME: *30 min*
INGREDIENTS *(for 6):*
1 lb (450 g) tart red dessert apples
2 tablespoons lemon juice
1 level teaspoon caster sugar
¼ pint (150 ml) mayonnaise (page 85)
½ head celery
2 oz (50 g) shelled walnuts
1 lettuce

Wash and core the apples, slice one apple finely and dice the remainder. Dip the apple slices in a dressing of lemon juice, caster sugar and 1 tablespoon of the mayonnaise. Set aside. Toss the diced apple in the dressing and let it stand for 30 minutes.

Scrub and chop the celery and chop the walnuts. Add the celery and walnuts to the diced apple, with the rest of the mayonnaise, and mix thoroughly. Line a serving bowl with the cleaned and chilled lettuce leaves, pile the salad into the centre and garnish with the apple slices.

FASOULIA

In Greece, this regional dish of haricot beans is usually served as a vegetable course on its own. It can accompany any kind of meat and is particularly good with lamb. Preparations should begin 12 hours in advance.

PREPARATION TIME: *8 min*
COOKING TIME: *3¼ hours*
INGREDIENTS *(for 4):*
½ lb (225 g) dried haricot beans
1 large onion
¼ pint (150 ml) olive oil
2 cloves garlic
1 bay leaf
½ level teaspoon powdered thyme
1 tablespoon tomato paste
Juice of a lemon
Salt and black pepper*
GARNISH:
Coarsely chopped parsley

Soak the haricot beans in plenty of cold water for 12 hours. The following day, peel and coarsely chop the onion; fry it in the olive oil in a deep sauté pan until it takes colour. Strain the beans and add to the onion, together with the peeled and crushed garlic, the bay leaf, thyme and tomato paste. Cook over a moderate heat for 10 minutes, then add boiling water to cover the beans by about 1 in (2½ cm). Continue cooking, covered, at a gentle simmer for about 3 hours or until the beans are quite tender, but not mushy. Add the lemon juice and season to taste. Allow the beans to cool in the liquid which should have the consistency of a thick sauce.

Serve the cold beans in their liquid garnished with parsley.

NAPOLEON'S BEAN SALAD

In exile on St Helena, Napoleon was still emperor at his own table. This salad of haricot beans is said to have been a favourite of his and was served every day at lunchtime. The beans should be soaked for at least 8 hours before they are cooked.

PREPARATION TIME: *10 min*
COOKING TIME: *2–3 hours*
CHILLING TIME: *1 hour*
INGREDIENTS *(for 6):*
½ lb (225 g) dried haricot beans
1 onion
1 carrot
Bouquet garni (page 99)
Salt and black pepper*
½ cup of finely chopped parsley, chervil, tarragon, chives or spring onions
5 tablespoons olive oil
1 tablespoon tarragon vinegar
1 rounded teaspoon prepared French mustard
½ level teaspoon caster sugar

Soak the beans in a bowl of water for 8 hours or overnight. Drain the beans and put them in a large pan or casserole. Peel and quarter the onion and carrot, and add them, with the bouquet garni and plenty of black pepper, to the beans. Pour over enough water to cover the beans by ½ in (1 cm). Put a lid on the pan and cook in the centre of a pre-heated oven, at 275°–300°F (140°–160°C, mark 1–2) for 3 hours, or on top of the stove at simmering point, for 2 hours. If necessary, top up with water during cooking so that the beans do not dry out.

Season the cooked beans to taste with salt and cook for another 5 minutes. Drain the beans through a colander, remove the onion, carrot and bouquet garni, and put the beans in a large serving bowl. Add the chopped herbs, oil, vinegar, mustard and sugar to the beans. Stir to blend the ingredients thoroughly and leave to chill in the refrigerator for about 1 hour.

LETTUCE AND CELERY SALAD

Most rich meat dishes, especially those with sweet stuffings, are better accompanied by a side salad than by a vegetable dish.

PREPARATION TIME: *10 min*
INGREDIENTS *(for 4–6):*
4 lettuces
4 celery sticks
DRESSING:
1 level teaspoon Dijon mustard
*½ level teaspoon salt**
1 level teaspoon caster sugar
¼ pint (150 ml) single cream
¼ pint (150 ml) olive oil
3 tablespoons tarragon vinegar
GARNISH:
Celery leaves

Strip the outer leaves off the lettuce and cut each into four. Trim off roots and coarse leaves from the celery, scrub and chop the sticks coarsely. Place these ingredients in a serving bowl.

To make the dressing, blend the mustard, salt and sugar in a mixing bowl; stir in the cream. Beat in the olive oil, drop by drop, and when all the oil is absorbed, gradually beat in the vinegar until the dressing has the consistency of thick cream. Pour the dressing over the celery and lettuce, toss and serve garnished with a few celery leaves.

FASOULIA

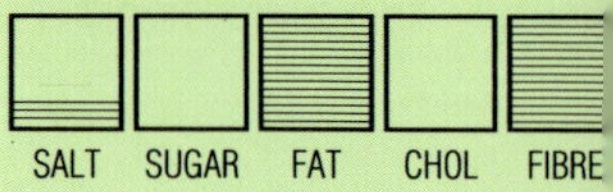

GLUTEN-FREE WHOLEFOOD VEGETARIA
TOTAL CALORIES: ABOUT 2000

Boil haricot beans rapidly for 10 minutes before covering them and continuing the cooking. This ensures that any poisonous chemicals are destroyed.
Reduce the **fat** level to low by cooking the onion in a pan lightly brushed with oil. Keep the pan covered so that the onion cooks by a mixture of frying and steaming. If wished add a little more good-quality oil at the end to give the characteristic Mediterranean flavour. (Calories lost: up to 1079.)

NAPOLEON'S BEAN SALAD

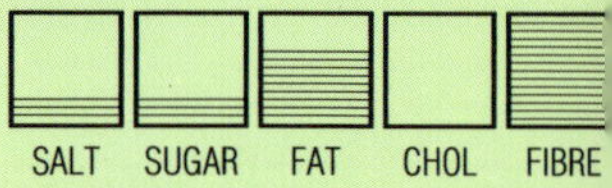

GLUTEN-FREE WHOLEFOOD* VEGETARIA
TOTAL CALORIES: ABOUT 1325

Boil haricot beans rapidly for 10 minutes before covering them and continuing the cooking. This ensures that any poisonous chemicals are destroyed.
For a low **fat** dish, reduce the amount of oil to 2 tablespoons. (Calories lost: up to 405.)

Pressure cooker: ✓ for the beans.

ETTUCE AND CELERY ALAD

SALT	SUGAR	FAT	CHOL	FIBRE

LUTEN-FREE* WHOLEFOOD* VEGETARIAN
OTAL CALORIES: ABOUT 1800

or a low **fat** dish, the dressing an be changed to use only 1 ablespoon oil, with ¼ pint 150 ml) low-fat yogurt, ultured buttermilk or a nixture of either of these with metana. (Calories lost: up to 474.)

Check that the mustard is **luten-free**.

SPINACH RAMEKINS

This unusual appetiser is a creamy pâté of spinach, sardines and eggs. Serve it with grissini (Italian bread sticks) or toast.

PREPARATION TIME: *10–15 min*
CHILLING TIME: *½–1 hour*
INGREDIENTS *(for 4):*
1 lb (450 g) spinach
1 onion
½ level teaspoon dried tarragon
1–2 tablespoons finely chopped parsley
1 hardboiled egg
4 sardines
2 tablespoons double cream
Salt and black pepper*
GARNISH:
1 hardboiled egg
4 anchovy fillets

Pull the spinach leaves off the stalks and wash in several lots of cold water to remove all traces of soil. Peel and finely chop the onion. Put the wet spinach in a large saucepan with the onion, tarragon and parsley; cover with a lid. Cook over low heat for 7–10 minutes, or until softened, then drain thoroughly.

Chop one hardboiled egg and the boned sardines and blend with the spinach. Rub the mixture through a coarse sieve, or liquidise it to a purée. Stir in the cream and season to taste with salt and freshly ground pepper. Spoon the creamed spinach into individual ramekins or small serving dishes and chill in a refrigerator until set.

For the garnish, separate the white and yolk of the hardboiled egg; chop the white finely and sieve the yolk. Decorate each ramekin with alternate rows of white and yolk. Split the anchovy fillets in half and lay them on top in a criss-cross pattern.

PEPPER, ANCHOVY AND TOMATO SALAD

This unusual and tasty salad goes perfectly with grilled veal chops and with most chicken dishes. It can also be served on its own as a light beginning to a substantial meal.

PREPARATION TIME: *35 min*
CHILLING TIME: *30 min*
INGREDIENTS *(for 4):*
2 large sweet red peppers
3 large tomatoes
2 small tins anchovy fillets
1 small clove garlic
3–4 tablespoons olive oil
Juice of half lemon
Salt and black pepper*

Put the peppers under a hot grill, turning them frequently until the skins are charred and black all over. The black outer skin then rubs off easily under cold running water. Remove the stalk ends and seeds from the peppers and cut out any white pith. Cut the flesh into wide strips with scissors. Skin the tomatoes (page 92), cut them into slices and remove the seeds. Drain the anchovy fillets and rinse them in cold water to remove excess oil and salt; ease them carefully apart.

Arrange the pepper strips on a flat serving dish with the sliced tomatoes, and lay the anchovy fillets on top in a lattice pattern.

Peel and crush the garlic and mix with the oil. Pour this dressing over the salad and sprinkle with lemon juice, salt and very little freshly ground pepper. Chill for at least 30 minutes before serving.

SPINACH RAMEKINS

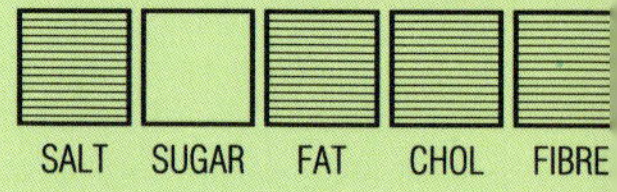

GLUTEN-FREE WHOLEFOOD
TOTAL CALORIES: ABOUT 600

The high level of **salt** comes from the anchovy fillets plus th tinned sardines. To reduce the level to low, omit the anchovie (garnish with strips of pepper instead) and use only 2 sardine The **fat** and **cholesterol** can be reduced to moderate, despite the natural oils of sardines, by the following steps: drain sardines tinned in oil thoroughly, replace the cream with quark or smetana, and omit the egg used for garnish, replacing with egg white only or with finely diced red pepper (Calories lost: up to 177.)

Food Processor: √
Freezing: √ up to 3 months.
Microwave: √

PEPPER, ANCHOVY AND TOMATO SALAD

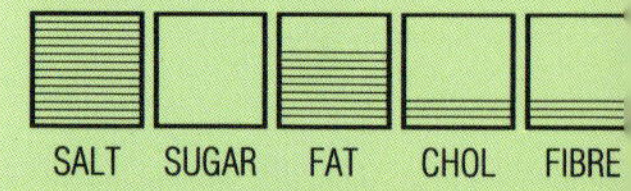

GLUTEN-FREE WHOLEFOOD
TOTAL CALORIES: ABOUT 750

Anchovies are saturated in **salt** even after rinsing in water. For a low salt level, replace the anchovies with 6 oz (175 g) monkfish, lightly poached in stock for 6–8 minutes, then cut into cubes or strips.
To reduce **fat** level to low, simply use only 1 or 1½ tablespoons oil, adding some low-fat yogurt if more bulk is wanted for the dressing. (Calories lost: up to 405.)

'EPERONATA

SALT SUGAR FAT CHOL FIBRE

.UTEN-FREE WHOLEFOOD* VEGETARIAN
)TAL CALORIES: ABOUT 650

'o reduce the **fat** level to low, ɔok the onion and peppers in ınly 2 teaspoons butter (about oz, 10 g) or the same amount f oil, covering the pan so that ıe juice from the vegetables ıoistens the dish without vaporating. (Calories lost: up ɔ 381.)

'reezing: ✓ up to 3 months.

ficrowave: ✓

:ELERIAC SALAD WITH 'ARMA HAM

SALT SUGAR FAT CHOL FIBRE

LUTEN-FREE WHOLEFOOD
)TAL CALORIES: ABOUT 865

'he **salt** comes almost entirely :om the ham, and even halving ıe amount will still leave the :vel high. If wished, keep very mall portions, say 1 oz (25 g) er person (still moderately igh) and complete the salad ,ith slices of apple tossed in range juice, or cubes of melon. f the fat from the ham is not aten, most of the **fat** comes :om the mayonnaise, which is 0% oil. To avoid this, replace : with quark or smetana, ıinning with a little lemon ıice if necessary. The fat level ,ill then be low but the **holesterol** level still remains igh, due to the ham. (Calories ɔst: up to 429.)

PEPERONATA

This spicy casserole of sweet peppers and tomatoes is of Italian origin. It is served hot with grilled meat and fish, or cold as a side salad or a starter.

PREPARATION TIME: *10 min*
COOKING TIME: *30–35 min*
INGREDIENTS *(for 4)*:
4 large red or green peppers
1 onion
8 large tomatoes
1 clove garlic
Salt and black pepper*
1 oz (25 g) unsalted butter
2 tablespoons olive oil
2 level teaspoons caster sugar (optional)

Peel and finely chop the onion. Remove the stalks and wash the peppers; cut them in half lengthways and remove the inner ribs and the seeds. Cut the peppers into narrow strips. Skin the tomatoes (page 92) and chop them coarsely. Peel the garlic and mash it to a paste with a little salt.

Heat the butter and oil in a heavy-based pan; add the onion and peppers. Cover the pan with a lid and fry the vegetables gently until soft, but not brown. Add the tomatoes and garlic and season to taste with freshly ground pepper and sugar. Put the lid back on the pan and continue cooking over very low heat, stirring occasionally, for 25–30 minutes. The mixture should now be soft, and the juices from the tomatoes should have evaporated. Correct seasoning if necessary.

Spoon the mixture into a serving dish and serve hot or cold.

CELERIAC SALAD WITH PARMA HAM

The large celery root – or celeriac – is becoming a popular vegetable in Britain. It can also be served raw in a salad, with Parma ham or thinly sliced salami.

PREPARATION TIME: *10–15 min*
COOKING TIME: *2–3 min*
INGREDIENTS *(for 4)*:
1 large celeriac
2–3 rounded tablespoons mayonnaise (page 85)
¼ teaspoon French mustard
12 slices Parma ham

Peel the celeriac. Cut it into narrow slices and then into matchstick-thin pieces. Add to a pan of boiling salted water and blanch for 2–3 minutes; drain in a colander and allow to cool. Blend together the mayonnaise and French mustard and toss the celeriac in this dressing.

Arrange the Parma ham on individual plates, allowing three thin slices per person. Divide the salad between the portions.

TOMATO SALAD

Tomatoes can make a refreshing starter to a meal, or they can be served as a side dish with cold meats.

PREPARATION TIME: *20 min*
CHILLING TIME: *1 hour*
INGREDIENTS *(for 6):*
12 tomatoes
2 level teaspoons caster sugar
Salt and black pepper*
4 tablespoons olive or corn oil
4 teaspoons white wine vinegar
1 level tablespoon chopped chives or tarragon

Skin and thinly slice the tomatoes (page 92) and place them in a shallow serving dish. Sprinkle over the sugar, and season to taste with salt and freshly ground pepper.

Mix the oil and vinegar together, and sprinkle over the tomatoes. Add chopped chives or tarragon and leave the salad to chill in the refrigerator for at least 1 hour before serving. Turn the tomato slices once or twice.

MUSHROOM SALAD

Mushrooms should be used as soon as possible after gathering. They tend to go limp when exposed to the air and should on no account be stored in the refrigerator.

PREPARATION TIME: *15 min*
STANDING TIME: *1 hour*
INGREDIENTS *(for 4–6):*
1 lb (450 g) large mushrooms
Salt and black pepper*
2 teaspoons Worcestershire sauce
1 tablespoon soya sauce

Wash and trim the mushrooms, and slice them as thinly as possible into a deep serving dish. Season to taste with salt and freshly ground pepper, and sprinkle over the Worcestershire and soya sauces. Mix the salad well and set aside for about 1 hour, turning the mushroom slices from time to time in the dressing.

The mushrooms will have made quite a lot of juice by the time they are ready for serving; this is an essential part of the dressing and should not be drained off.

COURGETTE AND CHIVES SALAD

Baby marrows, known as courgettes or zucchini, are very popular as a cooked vegetable. They are also suitable for a fresh chilled salad to serve with cold meat and poultry.

PREPARATION TIME: *10 min*
COOKING TIME: *5 min*
CHILLING TIME: *1 hour*
INGREDIENTS *(for 4):*
$\frac{3}{4}$ lb (350 g) courgettes
1 tablespoon olive or corn oil
Juice of half lemon
Salt and black pepper*
1 heaped tablespoon chopped chives.

Wash the courgettes thoroughly and top and tail them. Bring a large pan of lightly salted water to the boil, drop in the courgettes and boil for 5 minutes to soften them slightly and reduce the bitterness of the skin. Drain the courgettes immediately in a colander and rinse in cold water.

Cut the drained courgettes crossways into $\frac{1}{2}$ in (1 cm) thick slices and put them in a shallow serving dish. Make a dressing from the oil and lemon juice, season with salt and freshly ground pepper and pour over the courgettes. Add the chopped chives and blend thoroughly before chilling the salad.

SALAD ELONA

This unusual salad of cucumber and strawberries is an ideal side dish to serve with cold chicken and turkey, or with delicately flavoured fish such as salmon and turbot.

PREPARATION TIME: *15 min*
CHILLING TIME: *1 hour*
INGREDIENTS *(for 4–6):*
1 small cucumber
12 large strawberries
Salt and black pepper*
1–2 tablespoons dry white wine or white wine vinegar

Peel the cucumber and slice it thinly. Wash and hull the strawberries, drain them in a colander and then cut them into thin, even slices. Arrange the slices in a decorative pattern in a shallow serving dish – an outer circle of cucumber, slightly overlapped by a circle of strawberry, then more cucumber, finishing with a centre of strawberry slices. Season lightly with salt and freshly ground pepper. Sprinkle the wine or vinegar over the salad and chill in the refrigerator before serving.

TOMATO SALAD

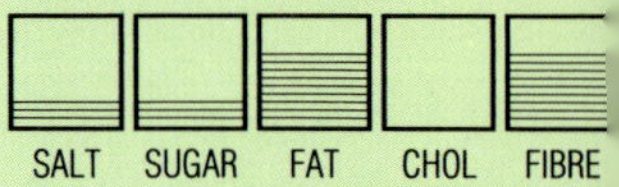

GLUTEN-FREE WHOLEFOOD* VEGETARIA
TOTAL CALORIES: ABOUT 665

To reduce the **fat** level to low, use only 1–2 tablespoons good quality oil for flavour, mixed with the same amount of low-fa yogurt, smetana or quark. (Calories lost: up to 250.)

MUSHROOM SALAD

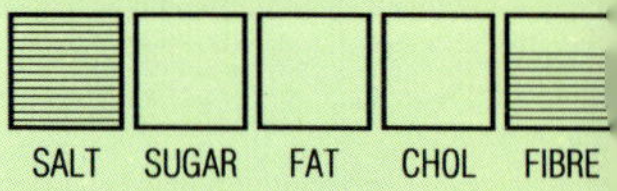

GLUTEN-FREE WHOLEFOOD VEGETARIAN
TOTAL CALORIES: ABOUT 70

To reduce the **salt** level to low, replace the soya sauce with 2–3 tablespoons of lemon juice, adding a very little honey to it first if you like to reduce the tartness.
For a **gluten-free** dressing, make sure the soya sauce contains no gluten. Many makes do, but the Japanese equivalent, tamari, should not contain any wheat derivatives. Alternatively, replace the soya sauce as suggested above.

COURGETTE AND CHIVES SALAD

SALT SUGAR FAT CHOL FIBRE

GLUTEN-FREE WHOLEFOOD VEGETARIAN
TOTAL CALORIES: ABOUT 185

The **salt** level is low assuming that you have not salted the water for cooking the courgettes.
This recipe needs no changes to fit healthy eating guidelines. However, the courgettes may retain more nutrients and flavour if steamed or cooked in ½ in (1 cm) stock or water, tightly covered, rather than being boiled.

SALAD ELONA

SALT SUGAR FAT CHOL FIBRE

GLUTEN-FREE WHOLEFOOD VEGETARIAN
TOTAL CALORIES: ABOUT 100

This dish needs no changes at all to fit healthy eating guidelines. Strawberries, like other soft fruit, are higher in fibre than many salad vegetables.

IMAM BAYILDI

This Turkish dish takes its name from the Imam, or Muslim holy man. He is said to have swooned with pleasure – or from overeating – after being served this aubergine dish.

PREPARATION TIME: *30 min*
COOKING TIME: *40 min*
INGREDIENTS *(for 6):*
3 large aubergines
Salt and black pepper*
Olive oil
3 large onions
12 oz (350 g) tomatoes
1 clove garlic
$\frac{1}{2}$ level teaspoon ground cinnamon
1 level teaspoon caster sugar
1 level tablespoon chopped parsley
1 heaped tablespoon finely chopped pine kernels (optional)

Cut the leaf bases from the aubergines, wipe them and put them in a large saucepan. Add boiling water and cover with a lid; cook the aubergines for 10 minutes. Drain the aubergines, plunge them into cold water and leave for 5 minutes. Cut them in half lengthways and scoop out most of the flesh, leaving a $\frac{1}{2}$ in (1 cm) thick shell. Set aside the scooped-out flesh. Arrange the shells in a buttered ovenproof dish and sprinkle them with a little salt and freshly ground pepper. Pour 4 teaspoons of olive oil in each shell and cook the aubergines, uncovered, in the centre of an oven pre-heated to 350°F (180°C, mark 4) for 30 minutes.

While the aubergine shells are cooking, peel and finely chop the onions; skin the tomatoes (page 92) and chop them. Peel and crush the garlic. Heat two tablespoons of oil in a frying pan, add the onions and garlic and fry gently for 5 minutes, then add the tomatoes, cinnamon, sugar and parsley; season to taste with salt and pepper. Continue simmering this mixture until the liquid has reduced by half, after about 20 minutes. Chop the aubergine flesh and add to the frying pan, with the chopped pine kernels (if used), and cook for a further 10 minutes.

Remove the aubergine shells from the oven, stuff them with the tomato mixture and serve hot or cold, on its own, or with roast and grilled meat.

IMAM BAYILDI

SALT SUGAR FAT CHOL FIBRE

GLUTEN-FREE WHOLEFOOD* VEGETARIA
TOTAL CALORIES: ABOUT 850

To reduce the **fat** content to low, omit the olive oil added to each shell. Cook the onions and garlic in a heavy-based pan brushed lightly with oil. (Calories lost: up to 404.)

Freezing: √ up to 2 months.

AUBERGINES WITH HAM

SALT SUGAR FAT CHOL FIBRE

GLUTEN-FREE WHOLEFOOD
TOTAL CALORIES: ABOUT 2715

The high **salt** level is due to the ham. If only half the amount is used, the level will be moderate To reduce the overall **fat** to low choose lean ham, and do not fry the aubergine shells. Brush them lightly with oil and grill on either side for about 4–6 minutes or until tender. Cook the aubergine flesh in a pan lightly brushed with oil, using the same method for the ham. Make the sauce without adding extra fat, although a teaspoonful or two of butter added to the pan at this stage could be allowed. Use skim milk. Do not dot the dish with butter, but cover it with foil for a few minutes to keep moist before uncovering to brown. This gives low fat and, if half the quantity of ham is used, fairly low **cholesterol**. (Calories lost: up to 1545.)

Freezing: √ up to 1 month.

RAISED CELERY

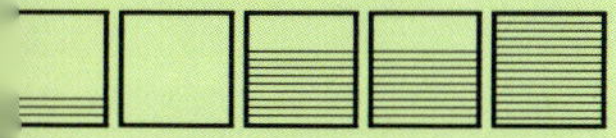

LUTEN-FREE* WHOLEFOOD*
OTAL CALORIES: ABOUT 550

'o give a low **fat** and **holesterol** content, add no ıore than a level teaspoon of utter per person in the form of eurre manié. Alternatively, eplace this thickening method vith 2 teaspoons of arrowroot, aked to a smooth paste with a ttle cold water, then blended ıto the mixture for the last few ninutes of cooking. (Calories ost: up to 253.) This also ıakes the recipe **gluten-free**. 'or a **vegetarian** dish, ubstitute water or vegetable tock for the chicken stock.

'reezing: ☑ up to 6 months.

Aicrowave: ☑

AKED CABBAGE

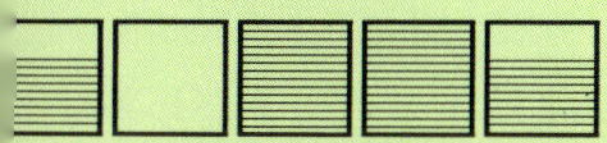

LUTEN-FREE* WHOLEFOOD* VEGETARIAN
OTAL CALORIES: ABOUT 1490

'or a low **salt** level, use nsalted nuts and only 2 oz 50 g) cheese.
'or low **fat** and **cholesterol** evels, make the sauce by the lending method (page 84), mitting the butter. Use skim nilk and only half the amount f peanuts and cheese. (Calories ost: up to 763.)
Gluten-free rice flour can be sed to make the sauce.

'reezing: ☑ up to 2 months.

Aicrowave: ☑

AUBERGINES WITH HAM

For this hot lunch or supper dish, the aubergines are filled with a ham stuffing.

PREPARATION TIME: *25 min*
COOKING TIME: *20 min*
INGREDIENTS *(for 4):*
4 aubergines
6 oz (175 g) ham, in ¼ in (½ cm) thick slices
¼ pint (150 ml) olive oil
2 oz (50 g) unsalted butter
1 level tablespoon plain flour
½ pint (300 ml) milk
Salt and black pepper*
Juice of half lemon
3–4 oz (75–100 g) dry breadcrumbs

Remove the stalk ends from the aubergines and wipe them with a damp cloth. Cut each fruit in half lengthways with a sharp knife, and carefully scoop out the flesh without breaking the skin. Finely dice the aubergine flesh and the ham.

Heat the oil in a heavy-based pan over moderate heat and fry the aubergine shells until brown, turning them over with a fish slice. Remove and drain on crumpled kitchen paper. Cook the diced aubergine flesh in the oil in the pan and, when softened and lightly browned, remove from the pan and drain. Melt half the butter in another pan and cook the ham until brown.

Sprinkle the flour into the pan in which the aubergine was cooked and blend until the oil is absorbed. Gradually add enough milk to make a thick white sauce (page 84), stirring all the time. Mix in the cooked ham and aubergine; add lemon juice and season to taste.

Spoon this mixture into the aubergine shells and set them in a buttered baking dish. Sprinkle breadcrumbs over the stuffing and dot with the remaining butter. Bake near the top of the oven, pre-heated to 400°F (200°C, mark 6) until brown. Serve at once.

BRAISED CELERY

This can be made ahead of time: if you do this, cook it for only 30 minutes and reheat gently when needed for about 10 minutes.

PREPARATION TIME: *20 min*
COOKING TIME: *40 min*
INGREDIENTS *(for 12):*
6 heads of celery
1 Spanish onion
6 small carrots
½ pint (300 ml) chicken stock
Salt and black pepper*
Beurre manié (page 84)
Parsley

Peel the onion, scrape the carrots, and slice them thinly. Trim the roots off the celery and remove any damaged stalks; scrub thoroughly, then cut each celery in half lengthways, and remove the green leafy tops. Blanch the celery for 10 minutes in boiling water, drain carefully in a colander, and put in a large fireproof dish. Cover with the thinly sliced onion and carrots; pour over the stock and season to taste.

Cover the pan with a lid or foil and simmer the celery over low heat, until tender, after about 40 minutes. About 5 minutes before the end of cooking time, add knobs of beurre manié to thicken the stock as desired. Serve the celery sprinkled with finely chopped parsley.

BAKED CABBAGE

Firm white winter cabbage is one of the least expensive vegetables. Baked in a cheese sauce, it goes well with sausages and bacon.

PREPARATION TIME: *30 min*
COOKING TIME: *15 min*
INGREDIENTS *(for 6):*
1½ lb (700 g) white cabbage
2 oz (50 g) butter
2 oz (50 g) plain flour
¼ pint (150 ml) milk
Salt and black pepper*
Ground mace or nutmeg
2 oz (50 g) salted chopped peanuts
2–4 oz (50–100 g) grated Cheddar cheese

Discard any damaged outer leaves and cut the cabbage into quarters. Cut out the centre stalk and shred the cabbage finely.

Heat ½ in (1 cm) of water in a large heavy-based saucepan and add 1 teaspoon of salt. Put in the washed cabbage, a handful at a time, seasoning each layer with freshly ground black pepper.

Cover the pan with a lid and cook over low heat for about 10 minutes, or until the cabbage is cooked, but still crisp.

Meanwhile, make a thick white sauce (page 84). Season to taste.

Butter an ovenproof dish lightly and arrange a layer of cabbage over the base. Cover with some of the sauce and sprinkle with nuts and cheese. Fill the dish with layers of cabbage, sauce, nuts and cheese, finishing with cheese. Bake in the centre of an oven pre-heated to 425°F (220°C, mark 7) for 15 minutes, or until the cheese is golden brown.

Serve the cabbage at once.

CALABRESE WITH POULETTE SAUCE

Green broccoli, or calabrese, is also known as Cape broccoli. In this recipe, it is served with a classic French vegetable sauce whose creamy-white colour contrasts well with the curds.

PREPARATION TIME: *10 min*
COOKING TIME: *30 min*
INGREDIENTS *(for 4–6):*
2 lb (900 g) calabrese (green broccoli)
Salt and black pepper*
2 oz (50 g) butter
1 level tablespoon plain flour
1 egg yolk
Juice of half lemon
2 tablespoons double cream

Trim the tough stalk and any leaves off the broccoli head or heads. Wash thoroughly in cold water. Put the broccoli in a large pan of boiling salted water. Cover the pan with a lid and simmer over low heat for about 15 minutes or until just tender. Lift the broccoli carefully into a colander to drain; cover it with a dry cloth to keep it warm and set the liquid aside.

Melt the butter in a small saucepan, then take the pan off the heat. Stir in the flour to make a roux (page 84), and gradually blend in ½ pint (300 ml) of the broccoli liquid. Bring this sauce to the boil over low heat and simmer for about 10 minutes. Beat the egg yolk with 2 teaspoons of lemon juice and 2 tablespoons of the hot sauce. Remove the sauce from the heat and blend in the egg mixture.

Stir in the cream. Keep the sauce warm, but do not allow it to boil or the egg and cream will curdle. Season to taste with salt, freshly ground pepper and more lemon juice. Put the broccoli in a warm deep serving dish and pour over the sauce.

BAKED CAULIFLOWER CHEESE

In this dish the strong, smooth flavour of Gruyère cheese contrasts well with crisp cauliflower. The more usual Cheddar, perhaps mixed with a little Parmesan, can replace it but is less subtle. The Gruyère is particularly good in this rich, egg-based sauce, much more of a party piece than the usual béchamel. It can be served with grilled or roasted meats.

PREPARATION TIME: *20 min*
COOKING TIME: *50 min*
INGREDIENTS *(for 6):*
1 large cauliflower
1 onion
2 oz (50 g) unsalted butter
3 oz (75 g) fresh breadcrumbs
½ pint (300 ml) milk
2 oz (50 g) grated Gruyère cheese
Salt and black pepper*
Ground nutmeg
5 beaten eggs

Cut away the coarse outer leaves from the cauliflower and break off the florets. Bring a large pan of lightly salted water to the boil. Add the florets, cover the pan with a lid, and boil gently for 5–8 minutes. Drain.

Meanwhile, finely chop the onion. Melt half the butter and fry the onion for 10 minutes. Butter the inside of a 3½ pint (2 litre) baking dish and line it with 1 oz (25 g) of breadcrumbs.

In a saucepan, bring the milk to the boil and add the Gruyère and the remaining butter. Season to taste with salt, pepper and a little nutmeg. Stir in the remaining breadcrumbs and the fried onion. Remove from the heat and blend in the beaten eggs. Fold the

CALABRESE WITH POULETTE SAUCE

SALT SUGAR FAT CHOL FIBRE

GLUTEN-FREE* WHOLEFOOD* VEGETARIA
TOTAL CALORIES: ABOUT 830

To reduce the **fat** and **cholesterol** levels to low, mak the sauce with only 1 oz (25 g) butter and half the flour. Mix the remaining flour to a smoot paste with a very little cold water, and add to the roux afte you have worked in some of th liquid. Replace the double cream with single cream, sour cream, smetana or quark. (Calories lost: up to 286.)

Microwave: ☑ for the broccoli.

BAKED CAULIFLOWER CHEESE

SALT SUGAR FAT CHOL FIBRE

GLUTEN-FREE* WHOLEFOOD* VEGETARIA
TOTAL CALORIES: ABOUT 1360

The **salt** comes mainly from th breadcrumbs and cheese, so th only way of significantly reducing it is to use less cheese and breadcrumbs made from bread with little or no added sa The **fat** level can be reduced tc medium by frying the onion in a pan lightly brushed with oil, omitting the butter. Keep the pan covered, but if the onion gets dry, add a spoonful or twc of stock or water. Use skim milk, and only 3 eggs. (Calorie lost: up to 511.) **Cholesterol** content will also be medium.

Microwave: ☑ for the cauliflower.

:AULIFLOWER WITH ıLMONDS

SALT SUGAR FAT CHOL FIBRE

.UTEN-FREE WHOLEFOOD VEGETARIAN
)TAL CALORIES: ABOUT 780

'o reduce the **fat** level to low, ınd eliminate **cholesterol**, toast ıe almonds on a baking tray .ghtly brushed with oil under a ıedium grill, omitting the ·utter. (Calories lost: up to 85.)
'he **salt** level is low assuming ıat the cauliflower is cooked ·ithout salt, and that unsalted ·utter is used.

Aicrowave: ✓ for the auliflower.

:AULIFLOWER 'OLONAISE

SALT SUGAR FAT CHOL FIBRE

LUTEN-FREE* WHOLEFOOD* VEGETARIAN
)TAL CALORIES: ABOUT 800

'he low **salt** level assumes that ou cook the cauliflower in nsalted water, use unsalted utter and, if possible, low-salt read for the crumbs. If you annot find low-salt bread, the alt level will be low to ıedium, given that eggs also rovide some sodium.
f wished, use only 1 egg. This ·ill reduce the **fat** and **holesterol** levels to low if you lso use only half the amount of utter to crisp the crumbs. Calories lost: up to 275.)

Aicrowave: ✓ for the auliflower.

cauliflower into the sauce and spoon the mixture into the baking dish.

Bake on the lower shelf of an oven pre-heated to 325°F (170°C, mark 3) for 50 minutes or until firm.

CAULIFLOWER WITH ALMONDS

Crisp roasted almonds complement the delicate flavour and texture of lightly cooked cauliflower, making this an ideal accompaniment for a fish or meat dish in a rich sauce.

PREPARATION TIME: *10 min*
COOKING TIME: *12 min*
INGREDIENTS *(for 4)*:
1 large white cauliflower
*Salt**
2 oz (50 g) clarified butter (page 95)
2 oz (50 g) flaked almonds

Dissolve two tablespoons of salt in a large bowl of cold water. Cut away the coarse outer leaves from the cauliflower and break the individual florets from the central stem, leaving a short stalk on each. Drop the florets in the salted water, together with the inner pale green leaves.

Bring a large pan of salted water to the boil; cook the drained cauliflower, covered, over low heat for 5–8 minutes. Drain through a colander.

Meanwhile, fry the almonds in the clarified butter over low heat until deep brown. Put the cauliflower in a dish and spoon over the almonds and butter.

CAULIFLOWER POLONAISE

Plainly cooked cauliflower is an excellent accompaniment to meat or poultry served in a rich sauce. The attractive garnish makes the dish particularly appetising.

PREPARATION TIME: *15 min*
COOKING TIME: *20 min*
INGREDIENTS *(for 4–6)*:
1 cauliflower
2 oz (50 g) butter
2 hardboiled eggs
2 oz (50 g) dried breadcrumbs
2 level tablespoons chopped parsley
Salt and black pepper*
Lemon juice

Cut off the tough outer leaves and thick stalk base of the cauliflower. Wash thoroughly. Cook the cauliflower whole in boiling salted water for 10–15 minutes or until just tender. Drain in a colander and cover with a dry cloth to keep warm.

Meanwhile, shell the eggs, remove the yolks and rub them through a sieve; chop the whites finely with a stainless steel knife. Melt the butter in a small pan and fry the breadcrumbs until crisp. Remove the pan from the heat, stir in the parsley and season with salt, freshly ground pepper and lemon juice.

Place the cauliflower in a warm serving dish, sprinkle with the roasted breadcrumbs, and garnish with the egg yolks and whites in an attractive pattern.

TURKISH FRIED CARROTS

In Turkey, cold or warm yogurt is often used to dress vegetables and salads. Young or maincrop carrots are equally suitable for this dish, which goes well with lamb.

PREPARATION TIME: *15 min*
COOKING TIME: *20 min*
INGREDIENTS *(for 4):*
1 lb (450 g) carrots
Salt and black pepper*
1 level tablespoon seasoned flour (p. 100)
2 tablespoons olive oil
½ pint (300 ml) natural yogurt
GARNISH:
1 level tablespoon chopped mint or 1 level teaspoon caraway seeds

Peel or scrape the carrots and wash them. Cut them across into ¼ in (½ cm) thick slices. Bring a pan of salted water to the boil and cook the carrots for about 10 minutes or until nearly tender. Drain in a colander, then spread the carrots on absorbent paper so as to dry thoroughly.

Toss the carrots in seasoned flour, shaking off any surplus. Heat the oil in a heavy-based pan and fry the carrots over moderate heat until golden brown. Season to taste with salt and freshly ground pepper. Put the yogurt in a separate pan over low heat, and let it warm through. Do not let it reach boiling point or it will curdle.

Spoon the carrots into a hot serving dish, pour over the yogurt, and sprinkle with mint or caraway seeds.

CARROTS PAYSANNE

In cookery, *paysanne* refers to vegetables cooked in butter and used to garnish meat and poultry. Young carrots make a good accompaniment to grilled meat.

PREPARATION TIME: *15 min*
COOKING TIME: *30 min*
INGREDIENTS *(for 4–6):*
1 lb (450 g) small carrots
1 large onion
2 rashers lean bacon
2½ oz (65 g) unsalted butter
¼–½ pint (150–300 ml) chicken stock or water
1 teaspoon caster sugar
4 tablespoons double cream
*Salt**
GARNISH:
Finely chopped parsley

Trim the tops and roots from the carrots, scrape them and wash thoroughly. Blanch the carrots for 5 minutes in boiling salted water, then drain in a colander.

Peel and thinly slice the onion. Cut off the rinds and dice the bacon. Melt the butter in a wide shallow pan over low heat, and cook the onion and bacon until just soft and beginning to colour.

Add the carrots to the bacon and onion, and pour over enough stock or water to barely cover the vegetables. Cover the pan with a lid and cook over moderate heat until the carrots are tender. Lift out the carrots and keep them hot.

Boil the liquid over high heat until it has reduced to a few tablespoons. Add the sugar and cream, and season to taste with salt. Simmer the liquid, uncovered, until the sauce has thickened slightly.

Pour the cream sauce over the carrots and sprinkle with parsley.

TURKISH FRIED CARROTS

SALT SUGAR FAT CHOL FIBRE

GLUTEN-FREE* WHOLEFOOD* VEGETARIA
TOTAL CALORIES: ABOUT 580

Microwave: √ for the carrots.

CARROTS PAYSANNE

SALT SUGAR FAT CHOL FIBRE

GLUTEN-FREE WHOLEFOOD
TOTAL CALORIES: ABOUT 1120

The high **salt** level comes almost entirely from the bacon. To reduce it to low, use only ½ oz (10–15 g) bacon. If, as well, the butter is omitted and the onion is cooked in a heavy pan brushed lightly with oil together with the bacon, and the double cream replaced with sour cream, smetana or low-fat yogurt, the dish will have a low fat and **cholesterol** level. (Calories lost: up to 745.)

GLAZED CARROTS

SALT SUGAR FAT CHOL FIBRE

GLUTEN-FREE WHOLEFOOD VEGETARIAN
TOTAL CALORIES: ABOUT 310

To avoid raising the **salt** level, do not sprinkle the carrots with salt before serving. If wished, add a generous amount of extra parsley and pepper instead.

Microwave: √

RAGOÛT OF LETTUCE AND PEAS

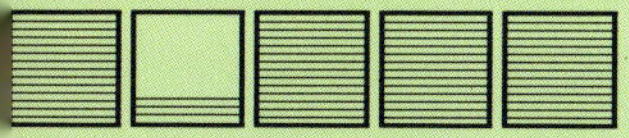

SALT SUGAR FAT CHOL FIBRE

GLUTEN-FREE* WHOLEFOOD*
TOTAL CALORIES: ABOUT 1900

The **salt** level is high because of the ham. To reduce the level to low, use not more than 2 oz (50 g). If wished, some more onions can be added to the dish to restore the bulk.
The high **fat** level comes mainly from the butter, if lean ham is used, and from the fried bread garnish. For low fat, toss the vegetables in only 1 oz (25 g) butter, or a mixture of butter and oil. Garnish the dish with spring onion, cut in long slivers, or with poached whole mushrooms. If only 2 oz (50 g) ham or bacon is used the cholesterol will also be low. (Calories lost: up to 880.) This will also make the dish **gluten-free**.

Microwave: ☑

PEAS AND SPRING ONIONS

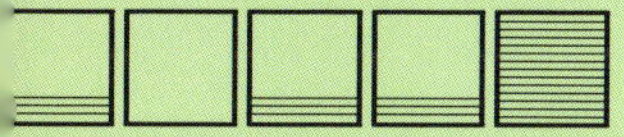

SALT SUGAR FAT CHOL FIBRE

GLUTEN-FREE* WHOLEFOOD*
TOTAL CALORIES: ABOUT 1075

For a **gluten-free** dish, make the beurre manié with rice, maize, buckwheat or other gluten-free flour.
For a **vegetarian** dish, use water or vegetable stock instead of chicken stock.

Microwave: ☑

GLAZED CARROTS

The full flavour of tender carrots is retained by cooking them in a buttery glaze. They are suitable for serving with thick meat casseroles, and with roast lamb and pork as well as with grilled chops.

PREPARATION TIME: *10 min*
COOKING TIME: *20–25 min*
INGREDIENTS *(for 4):*
1 lb (450 g) young carrots
1 oz (25 g) unsalted butter
Salt and black pepper*
1 level teaspoon caster sugar
1 heaped teaspoon chopped parsley

Scrub and scrape the carrots and cut them into slices about $\frac{1}{4}$ in ($\frac{1}{2}$ cm) thick. Melt the butter in a saucepan, add the carrot slices and season with the freshly ground pepper and the sugar. Add sufficient cold water to just cover the carrots. Bring to the boil, cover the pan with a lid and simmer gently for 15–20 minutes or until the carrots are tender.

Remove the lid; increase the heat and cook the carrots until the liquid has evaporated and only the butter remains – do not allow the carrots to brown. Draw the pan off the heat; add the parsley and toss with the carrots in the butter glaze. Sprinkle with salt and turn the carrots into a hot serving dish.

RAGOÛT OF LETTUCE AND PEAS

Peas that are no longer quite young are the main components of this French vegetable stew. It makes a filling dish on its own, but can also be served with roast meat and poultry.

PREPARATION TIME: *25 min*
COOKING TIME: *45 min*
INGREDIENTS *(for 4):*
2 large cabbage lettuces
2 lb (900 g) fresh peas
12–16 large spring onions
6 oz (175 g) lean cooked ham or boiled bacon
3 oz (75 g) butter
Salt and black pepper*
1–2 sugar cubes
GARNISH:
Fried bread triangles

Shell the peas, setting aside about a dozen of the smaller pods. Remove the coarse outer leaves from the lettuce, and cut the heads into quarters lengthways; wash and drain thoroughly. Trim the roots and stems from the spring onions. Cut the ham or bacon into $\frac{1}{2}$ in (1 cm) cubes.

Melt $2\frac{1}{2}$ oz (65 g) of the butter in a large, heavy-based pan over moderate heat. Put the lettuce, peas, pea pods and spring onions into the pan and coat them carefully in the butter. Season to taste with salt and freshly ground pepper. Add the ham or bacon and 3 tablespoons of hot water; cover the pan with a tight lid.

Cook over very low heat for 35–45 minutes depending on the age of the peas; they should be tender but not mushy when cooked. Shake the pan from time to time to prevent sticking.

Before serving, remove the pea pods and stir in the sugar lumps and remaining butter.

Serve the ragoût hot, garnished with triangles of fried bread.

PEAS AND SPRING ONIONS

It is a happy coincidence that spring onions and young garden peas both appear at the same time in early summer. They make an excellent combination to serve with roast lamb or chicken.

PREPARATION TIME: *15–20 min*
COOKING TIME: *20–30 min*
INGREDIENTS *(for 4–6):*
$2\frac{1}{2}$ lb (a generous kilo) fresh green peas
10–12 spring onions
$\frac{1}{2}$ pint (300 ml) chicken stock
Beurre manié (page 84)
Salt and black pepper*

Shell the peas. Trim the roots and outer leaves from the onions; wash them and cut the stems off the onions, leaving about 1 in ($2\frac{1}{2}$ cm) of green on each bulb. Put the onions in a pan with the stock and bring slowly to simmering point. Cook gently until they begin to soften, then add the peas and continue to cook over low heat until the peas are tender, after about 20 minutes.

When the peas are just cooked, crumble in the beurre manié and stir carefully, so that the peas do not break up, until the stock has thickened to a sauce. Season to taste with salt and freshly ground pepper. Serve hot.

WESTPHALIAN BEANS AND PEARS

A blending of sweet and sharp flavours is characteristic of German cookery. This recipe for French or runner beans makes a good vegetable dish with grilled or roast pork and ham.

PREPARATION TIME: *15 min*
COOKING TIME: *30 min*
INGREDIENTS *(for 4–6)*:
1 lb (450 g) French or runner beans
4 large cooking pears
¾ pint (425 ml) stock or bouillon
Lemon rind
4 rashers green streaky bacon
2 level tablespoons soft brown sugar
1 tablespoon tarragon vinegar

Peel the pears and cut them in half lengthways. Remove the cores and cut each half across into three or four pieces. Bring the stock to the boil, and drop in a thin piece of lemon rind, together with the pears. Simmer, uncovered, over low heat for 10 minutes.

Meanwhile, top and tail the beans (remove the strings as well from runner beans). Wash the beans and add them to the pears. Continue cooking over low heat.

Remove the rind and any gristle from the bacon and cut the rashers, crossways, into ½ in (1 cm) wide strips. Fry the bacon strips, with no additional fat, in a pan over low heat, until the fat runs and the bacon becomes crisp. Remove the bacon from the pan with a slotted spoon and keep it warm. Stir the sugar into the fat in the frying pan, blend in the vinegar and 2 tablespoons pear and bean liquid. Mix thoroughly, then add to the pan with the pears and beans. Simmer, uncovered, until the liquid has reduced to a syrupy sauce and the beans are tender. Remove the lemon.

Spoon the beans, pears and liquid into a hot serving dish and sprinkle with the bacon.

GREEN BEANS, TUSCANY STYLE

This spicy Italian method of cooking beans is a useful way of ringing the changes on runner beans towards the end of their season. French beans may also be cooked by this means, and both go well with roast or grilled meat and poultry.

PREPARATION TIME: *10 min*
COOKING TIME: *15 min*
INGREDIENTS *(for 4)*:
1 lb (450 g) runner beans
2 oz (50 g) butter
1 tablespoon olive oil
2 level teaspoons chopped fresh sage or 1 tablespoon chopped fresh parsley
1 large clove garlic
*Salt**
1 level tablespoon grated Parmesan cheese
Black pepper

Wash, top, tail and string the runner beans. Cut them into 2 in (5 cm) chunks, not finely sliced as in the English style. Cook the beans in boiling salted water over low heat until just tender. Drain the beans thoroughly and cover them with a cloth to keep them warm.

Heat the butter and oil over moderate heat; stir in half the sage or parsley and the peeled and crushed garlic. Fry for 1 minute, then add the beans. Season to taste with salt and freshly ground pepper and stir over low heat for 5 minutes.

Mix in the Parmesan cheese, and serve the beans at once, sprinkled with herbs.

COURGETTES GRATINÉES

The subtle flavour and light consistency of courgettes make them an excellent accompaniment to delicately flavoured fish, chicken or veal dishes.

PREPARATION TIME: *5 min*
COOKING TIME: *25–30 min*
INGREDIENTS *(for 4)*:
6 courgettes
2 oz (50 g) unsalted butter
*Salt**
1½ oz (40 g) Cheddar or Lancashire cheese
4 tablespoons double cream (optional)
Black pepper

Wipe the courgettes with a clean damp cloth; do not peel them, but cut off the stalk ends. Slice each courgette in half lengthways with a sharp knife.

Melt the butter in a shallow, flameproof dish and fry the courgettes, cut side downwards, until light golden. Turn the courgettes over, season them with salt and freshly ground pepper and sprinkle the grated cheese over them.

Cover the dish with a lid or foil and bake in the centre of a preheated oven at 375°F (190°C, mark 5), for 20 minutes.

Heat the cream in a small pan over moderate heat. Do not let it reach boiling point, and pour it over the courgettes just before serving.

WESTPHALIAN BEANS AND PEARS

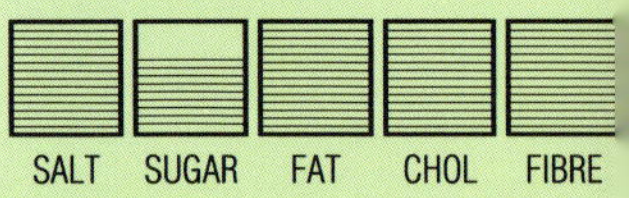

GLUTEN-FREE WHOLEFOOD
TOTAL CALORIES: ABOUT 660

Most of the **salt** comes from the bacon. To reduce it, substitute the same amount of ham, giving a medium level if serving 4 people, low if serving 6.
If wished, the amount of **sugar** can be reduced. Add half the amount, and check the flavour.
Substituting ham also makes the dish low in **fat** and **cholesterol**, provided the stock is not fatty. Heat the ham in a heavy pan lightly brushed with oil, as it will not produce enough fat, if lean, to lubricate itself. (Calories lost: up to 59.)

Microwave: ✓ for the beans and the pears.

GREEN BEANS, TUSCANY STYLE

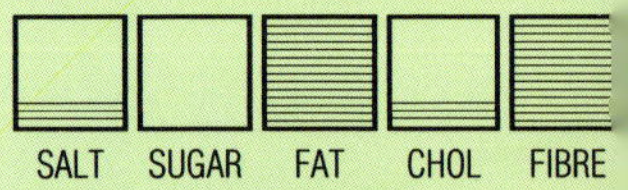

GLUTEN-FREE WHOLEFOOD VEGETARIAN
TOTAL CALORIES: ABOUT 650

The low **salt** level assumes that the butter is unsalted.
To reduce the **fat** level to low, use only 2 teaspoons butter and 1 of oil. To eliminate **cholesterol** from the dish, apart from a tiny amount from the cheese, substitute vegetable margarine for the butter. (Calories lost: up to 390.)

Microwave: ✓ for cooking the beans.

COURGETTES GRATINÉES

SALT SUGAR FAT CHOL FIBRE

GLUTEN-FREE WHOLEFOOD VEGETARIAN
TOTAL CALORIES: ABOUT 865

This type of cheese is less salty than some, and the amount used is not large enough to give a high level of **salt**.
The **fat** level can be cut to low and **cholesterol** to moderate by cooking the courgettes in a heavy pan brushed lightly with oil, omitting the remaining fat. The cream can be replaced with smetana or low-fat yogurt into which 1 teaspoon cornflour has been smoothly blended. (Calories lost: up to 463.)

Microwave: √

COURGETTES IN HOLLANDAISE SAUCE

SALT SUGAR FAT CHOL FIBRE

GLUTEN-FREE* WHOLEFOOD*
TOTAL CALORIES: ABOUT 2030

Hollandaise sauce is naturally extremely high in both **fat** and **cholesterol**. To achieve a low fat dish, therefore, involves using another dressing, such as a cheese sauce made by the blending method (see page 84) using skim milk and mature Cheddar or Parmesan. In this way a small amount of cheese, with its high fat and considerable salt level, will give enough flavour. (Calories lost: up to 1559.)

Microwave: √ for baking the courgettes.

COURGETTES IN HOLLANDAISE SAUCE

The delicate flavour of young marrows – or courgettes – is best preserved when served with melted butter or a simple sauce.

PREPARATION TIME: *30 min*
COOKING TIME: *30 min*
INGREDIENTS *(for 6)*:
1 lb (450 g) courgettes
1 oz (25 g) unsalted butter
Salt and black pepper*
Juice of half lemon
SAUCE:
7 oz (200 g) unsalted butter
3 egg yolks
1–2 tablespoons lemon juice
1 tablespoon water or dry white wine
*Salt**
3 tablespoons grated Parmesan cheese
Black pepper

Wash the courgettes and trim off the stalks; blanch in boiling water for 1–2 minutes. Drain, wipe dry and cut the courgettes in half lengthways. With a pointed teaspoon, take out a shallow groove in each half.

Arrange the courgettes, cut side up, in a large, shallow, lightly buttered flameproof dish. Sprinkle with salt, freshly ground pepper and the lemon juice. Cut the remaining butter into small pieces over the courgettes and cover the dish tightly. Bake in the centre of a pre-heated oven at 350°F (180°C, mark 4) for 25 minutes.

Meanwhile, cut 6 oz (175 g) of the butter into small pieces and let it melt slowly in a small, heavy-based pan over low heat. As soon as the butter has melted, remove the pan from the heat, and pour the butter into a jug. Put the 3 egg yolks into the same pan and beat thoroughly with a wire whisk. Add 1 tablespoon of lemon juice and 1 of water (or wine), with a good pinch of salt; beat again. Add $\frac{1}{2}$ oz (10 g) of cold butter to the egg yolk mixture and put the pan over low heat on an asbestos sheet. Cook, whisking steadily, until the egg yolks are creamy and beginning to thicken enough to coat the wires of the whisk. Remove the pan from the heat and beat in the remaining butter.

Add the melted butter to the egg mixture, drop by drop, whisking continuously. As the mixture thickens, the butter may be added more rapidly. When the sauce has the consistency of thick cream, season to taste with salt, pepper and lemon juice. If the sauce is too thick, it can be thinned with about a tablespoon of water or single cream. Finally, stir in 2 tablespoons of grated Parmesan cheese.

Spoon the sauce into the grooves of the cooked courgettes, and sprinkle with the remaining cheese. Put the dish under a hot grill until the cheese is lightly browned. Serve at once. They are especially good with roast chicken or lean roast meat.

STUFFED MARROW RINGS

Young, home-grown marrows stuffed and baked, make a good lunch or supper dish on their own.

PREPARATION TIME: *25 min*
COOKING TIME: *45 min*
INGREDIENTS *(for 2–4):*
1 short thick marrow (about 2 lb, 1 kilo)
3 oz (75 g) butter
2 oz (50 g) mushrooms
4 oz (100 g) lean cooked ham
2 level teaspoons chopped parsley
¼ level teaspoon dried summer savory
*Salt**
1–2 tablespoons fresh breadcrumbs
Black pepper

Wash the marrow and wipe it dry; cut it into rings 1½–2 in (4–5 cm) thick. Remove the peel unless the marrow is very young and tender. Spoon out the seeds. Butter a large ovenproof dish thoroughly and arrange the marrow rings in this in a single layer.

Trim the mushrooms and chop them roughly. Dice the ham. Heat 1 oz (25 g) of the butter in a pan and lightly fry the mushrooms and ham for 2–3 minutes. Add the parsley and savory, and season to taste with salt and freshly ground pepper. Stir in enough breadcrumbs to bind the stuffing.

Lightly sprinkle the marrow rings with salt and pepper before filling them with the stuffing. Dot with the remaining butter and cover the dish tightly with foil so that the marrow will cook in its own steam. Bake in the centre of a pre-heated oven at 375°F (190°C, mark 5) for 45 minutes or until the rings are tender.

Serve the marrow rings straight from the dish, with a hot cheese or tomato sauce.

MARROW EN CASSEROLE

Marrow has such a high water content that it loses most of its flavour if steamed or cooked in water. But firmness and taste is preserved by cooking marrow in butter in a casserole. It goes well with grilled meat and fish.

PREPARATION TIME: *10 min*
COOKING TIME: *30 min*
INGREDIENTS *(for 4–6):*
1 young marrow (about 2 lb, 1 kilo)
1½ oz (40 g) butter
2 level tablespoons mixed fresh herbs – tarragon, mint, parsley and chives
Salt and black pepper*

Cut the marrow into 1 in (2½ cm) thick slices; peel and cut them into rough chunks, discarding the seeds. Butter an ovenproof dish thoroughly. Add the marrow with the remaining butter cut into small knobs and sprinkle with the fresh, finely chopped herbs. Season with salt and freshly ground pepper.

Cover the dish with a lid or foil and bake in the centre of a pre-heated oven at 350°F (180°C, mark 4) until just tender, after about 30 minutes. Be careful not to overcook. Serve the marrow at once, straight from the dish.

STUFFED MARROW RINGS

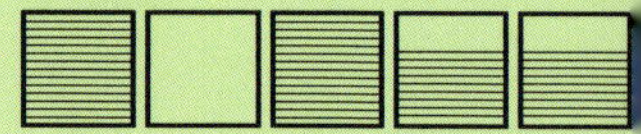

SALT SUGAR FAT CHOL FIBRE

GLUTEN-FREE* WHOLEFOOD*
TOTAL CALORIES: ABOUT 890

For a low **salt** level, use only 1 oz (25 g) ham and compensate by using 2 oz (50 g) pine nuts.
For low **fat** and **cholesterol** omit the butter and brush both the dish for the marrows and the pan for cooking the mushrooms very lightly with oil. (Calories lost: up to 420.)
Other possible substitutes for some or all of the ham: up to ½ oz (10 g) dried mushrooms, soaked for half an hour before using, or finely chopped Florence fennel.
Both these are low in salt and fat, and fennel is high in **fibre**.

Freezing: ✓ up to 6 months.
Microwave: ✓

MARROW EN CASSEROLE

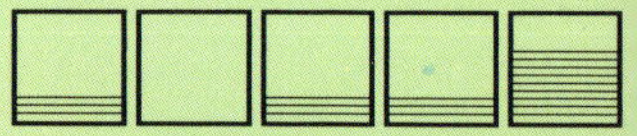

SALT SUGAR FAT CHOL FIBRE

GLUTEN-FREE WHOLEFOOD VEGETARIAN
TOTAL CALORIES: ABOUT 440

The low **salt** level assumes that the butter is unsalted or only slightly salted.
If wished, the amount of butter can be reduced by up to half, giving very low **fat** and **cholesterol**. (Calories lost: up to 148.)

Freezing: ✓ up to 6 months.
Microwave: ✓

BRAISED CHICORY

SALT SUGAR FAT CHOL FIBRE

GLUTEN-FREE WHOLEFOOD
TOTAL CALORIES: ABOUT 240

This recipe needs no changes to suit healthy eating guidelines, although some people will prefer to avoid all **cholesterol** by replacing the butter with vegetable margarine or oil. For a **vegetarian** dish, use vegetable stock.

Freezing: √ up to 2 months.
Microwave: √

CHAMPIGNONS À LA CRÈME

SALT SUGAR FAT CHOL FIBRE

GLUTEN-FREE* WHOLEFOOD* VEGETARIAN
TOTAL CALORIES: ABOUT 1155

To reduce the **fat** and **cholesterol** content to low is very difficult without abandoning the character of the recipe. To reduce to medium, cook the mushrooms in 1 teaspoon butter mixed with 1 teaspoon of oil, brushed over a heavy-bottomed pan, and replace the cream with sour cream. For a version lower in fat, use smetana, which has less than a quarter of the fat of double cream, but still enough to give a medium fat content in this quantity. (Calories lost: up to 640.)

Freezing: √ up to 3 months.

BRAISED CHICORY

The sharp, clean taste of chicory – or Belgian endive – goes particularly well with roast pork, goose or duck.

PREPARATION TIME: *15 min*
COOKING TIME: *35 min*
INGREDIENTS *(for 4):*
4 heads of chicory
1 small onion
1 oz (25 g) unsalted butter
Salt and black pepper*
¼ pint (150 ml) chicken or beef stock
GARNISH:
Chopped parsley

Wash the chicory, trim off the root ends and cut each head in half lengthways. Scoop out the small pieces of tough core at the base of each heart.

Peel and finely chop the onion. Melt the butter in a flameproof casserole over low heat and fry the onion in the butter until soft and transparent, but not browned. Add the chicory, fry until golden on both sides, then season to taste with salt and freshly ground pepper.

Remove the dish from the heat. Pour the stock over the chicory, cover the dish closely with a lid or foil and cook in the centre of an oven pre-heated to 350°F (180°C, mark 4) for 35 minutes.

Serve the braised chicory straight from the dish, sprinkled with finely chopped parsley.

CHAMPIGNONS À LA CRÈME

For this dish of mushrooms in cream sauce, choose small firm mushrooms which will not break up during cooking. Serve them with grilled meat or chicken, or on buttered toast as a quick snack.

PREPARATION TIME: *10 min*
COOKING TIME: *7 min*
INGREDIENTS *(for 4):*
1 lb (450 g) button mushrooms
2 oz (50 g) unsalted butter
Salt and black pepper*
Dried mixed herbs
1 level tablespoon plain flour
¼ pint (150 ml) double cream
1 rounded tablespoon chopped parsley
Juice of half lemon

Perfect button mushrooms need only to be rinsed in cold water, drained and patted dry on absorbent kitchen paper. Trim the stalks level with the caps. Melt the butter in a pan and fry the mushrooms for 1–2 minutes, tossing to coat them evenly with the butter. Season to taste with salt, freshly ground pepper and the mixed herbs. Cook for a few more minutes to draw out the juices of the mushrooms.

Sprinkle the flour into the pan and stir thoroughly with a wooden spoon to blend the ingredients. Gradually stir in all the cream; bring the sauce to the boil, stirring continuously until it has thickened. Allow to simmer over low heat for 1–2 minutes then add the parsley and lemon juice and serve immediately.

ROASTED ONIONS

The sweet flavour of large Spanish onions is particularly enhanced by roasting them whole. Serve as an accompaniment to meat dishes, or cook alongside baked potatoes as part of a vegetarian meal.

PREPARATION TIME: *5 min*
COOKING TIME: *$2\frac{1}{2}$–3 hours*
INGREDIENTS *(for 6):*
6 large Spanish onions
2–3 oz (50–75 g) butter
*Coarse salt**
GARNISH:
Parsley sprigs

Line a deep roasting tin with foil to prevent the sugar contained in the onions from sticking to the tin. Cut the roots from the unpeeled, washed onions, and stand them upright in the tin. Bake in the centre of the oven, pre-heated to 350°F (180°C, mark 4), for $2\frac{1}{2}$ hours or until the onions are tender when tested with a skewer.

Remove the tin from the oven, carefully peel off the onion skins, and set the onions on a hot serving dish. Open the tops slightly with a pointed knife blade and push a knob of butter into each. Sprinkle the onions with salt, and top each with a small sprig of parsley.

BROWN TOM

The name of this dish describes a casserole of fresh tomatoes with a crumble of bacon and brown breadcrumbs. Serve it on its own, or with grilled sausages for lunch or supper.

PREPARATION TIME: *20 min*
COOKING TIME: *30–35 min*
INGREDIENTS *(for 4):*
1 lb (450 g) tomatoes
1 large onion
2 rashers lean bacon
4 large slices wholemeal bread
1 level tablespoon chopped parsley
$1\frac{1}{2}$ level teaspoons chopped fresh basil
$1\frac{1}{2}$ oz (40 g) butter
Salt and black pepper*
Caster sugar

Peel and roughly chop the onion; cut the rind off the bacon and chop the rashers into pieces. Put the onion and bacon through the fine blade of the mincer. Remove the crust and crumble the bread into the bacon and onion mince. Now add the herbs. Skin and thinly slice the tomatoes (page 92).

Put a layer of the bacon and crumb mixture in the bottom of a buttered, shallow fireproof dish. Cover this with a layer of tomatoes and season with salt, freshly ground pepper and a little sugar. Repeat these layers until all the ingredients are used up, finishing with a layer of bacon crumbs.

Dot with the remaining butter and bake near the top of the oven at 400°F (200°C, mark 6) for 30–35 minutes or until brown and bubbling. Serve at once.

TOMATOES WITH GREEN PEAS

Large firm tomatoes are ideal for stuffing, and may be served with grilled or roast meats. They can also be served as a hot first course, allowing one tomato per person. The stuffing used in the recipe for marrow rings on page 46 can also be used – in fact both stuffings are interchangeable.

PREPARATION TIME: *20 min*
COOKING TIME: *15 min*
INGREDIENTS *(for 6):*
6 large firm tomatoes
1 small onion
$1\frac{1}{2}$ oz (40 g) butter
$\frac{1}{2}$ pint (300 ml) cooked peas
2 level teaspoons chopped fresh mint
Salt and black pepper*
1 egg yolk
GARNISH:
Black olives

Remove the leaf bases, and wash and dry the tomatoes thoroughly. Slice off the top of each with a sharp, serrated knife, and carefully take out the core and seeds with a pointed teaspoon. Turn the tomatoes upside-down to drain thoroughly while making the stuffing.

Peel and finely chop the onion. Melt 1 oz (25 g) of the butter in a small, heavy-based pan and cook the onion over moderate heat until soft, but not coloured. Add the cooked peas and chopped mint to the onion. Cook the mixture for 3 minutes, stirring all the time. Allow the mixture to cool slightly, then rub it through a coarse sieve or liquidise it to a purée.

Return the purée to the pan and season to taste with salt and

ROASTED ONIONS

SALT SUGAR FAT CHOL FIBRE

GLUTEN-FREE WHOLEFOOD VEGETARIAN
TOTAL CALORIES: ABOUT 730

To reduce the **fat** and **cholesterol** level to low, simply replace the knob of butter inserted in each cooked onion with a spoonful of sour cream, smetana, quark or thick low-fat yogurt. (Calories lost: up to 495.)

BROWN TOM

SALT SUGAR FAT CHOL FIBRE

GLUTEN-FREE* WHOLEFOOD*
TOTAL CALORIES: ABOUT 915

Most of the **salt** comes from the bacon, with some from the bread. To reduce the level to low, use only 1 oz (25 g) bacon and unsalted breadcrumbs. This will also reduce the level of **fat** and **cholesterol**, which can be further reduced to low by greasing the baking dish sparingly with oil or vegetable margarine, and omitting dots of fat on top of the dish. If concerned about the dish drying out during baking, cover with foil for first 20 minutes. (Calories lost: up to 268.)

Freezing: ✓ up to 2 months.

TOMATOES WITH GREEN PEAS

SALT SUGAR FAT CHOL FIBRE

GLUTEN-FREE WHOLEFOOD VEGETARIAN
TOTAL CALORIES: ABOUT 520

Those on a **cholesterol**-lowering regime can replace the butter with vegetable margarine or oil, or use a half-and-half mixture, and omit the egg yolk, thickening the vegetable mixture by gentle simmering or by adding a teaspoonful of arrowroot made into a smooth paste with a little water. (Calories lost: up to 65.) Otherwise, this recipe suits healthy eating guidelines.

Microwave: √

LEEKS IN YOGURT SAUCE

SALT SUGAR FAT CHOL FIBRE

GLUTEN-FREE WHOLEFOOD VEGETARIAN
TOTAL CALORIES: ABOUT 580

The **fat** and **cholesterol** content can be low if the yogurt used is low-fat, and if the number of egg yolks is reduced, using 1 whole egg and 1 teaspoon of arrowroot mixed to a smooth paste with cold water instead. (Calories lost: up to 105.)

freshly ground pepper. Beat the egg yolk lightly, then add it to the peas and onions. Stir over low heat until the mixture thickens. Remove from the heat and set the stuffing aside to cool and stiffen.

Season the inside of the drained tomatoes with salt and pepper and spoon in the prepared stuffing. Replace the tomato lids and secure each with a wooden cocktail stick.

Arrange the tomatoes in a well-buttered ovenproof dish and cover tightly with foil. Bake in an oven pre-heated to 375°F (190°C, mark 5) for 15 minutes or until the tomatoes are just tender, but still retaining their shape.

Serve the tomatoes hot, garnished with an olive on top of each cocktail stick.

LEEKS IN YOGURT SAUCE

The first young leeks come on the market in late summer. They can be served cold with chicken or fish.

PREPARATION TIME: *15 min*
COOKING TIME: *30 min*
INGREDIENTS *(for 4–6):*
8 slender leeks
Juice of a large lemon
1 level coffeespoon salt
12 black peppercorns
12 fennel seeds
6 coriander seeds
6 sprigs parsley
2 shallots
SAUCE:
8 fluid oz (225 ml) natural yogurt
3 egg yolks
2 teaspoons lemon juice
Salt and black pepper*
Dijon mustard
GARNISH:
Fresh chopped parsley

Prepare a broth from ¾ pint (425 ml) of water, the lemon juice, spices, herbs and peeled and sliced shallots. Bring to the boil and cook for 10 minutes.

Meanwhile, trim the leeks, slit them halfway down from the top and wash them thoroughly under cold running water.

Put the leeks in a frying pan, wide enough to take them in one layer; pour the strained broth over them. Cover the pan with a lid and simmer the leeks gently for 10–15 minutes, until soft. Leave them to cool in the liquid.

For the sauce, beat the yogurt, egg yolks and lemon juice together in a bowl, and place it over a pan of gently simmering water. Cook the sauce, stirring frequently, until it has thickened, after about 15 minutes. Season with salt, pepper and mustard, and set aside.

Before serving, drain the leeks thoroughly and cut each into two or three diagonal pieces. Arrange them in a serving dish, spoon the yogurt sauce over the leeks and sprinkle with parsley.

PARSNIPS MOLLY PARKIN

This vegetable casserole is an unusual combination of parsnips, tomatoes, cheese and cream. It goes well with plain roast lamb and pork.

PREPARATION TIME: *40 min*
COOKING TIME: *40 min*
INGREDIENTS *(for 6):*
2 lb (900 g) parsnips
1 lb (450 g) tomatoes
5 tablespoons oil
3 oz (75 g) butter
3 level tablespoons soft brown sugar
Salt and black pepper*
6 oz (175 g) grated Gruyère cheese
$\frac{1}{2}$ pint (300 ml) single or double cream
4 rounded tablespoons fresh breadcrumbs

Peel the parsnips, cut away and discard any hard central cores. Slice the parsnips thinly. Skin the tomatoes (page 92), remove the seeds and cut the flesh into slices. Heat the oil in a pan and lightly fry the parsnips for 4 minutes.

Grease a large casserole dish with half the butter, and place a layer of parsnips over the base. Sprinkle with a little sugar, salt, freshly ground pepper and add a little cream, before covering with a layer of tomatoes. Spread a little more cream and cheese over the tomatoes and repeat these layers until all the ingredients are used up, finishing off with cream and cheese. Top with the breadcrumbs and dot with the remaining butter.

Cook the parsnip casserole for 40 minutes in the centre of an oven pre-heated to 325°F (170°C, mark 3). Serve straight from the casserole.

GARLIC POTATOES

Mashed or creamed potatoes are given additional flavour by garlic. The bitterness is reduced if the garlic is boiled for a few minutes first.

PREPARATION TIME: *20 min*
COOKING TIME: *2 hours*
INGREDIENTS *(for 6):*
3 lb ($1\frac{1}{2}$ kg) potatoes
5 cloves garlic
4 oz (100 g) unsalted butter
1 oz (25 g) plain flour
$\frac{1}{2}$ pint (300 ml) milk
*1 level teaspoon salt**
Black pepper
3 tablespoons double cream
3 heaped tablespoons finely chopped parsley

Wash and dry the potatoes, prick them with a fork, and bake for $1\frac{1}{2}$ hours or until tender on the centre shelf of an oven pre-heated to 400°F (200°C, mark 6).

Put the garlic in a small pan, cover with water; boil for 2 minutes, then drain and peel. Melt half the butter in a heavy-based saucepan and add the garlic. Cover the pan, and cook the garlic gently for 10 minutes or until tender. Remove the garlic. Stir the flour into the butter in the pan and cook over low heat for 2 minutes. Gradually blend in the boiling milk, stirring constantly until the sauce is smooth and thick. Add the salt, a few twists of pepper and the garlic. Boil for 2 minutes.

Liquidise the sauce or rub it through a sieve, then return it to the pan and heat through. Set aside.

Scoop the flesh from the baked potatoes, rub it through a sieve and beat in the remaining butter,

PARSNIPS MOLLY PARKIN

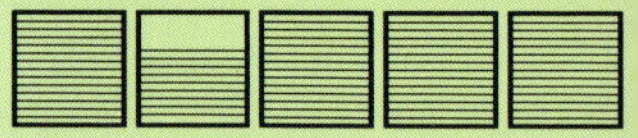

SALT SUGAR FAT CHOL FIBRE

GLUTEN-FREE* WHOLEFOOD* VEGETARIAN
TOTAL CALORIES: ABOUT 4000

The high **salt** content of the cheese can only be reduced by using less cheese, say half, giving a low/medium salt total.
The **sugar** content can be reduced to low by adding only 1 tablespoon.
The very high **fat** content can be reduced to low by using only 1 oz (25 g) butter (or vegetable margarine or a mixture) to grease and dot the dish; half the cheese; only 2 teaspoons of oil with a few spoonfuls of stock or water to brown the parsnips; and smetana mixed with low-fat yogurt, or yogurt alone, to layer. (Calories lost: up to 2495.)

Freezing: ✓ up to 2 months.

GARLIC POTATOES

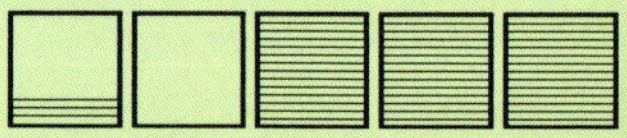

SALT SUGAR FAT CHOL FIBRE

GLUTEN-FREE* WHOLEFOOD* VEGETARIAN
TOTAL CALORIES: ABOUT 2400

The **fat** and **cholesterol** levels can be reduced to low by using only 1 oz (25 g) butter to cook the garlic and make the sauce; and replacing the butter and cream beaten into the potatoes and garlic sauce with quark or smetana. (Calories lost: up to 708.)

Microwave: ✓ for the initial cooking of the potatoes.

IMOGES POTATO PIE

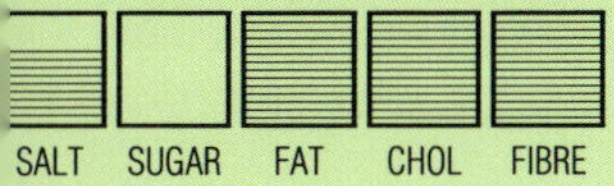

EGETARIAN
OTAL CALORIES: ABOUT 3430

or a low **salt** level, use pastry repared without salt.
he **fat** level is raised onsiderably by the puff pastry. o reduce this, use a yeast astry, or a cobbler topping uch as the scone dough on age 26.
Vithin the pie, the fat and **holesterol** levels can be educed to low by omitting the lots of butter and replacing the ream with low-fat yogurt. Calories lost: up to 1241.)
luten-free puff pastry is not uccessful; but you could use nstead a low-fat pastry. uff pastry is also difficult to nake well with wholemeal lour, so for a **wholefood** dish, topping as suggested above is referable.

reezing: ☑ up to 3 months.

ELERIAC AND POTATO URÉE

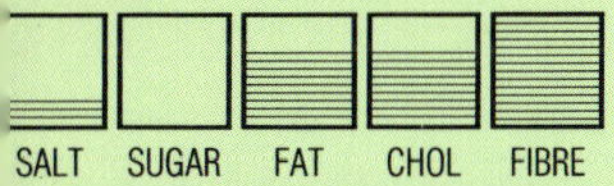

LUTEN-FREE WHOLEFOOD VEGETARIAN
OTAL CALORIES: ABOUT 1050

or low **fat** and **cholesterol** eplace the butter and cream vith the same amount of quark r smetana, with 2 teaspoons of utter for flavour if wished. Calories lost: up to 406.)

reezing: ☑ up to 3 months.

Microwave: ☑ for the eleriac.

a little at a time. Season to taste with salt and pepper. Stir the cream into the garlic purée, then beat the mixture into the potatoes. Stir in the parsley.

Heat the mashed potato through if necessary, pile it back into the potato skins and serve at once.

LIMOGES POTATO PIE

In spring the country round Limoges in France can be wet and cold. Consequently, the regional food tends to be warm and filling. This potato pie can be served as a supper dish on its own or as a first course.

PREPARATION TIME: *35 min*
COOKING TIME: *35 min*
INGREDIENTS *(for 6):*
1 lb (450 g) prepared puff pastry
1½ lb (700 g) new potatoes
3 oz (75 g) onion
3–4 cloves garlic
Salt and black pepper*
Nutmeg
2 oz (50 g) butter
3 fluid oz (75 ml) single cream
3 fluid oz (75 ml) double cream
1 egg
Bunch of fresh parsley, chives and chervil

Roll out half the puff pastry on a lightly floured board and use to line a 10 in (25 cm) flan ring or shallow cake tin. Wash and scrape the potatoes. Slice them thinly, using a mandolin slicer or the cucumber blade on a grater, into a bowl of cold water to prevent them turning brown.

Bring a pan of lightly salted water to the boil, put in the sliced potatoes and cook for 2 minutes only, after the water has returned to the boil. Drain the potatoes thoroughly through a colander. Peel and finely chop the onion and garlic.

Put a layer of potato slices on top of the pastry base, sprinkle with the onion and garlic and season with a little salt, nutmeg and freshly ground pepper. Repeat these layers, seasoning each, until all the vegetables are used up, finishing with a layer of potato. Dot the vegetables with the butter, cut into small knobs. Mix the creams together and pour about half over the potatoes.

Roll out the remaining pastry and cover the pie, sealing the edges firmly. Make a small hole in the centre of the pastry lid for the steam to escape. Beat the egg into the remaining cream and brush a little of this mixture over the pastry to glaze it while cooking. Score the pastry lightly into sections with a sharp knife – this makes it easier to cut the finished pie into portions.

Bake the pie near the top of a pre-heated oven at 450°F (230°C, mark 8) for 30 minutes. Protect the pastry with a piece of buttered paper if the pastry browns too quickly.

Chop the fresh herbs finely and blend them into the remaining egg and cream mixture. When the pie is cooked, pour the cream and egg mixture into the centre hole using a small kitchen funnel. Do this slowly in case there is not room for all the cream. Return the pie to the oven for 5 minutes then serve at once.

CELERIAC AND POTATO PURÉE

Celeriac, or celery root, is a turnip-shaped, knobbly root vegetable, popular in Europe. It has a strong celery flavour, and the leaves can be used for flavouring soups and stews. As a purée, it is particularly good served with game.

PREPARATION TIME: *10 min*
COOKING TIME: *45 min*
INGREDIENTS *(for 4–6):*
1 lb (450 g) celeriac
¾ lb (350 g) cooked mashed potatoes
1½ oz (40 g) butter
3 tablespoons double cream
Salt and black pepper*

Scrub the celeriac thoroughly in cold water to remove all traces of dirt. Put it in a pan of boiling salted water and cook, unpeeled, for 35–40 minutes or until quite tender. Leave to cool slightly, then peel the celeriac and chop it finely. Purée it through a sieve, or in a mouli.

Blend the celeriac purée with the mashed potatoes, add the butter and cream, and season to taste with salt and freshly ground black pepper. Heat the purée through over low heat before serving.

NOISETTE POTATOES

Small golden balls of fried potatoes make an attractive garnish for steaks, chops or sautéed meat. They should be left to soak for a few hours to remove excess starch. The cooked potatoes can be tossed in dissolved meat jelly and sprinkled with parsley. They are then known as *pommes de terre à la parisienne*.

PREPARATION TIME: *20 min*
COOKING TIME: *10 min*
INGREDIENTS *(for 6):*
2 lb (900 g) potatoes
*3 level tablespoons salt**
3 oz (75 g) unsalted butter

Peel the potatoes and leave them to soak for 2 hours in cold water in which 2 tablespoons salt have been dissolved. Drain and dry the potatoes. Using a ball scoop, take out small balls, about the size of walnuts, from the potatoes.

Bring a pan of water to the boil, add 1 tablespoon salt and cook the potato balls over low heat for 3 minutes. Drain through a colander and dry on a clean tea-towel.

Melt the butter over gentle heat in a sauté pan. Toss the potatoes in the butter for about 5 minutes until golden and cooked through.

Using a slotted spoon, lift the potato balls into a warm serving dish, sprinkle with a little salt and serve.

SCALLOPED POTATOES

For this recipe, choose firm, waxy potatoes which will not break up during long, slow cooking. The potato gratin can be served with any type of grilled or roast meat, or it can be made into a main dish by adding minced ham or flaked cooked fish between the potato layers.

PREPARATION TIME: *15–20 min*
COOKING TIME: *$1\frac{1}{2}$ hours*
INGREDIENTS *(for 6):*
$1\frac{1}{2}$ lb (700 g) potatoes
1 onion
4 oz (100 g) Cheddar or Gruyère cheese
2 oz (50 g) butter
Salt and black pepper*
1 egg
$\frac{1}{2}$ pint (300 ml) milk

Peel and wash the potatoes, and cut them into thin slices. Peel and finely chop the onion, and grate the cheese. Use a little of the butter to grease a shallow, ovenproof dish. Arrange the potato slices in layers in the dish, sprinkling each layer with onion, cheese, salt and freshly ground pepper. Finish with a thick layer of cheese and dot with the remaining butter.

Beat the egg and milk together and pour this mixture carefully over the potatoes. Cover the dish with buttered greaseproof paper or foil. Bake in the centre of an oven pre-heated to 350°F (180°C, mark 4) for $1\frac{1}{2}$ hours, or until the potatoes are tender, and the topping is golden. If cooked too quickly, the egg and milk will curdle.

NOISETTE POTATOES

SALT SUGAR FAT CHOL FIBRE

GLUTEN-FREE WHOLEFOOD VEGETARIAN
TOTAL CALORIES: ABOUT 1340

To reduce the **salt** level to low, omit the soaking in salt water and choose the driest potatoes possible. This will also avoid the loss of vitamin C and some minerals from the potatoes to the water during soaking. Cook the potato balls in unsalted water.
For a low **fat** and **cholesterol** level, toss in 1 oz (25 g) butter or vegetable margarine or oil, before grilling under medium heat for several minutes until cooked through. (Calories lost: up to 370.)

SCALLOPED POTATOES

SALT SUGAR FAT CHOL FIBRE

GLUTEN-FREE WHOLEFOOD VEGETARIAN
TOTAL CALORIES: ABOUT 1690

Most of the **salt** (assuming you are using unsalted butter) comes from the cheese, and the only way to reduce this is to use less cheese, say half the amount. Grate it finely and use the strongest flavoured cheese available, so that a smaller amount gives maximum flavour.
This will also help to reduce the high **fat** and **cholesterol** together with using only $\frac{1}{2}$ oz (10 g) butter to grease and dot the dish, and skim milk. These changes will give a low fat and cholesterol level. (Calories lost: up to 595.)

;ALETTE LYONNAISE

SALT SUGAR FAT CHOL FIBRE

.UTEN-FREE WHOLEFOOD VEGETARIAN
)TAL CALORIES: ABOUT 1045

'he low **salt** level assumes you re using unsalted butter.
'o reduce the **fat** and **holesterol** levels to low, cook ie onions in 2 teaspoons butter nd 2 of oil, omitting the emaining butter dotted on top. :educe the amount of holesterol further if wished by dding only the white of the gg, although 1 yolk between 4 ; not a high cholesterol level. Calories lost: up to 397.)

'reezing: ✓ up to 3 months.

OUFFLÉ POTATOES

SALT SUGAR FAT CHOL FIBRE

.UTEN-FREE WHOLEFOOD VEGETARIAN
)TAL CALORIES: ABOUT 1870

'o reduce the **fat** and **holesterol** levels to low, use nly 2 egg yolks (but 3 whites), nd replace the butter and ream beaten into potatoes with ie same amount of smetana or uark, or a mixture. This will ctually produce a lighter oufflé, but as it will have less olidity, serving immediately ecomes even more vital. Calories lost: up to 751.)

1icrowave: ✓ for the initial aking of the potatoes.

GALETTE LYONNAISE

This savoury potato dish with its classic Lyonnaise flavouring of onion and cheese is excellent with both fish and meat. Extra cheese may be mixed with the potato in addition to the topping.

PREPARATION TIME: *35 min*
COOKING TIME: *25 min*
INGREDIENTS *(for 4):*
1 lb (450 g) potatoes
½ lb (225 g) onions
2½ oz (65 g) butter
1 egg
Salt and black pepper*
Pinch nutmeg
2 tablespoons grated Cheddar, Gruyère or Parmesan cheese
GARNISH:
Parsley sprigs

Peel the potatoes, cut them into even pieces and boil them in lightly salted water. Rub the potatoes through a coarse sieve. Peel and finely chop the onions. Heat 2 oz (50 g) of butter and cook the onions over low heat until they are soft and golden. Stir the contents of the pan into the potatoes. Add the beaten egg and season to taste with salt, freshly ground pepper and nutmeg.

Spoon the potato mixture into a greased, shallow ovenproof dish; smooth the top, sprinkle over the grated cheese and dot with the remaining butter. Bake the potatoes in the centre of a preheated oven, at 400°F (200°C, mark 6), for about 20 minutes or until golden brown on top.

Serve the potatoes straight from the dish, garnished with sprigs of parsley.

SOUFFLÉ POTATOES

With just a little extra trouble, plain baked potatoes can be transformed into light and fluffy individual soufflés. They are ideal with all meats, particularly so with steak.

PREPARATION TIME: *15 min*
COOKING TIME: *1¾ hours*
INGREDIENTS *(for 6):*
6 large potatoes
2 oz (50 g) unsalted melted butter
4 fluid oz (100 ml) double cream
3 eggs
Salt and black pepper*

Wash and dry the potatoes, prick them lightly with a fork and bake for 1½ hours or until tender on the middle shelf of an oven preheated to 400°F (200°C, mark 6). Cut a lid lengthways off the baked potatoes, scoop the flesh out into a bowl and mix in with it the melted butter and cream. Separate the eggs and stir the yolks into the potato mixture. Beat the egg whites with a little salt until stiff and fold into the potato mixture. Season to taste with freshly ground pepper.

Pile this soufflé mixture back into the hollow potato skins, return to the oven and bake at the same temperature for 15 minutes, or until the soufflés are well risen.

Serve immediately, before the soufflés have time to collapse and go flat.

CREAMED SPINACH

Young crisp spinach leaves should be cooked as soon as possible after buying or gathering them. This dish goes well with most roast meats, particularly with ham and gammon.

PREPARATION TIME: *10 min*
COOKING TIME: *10–15 min*
INGREDIENTS *(for 4):*
2 lb (1 kilo) spinach
*½ level teaspoon salt**
1 oz (25 g) butter
¼ level teaspoon grated nutmeg
3 fluid oz (75 ml) double cream

Remove the stalks and coarse midribs from the spinach and throw away any bruised leaves. Wash the spinach thoroughly in several lots of cold water to get rid of all sand and grit. Put the spinach in a large saucepan with only the water clinging to the leaves. Cook over low heat, shaking the pan, until the spinach has reduced in volume and made its own liquid. Add the salt and cover the pan with a lid.

Cook gently for 5–8 minutes, then drain the spinach thoroughly through a fine sieve, squeezing out as much liquid as possible with a potato masher.

Chop the spinach roughly on a board. Melt the butter in the saucepan, add the spinach and nutmeg and heat through before stirring in the cream. Spoon into a hot serving dish.

SPINACH ROLL

Late summer spinach or even the frozen variety is ideal for this Yugoslavian puff pastry dish. It will serve as a light meal on its own, or it can be part of a packed lunch or picnic.

PREPARATION TIME: *45 min*
COOKING TIME: *30 min*
INGREDIENTS *(for 4):*
2 lb (900 g) fresh spinach
12 oz (350 g) prepared puff pastry
3 oz (75 g) cottage cheese
3 eggs
1 oz (25 g) grated Parmesan cheese
Salt and black pepper*
1 egg yolk

Roll the puff pastry out on a floured surface to a rectangle 12 in (30 cm) long by 8 in (20 cm) wide, and ¼ in (½ cm) thick. Lightly grease and flour a baking tray.

Wash the spinach thoroughly, discarding any stalks and tough midribs. Put it, still wet, in a large saucepan. Cover with a lid and cook over low heat for 5–7 minutes, or until just tender. Drain the spinach thoroughly in a colander. Chop it finely, and drain again (do not squeeze it completely dry).

Rub the cottage cheese through a sieve to remove any lumps. Separate the eggs. Lightly beat the yolks and add them to the spinach in a mixing bowl. Blend in the cottage and the Parmesan cheese, season with salt and freshly ground pepper. Beat the egg whites until stiff and fold into the mixture.

Moisten the edges of the pastry with cold water and spoon the spinach mixture down the centre of the rectangle and to within 1 in

CREAMED SPINACH

SALT SUGAR FAT CHOL FIBRE

GLUTEN-FREE WHOLEFOOD VEGETARIAN
TOTAL CALORIES: ABOUT 745

To reduce the level of **fat** and **cholesterol** to low, add only ½ oz (10 g) butter and 1 tablespoon of single cream to the spinach. (Calories lost: up to 414.)

Freezing: ✓ without cream up to 1 year; with cream up to 2 months.

Microwave: ✓

SPINACH ROLL

SALT SUGAR FAT CHOL FIBRE

VEGETARIAN
TOTAL CALORIES: ABOUT 2170

The **salt** level comes mainly from the cheese. If wished, unsalted quark can be used in place of the cottage cheese, giving a low salt level. This assumes there is no salt added to the pastry. If you use bought puff pastry, the salt level will probably be quite high.
To reduce the **fat** and **cholesterol** levels to low, the puff pastry needs to be replaced with a lower-fat wrapping such as yeast or strudel dough, and 2 yolks should be omitted from the mixture. Use a little of the egg white only to glaze. (Calories lost: up to 430.)

Freezing: ✓ up to 3 months.

Microwave: ✓ for cooking the spinach.

EPPERS WITH MINCE TUFFING

SALT SUGAR FAT CHOL FIBRE

LUTEN-FREE* WHOLEFOOD*
OTAL CALORIES: ABOUT 950

o keep the **salt** level low, cook he peppers in unsalted water nd use unsalted bread.
he **fat** level can be reduced by hoosing very lean meat, ideally uying a lean piece and nincing at home. The amount f oil can also be reduced to alf. If wished, the egg can be mitted to give a low **holesterol** level. (Calories ost: up to 191.)

reezing: ✓ up to 2 months.

Aicrowave: ✓

HESTNUT AND POTATO URÉE

SALT SUGAR FAT CHOL FIBRE

LUTEN-FREE WHOLEFOOD
OTAL CALORIES: ABOUT 1470

he low **salt** level depends on here being no salt in the stock.
o reduce the **fat** and **holesterol** levels to low, eplace the cream with quark or metana, and reduce the mount of butter added to 1 oz 25 g). (Calories lost: up to 64.)
or a **vegetarian** dish, simmer he chestnuts in water or egetable stock.

reezing: ✓ up to 3 months.

(2½ cm) of the shorter edges. Quickly fold the pastry over the spinach, close the edges tightly, and seal all three sides firmly with the lightly beaten egg yolk. Roll out the pastry trimmings and use to decorate the top of the roll, brush with the remaining egg yolk to glaze the pastry.

Make two or three slits in the top of the pastry for the steam to escape. Carefully lift the pastry roll on to the baking tray.

Bake in the centre of a pre-heated oven, at 450°F (230°C, mark 8) for 20 minutes, then reduce the temperature to 350°F (180°C, mark 4) for another 10 minutes, or until the pastry is well risen and golden brown. Serve the roll, hot or cold, cut into thick slices.

PEPPERS WITH MINCE STUFFING

Large, squat peppers filled with a savoury meat stuffing make a light lunch or supper dish on their own. They can also be included in cold buffet or picnic fare.

PREPARATION TIME: *20 min*
COOKING TIME: *30 min*
INGREDIENTS *(for 4):*
4 even-sized peppers
1 onion
1½ tablespoons olive oil
6–8 oz (175–225 g) minced beef or pork
1 thick slice bread
1 egg
Salt and black pepper*
Summer savory

Wash and dry the peppers. Use a sharp knife to cut off the stalk ends with a small circle of pepper attached to each. Set the stalks aside and remove the seeds and ribs carefully from the peppers without breaking the skins. Scald the peppers for 5 minutes in a pan of boiling, lightly salted water. Lift out the peppers and drain them, upside down.

Peel and finely chop the onion, and cook it until transparent in 1 tablespoon of the oil in a heavy-based pan. Add the mince, stirring continuously until it has browned and separated into grains. Remove the pan from the heat.

Remove the crust from the bread and soak it in the lightly beaten egg. Mash the bread and egg with a fork and stir it into the mince; season to taste with salt, freshly ground pepper and summer savory. Blend thoroughly until the stuffing is firm, but still moist.

Brush the base of an ovenproof dish with oil. Spoon the stuffing loosely into the peppers and place them upright in the dish. Brush the skins lightly with oil and put 2 or 3 tablespoons of water in the bottom of the dish. Cover it tightly with foil and a lid and bake in the centre of a pre-heated oven, at 375°F (190°C, mark 5) for 30 minutes or until tender.

Arrange the peppers on a warmed serving dish and replace the stalk caps at an angle so that a little of the stuffing shows. Serve with hot crusty French bread and a tomato sauce (you can use the pizza topping given on pages 68–69) flavoured with paprika and soured cream.

CHESTNUT AND POTATO PURÉE

Chestnuts are traditionally served as stuffing or as garnishes with game birds. This purée of potato and chestnuts is an excellent vegetable to serve with game, turkey or roast ham.

PREPARATION TIME: *20 min*
COOKING TIME: *30 min*
INGREDIENTS *(for 6–8):*
¾ lb (350 g) fresh chestnuts or 8 oz (225 g) tin chestnut purée
1 pint (570 ml) stock or bouillon
¾ lb (350 g) mashed potatoes
*Salt**
2 oz (50 g) butter
4–5 tablespoons single cream
Ground nutmeg or black pepper
4 rounded tablespoons chopped celery heart

Make a small cut on the flat side of each chestnut and roast them on top of the stove in a chestnut pan or on a baking tray near the top of a hot oven. After 5–10 minutes, the skins will crack. Peel the two layers of skin from the chestnuts while still warm.

Put the stock in a saucepan, add the peeled chestnuts and cover the pan with a lid. Bring to the boil, then simmer the chestnuts for 20 minutes or until tender. Drain the chestnuts and rub them through a coarse sieve.

Blend the chestnut purée with the mashed potato, stir in the butter and heat the mixture through over low heat. Blend in enough cream to give the purée a fluffy texture, and season with salt and ground nutmeg or pepper.

Blend in the chopped celery just before serving.

STUFFED GREEN PEPPERS

For this recipe, choose squat round peppers that will stand upright.

PREPARATION TIME: *20 min*
COOKING TIME: *50 min*
INGREDIENTS *(for 4)*:
4 even-sized green peppers
3 oz (75 g) long grain rice
1 small onion
2 oz (50 g) mushrooms
2 rashers lean bacon
1 oz (25 g) unsalted butter
4–6 chicken livers
Salt and black pepper*
1 rounded teaspoon chopped parsley
1 small egg
1–2 oz (25–50 g) Parmesan cheese
½ pint (300 ml) tomato sauce (use the pizza topping given on pages 68–69)

Cut a circle round the base of each green pepper to remove the stem and seeds. Place the peppers in a basin and cover with boiling water. Allow to stand for 5 minutes, then drain thoroughly and set the peppers aside.

For the stuffing, first cook the rice in a large pan of boiling salted water. Simmer for 8–10 minutes or until the rice is tender; drain through a colander. Peel the onion, wash and trim the mushrooms and chop both finely. Cut the rind from the bacon and dice the flesh. Melt the butter in a heavy-based pan and sauté the bacon, onion and mushrooms for a few minutes. Add the chicken livers whole and cook for a few minutes, then remove the livers and chop them into tiny pieces; return to the pan. Stir in the cooked rice, salt, pepper and parsley; remove the pan from the heat. Lightly beat the egg and use it to bind the rice and liver mixture.

Arrange the peppers, cut surface uppermost, in a buttered fireproof dish. Spoon the rice mixture into the peppers, and sprinkle them with half the grated cheese.

Spoon 2 tablespoons of cold water into the dish and set it above the centre of an oven pre-heated to 350°F (180°C, mark 4); cook for 35–40 minutes.

Immediately before serving, sprinkle the peppers with the remaining cheese. Serve a bowl of hot tomato sauce separately.

STUFFED GREEN PEPPERS

SALT SUGAR FAT CHOL FIBRE

GLUTEN-FREE WHOLEFOOD*
TOTAL CALORIES: ABOUT 1515

For low **salt** use only ½ oz (10 g) bacon and half the Parmesan. This will also reduce the **fat** and **cholesterol**. To reduce the fat further, to low, cook the bacon onion and mushrooms in a pan brushed with oil. For low cholesterol, replace the chicken livers with more mushrooms. (Calories lost: up to 250.)
Use brown rice for **wholefood** and to increase the **fibre** level. Cook it for about 40 minutes in 2¼ times its volume of water.

Freezing: ✓ up to 2 months.
Microwave: ✓

RICE SALAD WITH FLORENCE FENNEL

SALT SUGAR FAT CHOL FIBRE

GLUTEN-FREE WHOLEFOOD*
TOTAL CALORIES: ABOUT 2910

For moderate **salt**, use half the olives and tuna. Half or all the weight of fish can be replaced by a fresh fish such as monkfish, lightly poached and cut into cubes.
The high **fat** level comes from the mayonnaise, which also contains cholesterol to add to that from the egg garnish. To reduce fat and **cholesterol** to low, dress the salad with a mixture of yogurt and lemon juice, with fresh herbs and only 1 tablespoon of best quality oil,

ıd use tuna canned in brine.
ı place of the eggs, the salad
ın be garnished with toasted
mond flakes, say ½ oz (10 g),
hich will still provide a little
ıt, but no cholesterol.
Calories lost: up to 962.)

ASI GORENG

SALT SUGAR FAT CHOL FIBRE

.UTEN-FREE* WHOLEFOOD*
TAL CALORIES: ABOUT 3680

or low **salt** omit the soya
uce.
or low **fat** use only 1
blespoon of oil to cook the
nion and meat, covering the
ixture to prevent it drying
ut. Use only a light brushing
f oil in which to cook the
ring onions and omelette.
or moderate **cholesterol** make
alf the amount of omelette.
Calories lost: up to 1653.)
'amari, the Japanese soya
uce, is **gluten-free**.

reezing: ☑ up to 1 month.

LMOND RICE

SALT SUGAR FAT CHOL FIBRE

UTEN-FREE WHOLEFOOD*
TAL CALORIES: ABOUT 1200

or low **fat** use only ½ oz (10 g)
utter and half the almonds.
Calories lost: up to 233.)
educing the almonds will
ake this a low **fibre** dish;
sing brown rice will make it
igh in fibre and **wholefood**.
rown rice requires about half
s much stock again.

reezing: ☑ up to 3 months.

RICE SALAD WITH FLORENCE FENNEL

The sweet aniseed flavour of bulbous Florence fennel blends well with rice and Pernod-flavoured mayonnaise. The salad is usually served with cold meat or fish.

PREPARATION TIME: *30 min*
COOKING TIME: *20 min*
CHILLING TIME: *30 min*
INGREDIENTS: *(for 4–6):*
6 oz (175 g) long grain rice
2 Florence fennel roots
7–8 oz (200–225 g) tin of tuna fish
4 oz (100 g) stoned black olives
¼ pint (150 ml) mayonnaise (page 85)
1 tablespoon Pernod
GARNISH:
3 hardboiled eggs
6 spring onions

Bring a large pan of lightly salted water to the boil and cook the rice for 20 minutes. Rinse and drain the rice thoroughly in a sieve and set it aside to cool.

Trim the fennel, wash the roots in cold running water, then cut them into thin slices. Drain the oil from the tuna fish and break the flesh up with a fork. Mix the rice, fennel, tuna and olives together in a salad bowl. Stir the Pernod into the mayonnaise and fold this dressing into the salad.

Trim the spring onions and cut them in half lengthways. Shell and quarter the eggs. Garnish the salad with the onions and eggs and leave it to chill in the refrigerator for 30 minutes.

NASI GORENG

This Indonesian rice dish with omelette is an excellent way of using up cooked meat, poultry, fish, shellfish and vegetables.

PREPARATION TIME: *30 min*
COOKING TIME: *35 min*
INGREDIENTS *(for 6):*
8 oz (225 g) long grain rice
2 oz (50 g) dried shrimps
6 fluid oz (175 ml) peanut oil
2 onions
1 clove garlic
1 fresh chili or ½ level teaspoon chili powder
8 oz (225 g) cooked diced meat
Salt and black pepper*
OMELETTE:
1–2 tablespoons butter or vegetable oil
3–4 spring onions
1 tomato
Salt and chili powder*
3–4 tablespoons soya sauce
4 eggs
Cucumber slices

Peel and finely chop the onions and garlic and the spring onions for the omelette. Finely shred the fresh chili; skin and chop the tomato. Boil and drain the rice. Spread it on a dish to cool and meanwhile soak the shrimps in cold water.

Heat the oil in a large pan and fry the onions until transparent. Add the garlic and chili and fry for 3 more minutes. Stir in the meat and cook for 2 minutes, before adding the rice and the drained shrimps. Continue frying, stirring frequently, until the rice turns pale golden. Season to taste. Put the rice mixture on a warm serving dish.

For the omelette, fry the spring onions in the oil until soft. Add the tomato and cook for a further 2–3 minutes. Season with salt, chili powder and half the soya sauce. Cook for 3 minutes. Beat the eggs lightly and stir them into the pan, cover and cook the omelette, over low heat, until set. Remove from the pan, and shred the omelette finely.

Arrange the omelette over the rice, sprinkle with the remaining soya sauce and garnish with cucumber slices.

ALMOND RICE

Many rice dishes make good accompaniments to grilled poultry and gammon.

PREPARATION TIME: *5 min*
COOKING TIME: *25 min*
INGREDIENTS *(for 4):*
6 oz (175 g) long grain rice
1 onion
1 oz (25 g) unsalted butter
1 oz (25 g) stoned raisins
¾ pint (425 ml) chicken stock
*½ level teaspoon salt**
2 oz (50 g) roasted flaked almonds
GARNISH:
1 tablespoon chopped parsley

Peel and finely chop the onion. Melt the butter in a saucepan and add the onion; cover the pan with a lid and cook over low heat for about 5 minutes until the onion is soft. Add the rice and toss it with the onion and butter. Stir in the raisins and add the hot stock and the salt. Bring to the boil, lower the heat and cover the pan with a lid. Simmer the rice gently for 15–20 minutes or until it is tender.

When cooked, fluff the rice up with a fork, fold in the almonds and spoon it all into a hot serving dish. Sprinkle with parsley.

RISOTTO BIANCO

Rice is the staple food in northern Italy, as pasta is in the south. An Italian risotto is served quite plainly, with butter and cheese.

PREPARATION TIME: *10 min*
COOKING TIME: *20–25 min*
INGREDIENTS *(for 4–6)*:
8 oz (225 g) Italian rice
1 small onion
1 small clove garlic
3 oz (75 g) butter
2 teaspoons olive oil
$1\frac{1}{2}$ pints (900 ml) white stock
Salt and black pepper*
4 oz (100 g) grated Parmesan cheese

Peel and finely chop the onion and garlic. Heat 2 oz (50 g) of the butter with the oil in a deep sauté pan and cook the onion and garlic until soft and just beginning to colour. Add the cleaned rice to the pan. Cook over low heat, stirring continuously, until the rice is yellow and shiny.

Add a third of the hot stock to the rice; bring to the boil, stir, then cover the pan with a lid. Cook over moderate heat until all the liquid is absorbed, then gradually stir in the remaining stock. Cover the pan again, and simmer the rice, stirring occasionally, until all the stock has been absorbed, after about 15 minutes. The rice should then be creamy and firm. Watch the risotto carefully while cooking to see that it does not dry out.

Season the risotto to taste with salt and freshly ground pepper. Stir in the remaining butter and half the cheese. Spoon the risotto into a warm shallow dish, stir lightly with a fork, and sprinkle with the rest of the cheese.

RISOTTO ALLA MILANESE

There are several versions of Milanese rice, some being made with chicken broth, others with white wine or Marsala. The classic flavouring of saffron, however, is always included. The rice can be served as a course on its own, and is also the traditional accompaniment to *osso buco* (stewed shin of veal).

PREPARATION TIME: *20 min*
COOKING TIME: *20 min*
INGREDIENTS *(for 6)*:
1 lb (450 g) Italian or short grain rice
1 marrow bone
1 small onion
3 oz (75 g) unsalted butter
$\frac{1}{4}$ pint (150 ml) dry white wine
2 pints (1·2 litres) beef stock
$\frac{1}{2}$ level teaspoon powdered saffron
3 oz (75 g) grated Parmesan cheese

Ask the butcher to chop the bone into several pieces, so that the marrow can be easily extracted with a skewer – it should yield about 2 oz (50 g). Peel and finely chop the onion.

Melt half the butter in a large pan, add the marrow and onion and fry over moderate heat until transparent. Pour the wine over the onion and boil briskly until reduced by half. Add the rice and sauté, stirring continuously, until it begins to change colour.

Stir the boiling stock, a cupful at a time, into the rice, until completely absorbed. Blend in all the stock and finally stir in the saffron. The rice should be tender after 15–20 minutes. If necessary, add a little hot water to prevent the rice drying out.

Stir the remaining butter and grated Parmesan cheese into the rice and serve at once.

ORANGE RICE

Savoury rice, instead of potatoes, goes well with chicken or veal dishes in cream sauce. The rice can also be used cold as a base for a salad.

PREPARATION TIME: *10 min*
COOKING TIME: *30 min*
INGREDIENTS *(for 6)*:
1 lb (450 g) long grain rice
1 small onion
3 sticks celery
3 oz (75 g) unsalted butter
2 large oranges
Salt and black pepper*
2 sprigs thyme

Peel and finely chop the onion; wash the celery and cut into narrow slices. Melt the butter in a large, heavy-based pan and fry the onion and celery over low heat for about 5 minutes, until the onion is soft. Finely grate the rind from the oranges; squeeze the flesh and strain the juice. Add $1\frac{1}{2}$ pints (900 ml) of cold water to the pan, together with the orange rind and juice, a pinch of salt and the thyme. Bring this mixture to the boil.

Wash the rice and pour it into the orange mixture. Bring back to the boil and simmer, stirring occasionally, for about 25 minutes until the rice is tender and the liquid absorbed.

Before serving, remove the thyme and season with freshly ground pepper.

RISOTTO BIANCO

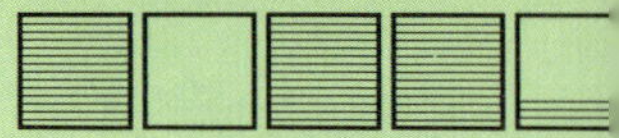

SALT SUGAR FAT CHOL FIBRE

GLUTEN-FREE WHOLEFOOD*
TOTAL CALORIES: ABOUT 1923

For low **salt**, replace the chees with mushrooms – dried mushrooms go very well in a risotto. Use about $\frac{1}{2}$ oz (10–15 g and soak them first for about half an hour. Their soaking water, strained, can be used fo cooking the rice.
To reduce the **fat** and **cholesterol** levels to low, softe the onion in the oil alone, covering the pan to prevent it drying out, and add a teaspoor of butter with the rice. When the rice is cooked add only 2 teaspoons more butter, an 1–2 oz (25–50 g) cheese. (Calories lost: up to 654.)
For a **vegetarian** dish, cook th rice in vegetable stock. Brown rice will need more liquid.

Freezing: ✓ up to 3 months.

RISOTTO ALLA MILANESE

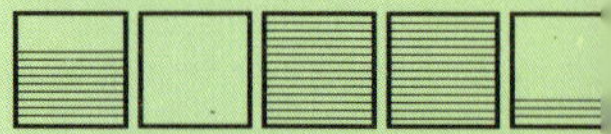

SALT SUGAR FAT CHOL FIBRE

GLUTEN-FREE WHOLEFOOD*
TOTAL CALORIES: ABOUT 2878

For low **salt** use only 2 oz (50 g Parmesan and unsalted stock.
To reduce the **fat** and **cholesterol** levels, cook the marrow and onion in a heavy pan brushed lightly with oil. Omit the remaining butter at the end, or add only 2–3 teaspoons so that each person gets about 2 teaspoonfuls fat. Together with reducing the Parmesan, as above, this will

ive a very moderate fat and
holesterol level. (Calories lost:
p to 472.)
f you are using brown rice for a
igh-**fibre** and **wholefood** dish,
t will need more liquid and will
ake a lot longer to cook.
'or a **vegetarian** dish omit the
narrow; use vegetable stock.

'reezing: √ up to 3 months.

)RANGE RICE

SALT SUGAR FAT CHOL FIBRE

.UTEN-FREE WHOLEFOOD* VEGETARIAN
)TAL CALORIES: ABOUT 2288

'o reduce the **fat** and
holesterol levels to low, cook
ne onion and celery in only ½ oz
10 g) butter, vegetable
nargarine or oil. Using either
ne margarine or oil will
liminate cholesterol from the
ish. (Calories lost: up to 481.)

'reezing: √ up to 3 months.

**:ICE WITH GARLIC AND
/ALNUTS**

SALT SUGAR FAT CHOL FIBRE

.UTEN-FREE WHOLEFOOD*
)TAL CALORIES: ABOUT 1604

'or low **fat** use 1 tablespoon
il and half the Parmesan.
Calories lost: up to 322.)
or a **vegetarian** dish, cook the
ce in a little more than its own
olume of water. Brown rice
ill need about 2¼ times its own
olume, and will give a high-
bre and **wholefood** dish.

'reezing: √ up to 2 months.

RICE WITH GARLIC AND WALNUTS

Plain boiled rice is a good substitute for potatoes and vegetables. Here the rice is given additional flavour, which makes it a good choice with goulash or curry.

PREPARATION TIME: *15 min*
COOKING TIME: *14 min*
INGREDIENTS *(for 4–6)*:
8 oz (225 g) Patna rice
2 heaped tablespoons finely chopped parsley
2 cloves garlic
1 oz (25 g) shelled walnuts
2 oz (50 g) grated Parmesan cheese
3 tablespoons olive oil
Salt and black pepper*
2 pints (1·2 litres) chicken stock
*1 level tablespoon salt**
Juice of half lemon

Pound the parsley in a mortar with the peeled garlic and nuts until a smooth paste is achieved. Beat in the cheese until the mixture is thick, then gradually beat in the oil. Season to taste with salt and freshly ground pepper.

Pour the stock into a large saucepan and bring to the boil. Add the salt, lemon juice and rice, stirring until it returns to the boil. Cover and boil for 14 minutes or until the rice is just tender, adding more water only if necessary. Drain in a colander and rinse the rice by running hot water through it.

Drain the rice thoroughly and stir with a fork to separate the grains. Spoon it into a hot serving dish; season with a good grating of pepper. Blend the nut mixture into the rice and serve.

GREEK RICE RING

Particularly attractive when moulded in a ring, this spicy rice dish, served hot or cold, makes a light meal on its own. Kebabs, shellfish or chicken make it even more substantial.

PREPARATION TIME: *20 min*
COOKING TIME: *20–40 min*
SETTING TIME: *1 hour*
INGREDIENTS *(for 6):*
8 oz (225 g) long grain rice
Salt and black pepper*
Lemon juice
2 large ripe tomatoes
1 tablespoon finely chopped chives
1 tablespoon finely chopped parsley
8 green olives
$\frac{1}{2}$ level teaspoon each, dried basil and marjoram
1 red pepper
4 tablespoons olive oil
2 tablespoons tarragon vinegar
GARNISH:
Black olives

Cook the rice in a large pan of boiling salted water, with a teaspoon of lemon juice, for about 15 minutes or until the rice is just tender. Drain the rice in a colander and cover with a dry cloth to absorb the steam and keep the rice dry and fluffy.

While the rice is cooking, skin the tomatoes (page 92). Chop them finely and put them in a large bowl together with the chives, parsley and finely chopped green olives. Blend in the dried herbs. Scald the pepper in boiling water for 5 minutes, cut off the stalk end and remove the seeds. Cut the pepper into narrow strips; set eight strips aside and chop the remainder finely. Add them to the tomato mixture.

Mix the still-warm rice into the tomato mixture. Blend the oil and vinegar together in a small bowl and season to taste with salt and freshly ground pepper. Add enough of this dressing to moisten the rice thoroughly; adjust seasoning and sharpen to taste with lemon juice. Press the rice firmly into a ring mould and leave to set in a cool place for at least 1 hour.

To serve hot, cover the rice mould with buttered foil or greaseproof paper and place it in a roasting tin containing about $\frac{1}{2}$ in (1 cm) of boiling water. Heat on top of the stove for 15–20 minutes, then remove the covering and place the serving dish over the mould. Turn it upside-down, and give a sharp shake to ease out the rice. Garnish with black olives and strips of red pepper.

Invert half a grapefruit in the centre and skewer grilled lamb kebabs in a fan arrangement in the grapefruit.

For a cold lunch, unmould the rice ring, as already described, without re-heating it. For a more substantial meal, fill the centre with cooked chicken, scampi or lobster in mousseline sauce.

FRIED RICE WITH LEEKS

This unusual rice dish is especially good with meat courses that contain a lot of sauce, such as casseroles and braised oxtail stews.

PREPARATION TIME: *15 min*
COOKING TIME: *20 min*
INGREDIENTS *(for 6):*
2 lb (900 g) leeks
6 oz (175 g) Patna rice
*2 level tablespoons salt**
2 oz (50 g) unsalted butter
$\frac{1}{2}$ level teaspoon curry powder
Black pepper

Set a pan holding about 6 pints ($3\frac{1}{2}$ litres) of water to boil for the rice, and a smaller one holding about 1 pint (570 ml) for the leeks. Remove the coarse outer leaves, roots and tops from the leeks, wash well under cold running water, flushing away any dirt trapped in the ends; cut into $\frac{1}{4}$ in ($\frac{1}{2}$ cm) thick slices. Add a tablespoon of salt to each saucepan of boiling water, put the leeks in one and the rice in the other. Stir the rice until it comes back to the boil, cover and boil for 14 minutes. Meanwhile, simmer the leeks for about 5 minutes, then drain them through a colander. Melt the butter in a frying pan, and fry the leeks for about 8 minutes or until just tender.

When it is cooked, turn the rice into a sieve and wash thoroughly under hot running water. Add the drained rice to the leeks in the frying pan, blend with the curry powder; fry for a few minutes, stirring all the time. Season with freshly ground pepper and serve.

GREEK RICE RING

SALT SUGAR FAT CHOL FIBRE

GLUTEN-FREE WHOLEFOOD* VEGETARIAN
TOTAL CALORIES: ABOUT 1430

The exact **salt** level depends or the number of black olives use for the garnish. For low salt, use not more than 6 or omit them entirely.
To reduce the **fat** level to low add only 2 or 3 tablespoons oil to the mixture, reducing the vinegar in proportion. (Calorie lost: up to 270.)
Brown rice will take longer to cook but contributes more **fibr** and makes the dish **wholefood**

Freezing: √ up to 3 months.

FRIED RICE WITH LEEKS

SALT SUGAR FAT CHOL FIBRE

GLUTEN-FREE*. WHOLEFOOD* VEGETARIA
TOTAL CALORIES: ABOUT 1280

The low **salt** level assumes the rice and leeks are cooked in unsalted water.
To reduce the **fat** level to low, change the method of cooking the leeks. Put them in a large saucepan with 1 tablespoon butter and 3 tablespoons stock and poach gently for about 8 minutes. (Calories lost: up to 265.)
Brown rice not only has more **fibre**, but more flavour even when cooked without salt. Check the curry powder is **gluten-free**.

Freezing: √ up to 2 months.

RAVIOLI WITH CHEESE

SALT SUGAR FAT CHOL FIBRE

WHOLEFOOD* VEGETARIAN
TOTAL CALORIES: ABOUT 2485

(To reduce the **salt** content to medium, use 12 oz (350 g) mushrooms, sliced and cooked in a heavy pan brushed with oil, then chopped, in place of half the ricotta cheese, and only 2 tablespoons of Parmesan, increasing the onion if wished. To reduce the **fat** and **cholesterol** content, use only 2 yolks to make the pasta and omit the yolks added to the filling, which should stick together enough without them. This will give low fat and cholesterol. Serve with smetana or quark instead of butter. Calories lost: up to 600.)

Freezing: ☑ up to 3 months.

RAVIOLI WITH CHEESE

This very rich pasta dough has a light filling, and is served simply with butter and grated cheese. Spinach is sometimes added to the ricotta.

PREPARATION TIME: *1 hour*
COOKING TIME: *10 min*
INGREDIENTS *(for 6–8):*
8 oz (225 g) plain flour
6 egg yolks
*¾ teaspoon salt**
4 fluid oz (100 ml) warm water
1 lb (450 g) ricotta cheese
4 oz (100 g) grated Parmesan cheese
2 tablespoons grated onion

Sift the flour onto a board; make a well in the centre and put 3 of the egg yolks in the well. Add ¼ teaspoon of the salt and 3 tablespoons of the water. Work it into the flour and knead until a stiff dough is formed, adding a little more warm water if necessary. Knead until smooth and elastic. Cover the dough and let it stand for 15 minutes.

Divide the dough in half, and roll out one half very thinly. In a bowl, mix the remaining egg yolks, the ricotta cheese, Parmesan cheese, onion, and remaining salt until well blended. Place 1 teaspoonful of the mixture on the centre of the dough; repeat, spacing teaspoonfuls 2 in (5 cm) apart in each direction.

Roll out the remaining half of the dough and carefully position it as a top layer, brushing the outside edges lightly with water to seal the layers. Press the layers of dough together around each mound of the cheese mixture.

Cut into squares with a pastry wheel or a sharp knife. Drop into boiling salted water, and simmer for 10 minutes. Drain well. Serve with melted butter and additional grated Parmesan cheese.

LOBSTER RAVIOLI

Ravioli – little egg pasta cushions – are usually bought ready made and then filled with a savoury stuffing. They bear little resemblance to fresh pasta, but here, for a special occasion, is a recipe for home-made ravioli, with a luxury filling. Crabmeat can be substituted for the lobster.

PREPARATION TIME: *$1\frac{1}{2}$ hours*
STANDING TIME: *2 hours*
COOKING TIME: *10 min*
INGREDIENTS *(for 4)*:
RAVIOLI:
8 oz (225 g) plain flour
*$\frac{1}{4}$ level teaspoon salt**
2 large eggs
$1\frac{1}{2}$ oz (40 g) butter
1 small egg
FILLING:
$\frac{1}{2}$–$\frac{3}{4}$ lb (225–350 g) lobster or crabmeat
1 tablespoon double cream
Squeeze of lemon
Cayenne pepper
SAUCE:
$\frac{1}{2}$ pint (300 ml) white sauce
3 tablespoons double cream
1 heaped teaspoon tomato purée
Juice of half lemon
Cayenne pepper
GARNISH:
Parmesan cheese

Sift the flour and the salt into a mixing bowl and make a well in the centre. Lightly beat the 2 eggs and pour into the flour; mix thoroughly. Melt the butter in a small saucepan and add to the flour. Knead the mixture to a stiff paste with a little cold water.

Turn the paste on to a floured surface and knead for 10 minutes until shiny. Set the paste aside to rest for at least 1 hour.

Meanwhile, make the filling for the ravioli; chop the lobster or crabmeat finely into a mixing bowl, add the cream and season to taste with lemon juice and cayenne pepper.

Roll out the paste, on a floured surface, to a paper-thin 24 in (60 cm) square. With a teaspoon, drop the filling over one half of the paste, at intervals of $1\frac{1}{2}$ in (4 cm). Brush between the fillings with lightly beaten egg. Turn over the other half of the paste and press down firmly with the fingers between the fillings. Cut through the filled squares with a pastry wheel. Dust the ravioli squares with flour and set them aside for about 1 hour before cooking.

When ready for cooking, bring a large pan of lightly salted water to the boil. Drop the ravioli into the water and cook for about 7 minutes. Drain on absorbent paper and keep them hot on a serving dish.

Serve the ravioli with a white sauce (page 84), enriched with cream and tomato purée. Season to taste with lemon and cayenne pepper. Heat the sauce through without boiling and serve in a sauce boat. Finally, grate Parmesan cheese into a separate bowl, and pass it round with the hot ravioli and sauce.

LOBSTER RAVIOLI

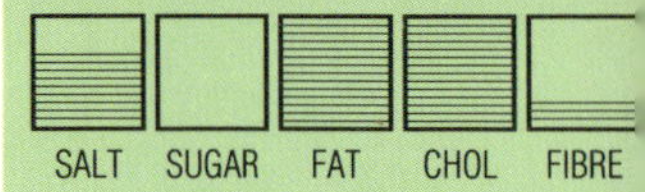

WHOLEFOOD*
TOTAL CALORIES: ABOUT 2685

The **salt** is natural to both lobster and crab. The only way to reduce it to low is to replace up to half with a less salty fish, such as monkfish.
The crab or lobster also accoun for much of the high **cholesterol** level, but this can be restricted to medium if some monkfish is used instead, as above, only 1 egg is used in making the pasta and the butter is replaced with 2 tablespoons oil. Omit the egg for brushing the pasta.
These moves will also reduce the **fat**. If, as well, the cream is replaced with smetana, quark or low-fat yogurt, and skim milk is used in the sauce, the total fat level will be low. (Calories lost: up to 685.)

TAGLIATELLE ALLA CARBONARA

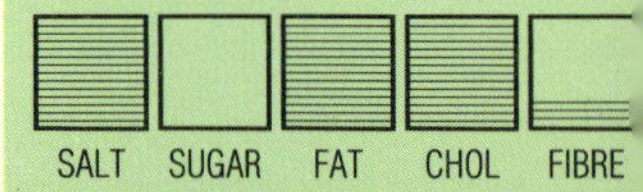

WHOLEFOOD*
TOTAL CALORIES: ABOUT 2045

The high **salt** content comes mainly from the bacon, with the ham, both cheeses, and eggs also contributing to the high total level. The only way to reduce it to moderate is to use half quantities of bacon, ham and cheese. You could omit the bacon which will almost halve the salt, giving a medium level, but green bacon is very characteristic of this dish. In addition, ensure that

'he pasta and butter are not ;alted.
\ny reduction in the bacon, :heese or eggs will also reduce he **fat** and **cholesterol** (ham is ıot high in either). Cooking the ›acon and ham in a pan lightly ›rushed with oil will save over ıalf the fat entailed in using ›utter and oil for this job. The ecipe will remain fairly high in :holesterol even if only 3 eggs ıre used. These changes can be nade to the degree that suits 'our taste, giving a medium fat, nedium salt and high 'holesterol dish. For a low-fat lish, it is necessary to cut the :ggs and cheese quite lrastically. (Calories lost: up to ›31.)

;PAGHETTI WITH \UBERGINE

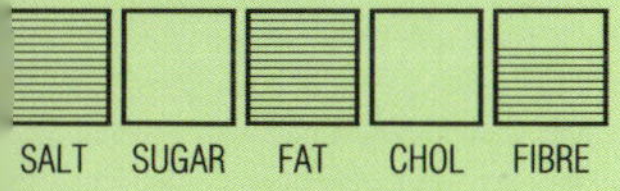

/HOLEFOOD* VEGETARIAN
'OTAL CALORIES: ABOUT 2265

'o reduce the **salt** level to low, ›mit the salting stage for the ıubergines. This is supposed to educe the bitter taste of ıubergines, but modern 'arieties seem not to need the reatment. What salting does do s reduce the need for so much ›il when aubergines are fried, ›ut grilling them as suggested ›elow avoids this problem too.
'or a low **fat** level, grill the ıubergine 'chips' on a ;enerously greased oven sheet or a few minutes, tossing ›ccasionally to coat with fat, ınder high heat. (Calories lost: ıp to 539.)

TAGLIATELLE ALLA CARBONARA

Alla carbonara means "in the style of the charcoal-burner's wife". She would probably have used fat belly pork, but streaky green bacon makes a good substitute. She would also have used all Parmesan or a mixture of Pecorino and Parmesan.

PREPARATION TIME: *10 min*
COOKING TIME: *15 min*
INGREDIENTS *(for 6):*
8 oz (225 g) tagliatelle
2 oz (50 g) streaky green bacon
2 oz (50 g) cooked ham
1 oz (25 g) butter
1 tablespoon olive oil
4 eggs
2 oz (50 g) grated Cheddar cheese
1 oz (25 g) grated Parmesan cheese
Salt and black pepper*

Remove the rind and gristle from the bacon and chop the rashers roughly; dice the ham. Cook the tagliatelle in plenty of well-salted boiling water for 10–15 minutes or until just tender. Drain thoroughly in a colander.

While the tagliatelle is cooking, heat the butter and oil in a pan over moderate heat and fry the bacon and ham until they are crisp. Beat the eggs and cheeses together in a bowl.

Add the drained pasta to the bacon and ham and stir carefully until evenly coated with fat. Pour in the beaten eggs and cheese and continue stirring over gentle heat until the eggs thicken. Be sure to remove the pan from the heat before the eggs scramble.

Spoon the mixture into a warm dish and serve at once, with a bowl of grated Parmesan cheese.

SPAGHETTI WITH AUBERGINE

In Italy, pasta – and in particular spaghetti – frequently forms the main meal of the day. Often oil and garlic are the only additions, but aubergine gives the pasta an unusual flavour.

PREPARATION TIME: *10 min*
COOKING TIME: *15 min*
INGREDIENTS *(for 4–6):*
¾ lb (350 g) spaghetti
1 large aubergine
2 level tablespoons salt
6 tablespoons olive oil
Seasoned flour (page 99)
Black pepper

Remove the stalk end and wipe the aubergine. Cut it into thin round slices and place these in layers in a colander. Sprinkle salt over each layer and leave for 1 hour to draw out the excess water. Wipe the slices dry on absorbent kitchen paper, cut them into ¼ in (½ cm) wide strips and coat them lightly with seasoned flour.

Heat 8 pints (4½ litres) of water in a large saucepan and, when boiling, add 1 level tablespoon salt and the spaghetti. Stir continuously until the water returns to the boil. Continue boiling and stirring occasionally for 9 minutes, when the spaghetti should be tender but still slightly undercooked (*al dente*). While the spaghetti is cooking, heat 3–4 tablespoons of olive oil in a frying pan and sauté the aubergine strips until crisp.

Drain the spaghetti, toss in a colander to remove the last of the water, and pepper well. Warm the remaining olive oil in a saucepan, transfer the spaghetti to a warm serving dish and pour over the oil. Toss well and blend the aubergine strips into the spaghetti.

SPAGHETTINI WITH MUSSEL SAUCE

Fine thin strands of spaghetti, known as spaghettini, make a lighter-than-usual pasta dish. It is here served in an unusual sauce for a main course.

PREPARATION TIME: *1 hour*
COOKING TIME: *15 min*
INGREDIENTS *(for 4–6):*
1 lb (450 g) spaghettini
4 pints ($1\frac{1}{2}$–2 kg) mussels
2 heaped tablespoons salt
8 tablespoons olive oil
3 cloves garlic
$\frac{1}{4}$ pint (150 ml) fish stock
Black pepper
1 level tablespoon finely chopped parsley

Wash the mussels under cold running water, scrubbing the shells and scraping off the beards. Leave the mussels in a pail of cold water to which has been added 2 tablespoons salt.

Set a large pan of lightly salted water to boil. Meanwhile, heat 3 tablespoons oil in large sauté pan. Add 2 peeled and crushed cloves of garlic and fry in the oil until brown. Remove the garlic. Put the mussels in the pan, place over high heat, cover with a lid, and shake the pan for 5 minutes, or until the shells have opened. Remove the pan from the heat and discard any mussels that remain closed. Turn the contents of the pan into a bowl and ease the mussels from the shells, retaining the liquid.

Put the spaghettini into the pan of boiling salted water, stirring until the water boils again. Cook the spaghettini for 7–10 minutes, stirring occasionally until just tender. Drain the spaghettini

SPAGHETTINI WITH MUSSEL SAUCE

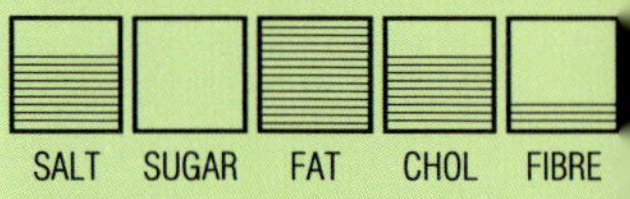

WHOLEFOOD*
TOTAL CALORIES: ABOUT 3375

The **salt** level comes mainly from the mussels, which are naturally high in sodium: $3\frac{1}{2}$ oz (100 g) shelled mussels yield over 200 mg, so even if no salt is added elsewhere to the pasta or stock, the level cannot be reduced below medium.
The high **fat** level can be reduced to moderate by using only 2 or 3 tablespoons oil. If top quality oil is used, the flavour will still be good. (Calories lost: up to 809.) The **cholesterol** level cannot be changed either as this is due to the mussels (but see also the notes on the next recipe).

LUMACHINE CON COZZE

SALT SUGAR FAT CHOL FIBRE

WHOLEFOOD*
TOTAL CALORIES: ABOUT 1785

The **salt** and **cholesterol** level are naturally present in the mussels, so cannot be reduced unless smaller portions are served. However, they are much lower than, for instance, in a bacon and egg breakfast. If a lower level of either is needed, replace half the mussels with mushrooms. This is, of course, a different dish, but still very good. (Calories lost: up to 238.)

Freezing: √ up to 3 months for the tomato sauce.

Microwave: √ for the tomato sauce.

SPAGHETTI WITH TUNA SAUCE

SALT SUGAR FAT CHOL FIBRE

WHOLEFOOD*
TOTAL CALORIES: ABOUT 2720

The **salt** level comes from the salt added to tinned tuna, whether in oil or brine. To give a low level, replace this with fresh tuna or monkfish.
The **fat** level can be reduced to low by cooking the garlic in a pan brushed with oil, omitting the remaining oil and butter. If wished, 1 oz (15 g) of butter can be tossed through the cooked pasta. Use tuna tinned in brine, not in oil. Again, using fresh fish means an even lower fat level. (Calories lost: up to 653.)

thoroughly in a colander.

Heat the remaining oil in the sauté pan over low heat. Peel and crush the remaining garlic and fry until golden. Pour half the contents of the pan over the spaghettini and toss until it gleams. Return the mussels and their liquid to the sauté pan and heat through gently. Add the fish stock and continue cooking for 1–2 minutes until thoroughly heated. Pepper well, and stir in the parsley.

Spoon the mussels and liquid over the spaghettini, toss and serve at once, with slices of warm crusty bread.

LUMACHINE CON COZZE

This is an Italian dish of egg pasta shells (lumachine) and mussels. When fresh mussels are not available, bottled mussels, without their brine, may be used. Spaghetti or spaghettini can be used instead of the pasta shells, and baby clams (also available bottled) can replace the mussels, making this into a version of the popular spaghetti alle vongole.

PREPARATION TIME: *30 min*
COOKING TIME: *25 min*
INGREDIENTS *(for 4):*
2 pints (1 kg) fresh mussels
1 lb (450 g) ripe tomatoes
1 clove garlic
1 tablespoon olive oil
1 level tablespoon chopped parsley
$\frac{1}{2}$ level teaspoon each, dried marjoram and basil
$2\frac{1}{2}$ fluid oz (75 ml) white wine
8 oz (225 g) lumachine
Salt and black pepper*
Lemon juice

Scrub and clean the mussels thoroughly. Remove the beards, and discard any mussels with broken or open shells.

Skin the tomatoes (page 92) and chop them roughly. Peel and finely chop the garlic. Heat the oil in a frying pan and lightly fry the garlic. Add the tomatoes, parsley and herbs and bring this mixture to simmering point.

Put the cleaned mussels and the wine in a pan and cover with a lid. Cook over moderate heat, shaking occasionally, until the mussels open. Remove the mussels from the shells and set them aside. Strain the cooking liquid through muslin to remove any sandy sediment, and stir it into the tomato mixture. Simmer over low heat for 20 minutes.

While the tomatoes are cooking, bring a large pan of water to the boil, add 2–3 teaspoons of salt and cook the pasta shells for 12 minutes or until tender, but not soft. Drain in a colander and cover with a clean cloth to keep the pasta warm.

Add the mussels to the tomato sauce and heat through. Season to taste with freshly ground pepper, adding salt only if necessary, and sharpen with lemon juice. Put the pasta shells in a warmed deep serving dish and pour the mussels and sauce over them. Serve at once, with crusty bread.

SPAGHETTI WITH TUNA SAUCE

Lighter and more summery than spaghetti with a tomato or meat sauce, this dish makes a good family meal. Serve it with crusty bread and a green salad, tossed in French dressing (page 85).

PREPARATION TIME: *10 min*
COOKING TIME: *15 min*
INGREDIENTS *(for 4–6):*
1 lb (450 g) spaghetti
1 clove garlic (optional)
2 tablespoons olive oil
2 oz (50 g) butter
8 fluid oz (225 ml) chicken stock
3 tablespoons dry white wine or vermouth
6 oz (175 g) tin of tuna fish
Salt and black pepper*
GARNISH:
2 tablespoons finely chopped parsley

Bring a large pan of salted water to the boil, add the spaghetti and bring back to the boil. Cook for 7–12 minutes or until the spaghetti is just resistant to the bite (*al dente*). Stir occasionally with a wooden spoon.

Peel and finely chop the garlic. Heat the oil and half the butter, and fry the garlic for 1–2 minutes, then stir in the stock and wine. Boil briskly over high heat until the liquid has reduced to about $\frac{1}{4}$ pint (150 ml). Drain the oil from the tuna fish, flake the meat and add it to the stock. Season with salt and freshly ground pepper.

When the spaghetti is cooked, drain it thoroughly in a colander and toss it in the remaining butter. Put the spaghetti in a serving dish, pour over the tuna sauce and sprinkle with the chopped parsley. Serve at once.

FETTUCCINE AL BURRO

This pasta dish is a speciality of many Roman restaurants and is ideally made from home-made noodles.

PREPARATION TIME: *8 min*
COOKING TIME: *10–15 min*
INGREDIENTS *(for 4–6):*
1 lb (450 g) ribbon noodles
*1 level tablespoon salt**
$\frac{1}{4}$ lb (100 g) unsalted butter
3 fluid oz (75 ml) double cream
6 oz (175 g) grated Parmesan cheese
Black pepper

Boil 8 pints ($4\frac{1}{2}$ litres) of water in a large saucepan, and add the salt and the noodles, stirring until the water returns to the boil, to prevent the noodles from sticking together. Cover and continue to boil for 8 minutes until the noodles are tender. Meanwhile beat the softened butter in a bowl until it fluffs; gradually beat in the cream and half the cheese. Drain the noodles and toss them in a colander to remove the last drops of water.

Put the noodles in a hot serving dish, pour over the cheese and cream sauce and toss to coat the noodles thoroughly. Pepper well and serve the remaining cheese in a bowl.

FETTUCCINE AL BURRO

SALT SUGAR FAT CHOL FIBRE

WHOLEFOOD* VEGETARIAN
TOTAL CALORIES: ABOUT 3430

The high **salt** level comes almost all from the cheese, assuming that the pasta is cooked and made without salt. This is a huge amount of Parmesan, and many people will find that 1 tablespoon per person is enough, giving a low to medium salt level.
If this is done, and if the butter is replaced with quark and the cream with low-fat yogurt or smetana, this will also give low overall **fat** and **cholesterol** levels. (Calories lost: up to 1159.)

RIGATONI WITH HARE SAUCE

SALT SUGAR FAT CHOL FIBRE

WHOLEFOOD*
TOTAL CALORIES: ABOUT 3500

The high **salt** level comes mainly from the bacon, with a substantial addition from the Parmesan. To reduce, use only 1 oz (25 g) bacon and 1–2 oz (25–50 g) cheese, giving a much lower though still medium/high level (325 mg per person from these items alone).
Hare is one of the leanest of all meats, and if the amount of bacon and cheese is reduced, as above, the dish will have a low **fat** level, especially if the lard is replaced with a brushing of oil in a heavy based pan. The **cholesterol** will also be low. (Calories lost: up to 582.)

Pressure cooker: √ for the sauce.

Freezing: √ up to 2 months for the sauce.

SCHINKENFLECKERL

SALT SUGAR FAT CHOL FIBRE

WHOLEFOOD*
TOTAL CALORIES: ABOUT 2600

The high **salt** level comes mainly from the ham, with some from the cheese. The only way to reduce this is to use less, but even if the amount of both is halved, the salt will still be high (just over 400 mg from these two ingredients alone). The **fat** level can be reduced by cooking the shallots in a heavy based pan brushed lightly with oil, omitting the butter, and using smetana, quark or low-fat yogurt (or any mixture of these) in place of the soured cream. To help stabilise these during baking, stir in a good teaspoonful of cornflour, mixed to a smooth paste with cold water, before adding the mixture. (Calories lost: up to 917.)
The **cholesterol** will stay high because of the eggs, but the fat level will be low to medium.

RIGATONI WITH HARE SAUCE

This rich pasta dish from Tuscany with a thick sauce of wine and hare is an ideal way of using up the remains of a hare.

PREPARATION TIME: *25 min*
COOKING TIME: *$1\frac{1}{4}$ hours*
INGREDIENTS *(for 4):*
12 oz (350 g) rigatoni or broad noodles
4 hare legs
4 oz (100 g) green streaky bacon
1 clove garlic
1 onion
1 stick celery
4 oz (100 g) mushrooms
1 tablespoon lard or bacon fat
1 tablespoon flour
4 fluid oz (100 ml) red wine or 2 fluid oz (50 ml) Marsala
Salt and black pepper*
Powdered thyme and marjoram
Rind and juice of half lemon
3–4 oz (75–100 g) grated Parmesan cheese

Slice the meat off the legs of the hare and remove the tough tendons. Chop the meat into $\frac{1}{2}$ in (1 cm) pieces and set aside. Remove the rind from the rashers and chop the bacon roughly. Peel and finely chop the garlic and onion. Scrub and chop the celery, and trim and slice the mushrooms.

Heat the lard or fat in a deep, heavy-based pan over moderate heat and fry the bacon, garlic, onion and celery for about 5 minutes, or until just taking colour. Add the hare meat and mushrooms and cook for a few minutes until lightly browned.

Remove the pan from the heat and stir in enough flour to absorb all the fat. Return the pan to the heat and fry the mixture until brown, stirring continuously. Add the wine and gradually blend in $\frac{3}{4}$ pint (425 ml) of water to make a thick sauce. Season to taste with salt, freshly ground pepper and a pinch of thyme and marjoram. Cover the pan with a lid and simmer over low heat for 1 hour. Add the grated lemon rind and sharpen with lemon juice.

Meanwhile, cook the rigatoni or noodles in a large pan of salted water for 12–15 minutes. Drain thoroughly in a colander. Arrange the rigatoni round the edge of a serving dish and spoon the hare sauce into the centre. Sprinkle a little cheese over the sauce and serve the remainder in a separate bowl. Serve a tossed green salad with the pasta.

SCHINKENFLECKERL

This recipe for noodles with ham is traditional both in Austria and in Switzerland.

PREPARATION TIME: *15 min*
COOKING TIME: *40–45 min*
INGREDIENTS *(for 4):*
8 oz (225 g) pasta squares or short cut noodles
2 teaspoons olive oil
2 tablespoons toasted breadcrumbs
Salt and black pepper*
8 oz (225 g) lean ham
2 shallots or 1 small onion
2 oz (50 g) butter
$7\frac{1}{2}$ fluid oz (200 ml) soured cream
2 eggs
2 oz (50 g) grated Gruyère or Cheddar cheese
GARNISH:
1 small green pepper

Grease a timbale mould or a round 6 in (15 cm) wide cake tin

with the oil and coat it evenly with the breadcrumbs.

Bring a large pan of salted water to the boil and add the pasta or noodles. Bring back to the boil and cook over high heat for 10 minutes. Drain well.

While the pasta is cooking, dice the ham, and peel and finely chop the shallots or the onion. Melt the butter in a small frying pan and cook the shallots over moderate heat for 5 minutes or until soft and transparent. Blend them into the pasta.

Blend the soured cream and eggs in a small bowl, stir in the ham and grated cheese, and add this mixture to the pasta. Blend well, and season to taste with salt and freshly ground pepper.

Spoon the pasta mixture into the prepared mould and put it in a roasting tin with enough cold water to reach 1 in ($2\frac{1}{2}$ cm) up the sides of the mould. Bake in the centre of an oven pre-heated to 400°F (200°C, mark 6) for 30 minutes, or until the mixture has set and is light brown on top.

Remove the mould from the oven and allow the mixture to cool and shrink slightly before unmoulding it on to a warmed serving dish.

Garnish with wedges or squares of grilled green pepper.

LASAGNE VERDI AL FORNO

The district round Bologna in Italy is famous for its lasagne – pasta squares often coloured with spinach (*pasta verde*). The pasta is usually baked in the oven with a Bolognese *ragù* or meat and vegetable sauce with alternating layers of thick béchamel sauce. This dish is an ideal main course for a small party as all the preparations can be done well in advance of baking.

PREPARATION TIME: *1 hour*
COOKING TIME: *20 min*
INGREDIENTS *(for 6):*

½ lb (225 g) green lasagne
2 oz (50 g) fat ham or bacon
1 small onion
1 carrot
2 oz (50 g) button mushrooms
1 oz (25 g) butter
6 oz (175 g) minced beef
2–3 oz (50–75 g) chicken livers (optional)
1 rounded tablespoon tomato concentrate
5 fluid oz (150 ml) dry white wine
½ pint (300 ml) beef stock or bouillon
1 level teaspoon caster sugar
*Salt**
¾ pint (425 ml) béchamel sauce
2 oz (50 g) grated Parmesan cheese

Chop the ham or bacon, having first removed rind and gristle. Peel and finely chop the onion and carrot and trim the mushrooms before slicing them thinly.

Melt half the butter in a large, heavy-based pan over low heat and fry the ham (or bacon) until the fat runs, then add the vegetables and fry them lightly. Crumble in the minced beef and add the cleaned and chopped chicken livers if used. Blend in the tomato concentrate. Continue frying, and stir continuously until the meat has browned. Add the wine and let the mixture bubble for a few minutes before adding the stock. Season to taste with sugar, and add salt if stock is used. Cover the pan with a lid and simmer over low heat for 30–40 minutes. Meanwhile make a thick béchamel sauce (page 84).

Cook the lasagne in a large pan of boiling salted water for 10–15 minutes or until just tender, stirring occasionally. Drain the pasta through a colander and drop it into a large basin of cold water to prevent it sticking together.

Thoroughly butter a shallow ovenproof dish, about 10 in (25 cm) by 8 in (20 cm). Cover the base with a thin layer of the meat mixture, then béchamel sauce and lastly the drained lasagne. Repeat these layers until all the ingredients are used up, finishing with béchamel sauce. Sprinkle the top with the Parmesan cheese.

Bake in the centre of the oven, pre-heated to 400°F (200°C, mark 6), for about 15–20 minutes or until the top is crisp and bubbly. Serve straight from the dish accompanied by a tossed green salad.

LUXURY PIZZA

The classic Italian pizza comes from Naples, and consists of a light yeast dough with a savoury topping. The cheese should by tradition be Mozzarella (buffalo cheese), but any quick-melting cheese, such as Bel Paese, Fontina or Gruyère, is suitable.

PREPARATION TIME: *1¾ hours*
COOKING TIME: *20–25 min*
INGREDIENTS *(for 6):*
8 oz (225 g) plain flour
*1 level teaspoon salt**
2½ fluid oz (75 ml) milk
¾ oz (20 g) fresh or ⅓ oz (10 g) dried yeast
1 level teaspoon caster sugar
1½ oz (40 g) unsalted butter
1 large egg
TOPPING:
2 large onions
2 small cloves garlic
1 lb (450 g) tomatoes
2 tablespoons olive oil
1 level tablespoon chopped fresh marjoram or ½ teaspoon dried oregano
Salt and black pepper*
GARNISH:
6 oz (175 g) quick-melting cheese
1 tin anchovy fillets
2–3 oz (50–75 g) black olives

Sift the flour and salt into a warm bowl and make a well in the centre. Heat the milk until tepid and use a few drops to cream together the yeast and sugar. (If using dried yeast, follow the manufacturer's instructions.) Pour the yeast mixture and the rest of the milk into the flour, together with the melted butter and beaten egg. Work the dough with the hand until it is smooth and leaves the sides of the bowl clean. Shape the dough into a ball

LASAGNE VERDI AL FORNO

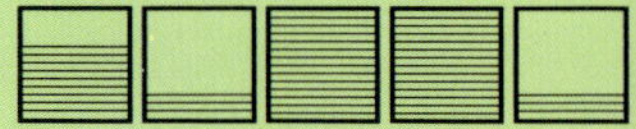

SALT SUGAR FAT CHOL FIBRE

WHOLEFOOD*
TOTAL CALORIES: ABOUT 2700

The **salt** level comes mainly from the ham or bacon and cheese. Ham has 33% less than most types of bacon. Using 1 oz (25 g) each of ham and cheese, the level will be low, assuming that the remaining ingredients, such as tomato concentrate, stock and béchamel, as well as the pasta itself, are unsalted.
To reduce the **fat** and **cholesterol** levels to low, choose lean ham, make the béchamel sauce with only ½ oz (25 g) butter and skim milk, and select lean beef. The beef itself will produce enough fat to brown itself in if heated gently, and 1 tablespoon olive oil will be enough to replace the butter at this stage. (Calories lost: up to 363.)
While not high in fat, chicken liver, like other liver, is high in cholesterol. The amount here is not large enough to give a high cholesterol count once other sources, such as bacon, butter and some of the cheese, are avoided, but strict low-cholesterol dieters will want to omit it. The amount of mushrooms can be increased to compensate.

Freezing: ✓ up to 2 months.

LUXURY PIZZA

SALT SUGAR FAT CHOL FIBRE

WHOLEFOOD*
TOTAL CALORIES: ABOUT 2320

To reduce the **salt** level to low, omit salt from the dough, use only 2 oz (50 g) of strong-flavoured cheese, and replace the garnish with slices of green or red pepper, sliced mushrooms and more fresh herbs, especially basil.
These changes will also reduce the **fat** level, which can be low if you add only ½ oz (10 g) butter to the pizza dough, omit the egg, and use only 1 tablespoon olive oil for the topping. (Calories lost: up to 905.)

Freezing: ✓ up to 3 months if uncooked, 2 months if cooked. The tomato sauce (topping) may be frozen separately for up to 3 months (up to 6 months if you omit the garlic).

CANNELLONI STUFFED WITH SPINACH

SALT	SUGAR	FAT	CHOL	FIBRE

WHOLEFOOD*
TOTAL CALORIES: ABOUT 2190

The **salt** comes almost all from the cheese, assuming that the pasta, tomato sauce and chicken are unsalted. To reduce the level to low, use only 2–3 tablespoons cheese.
This will also reduce the **fat** level, which can be low if the chicken is skinned, skim milk is used, and the tomato sauce is made using only 1 tablespoon oil. Make the white sauce by the low-fat blending method (see page 84), omitting the butter. (Calories lost: up to 345.)

Food Processor: ✓ for the filling.

Freezing: ✓ up to 1 month.

and put it into an oiled polythene bag. Leave it in a warm place until it has doubled in size.

Meanwhile, prepare the topping: peel and roughly chop the onions and garlic. Skin the tomatoes (page 92) and chop them roughly. Heat the olive oil in a heavy-based pan and cook the onion and garlic over moderate heat until soft and transparent. Add the tomatoes to the pan. Cook for about 10 minutes, then stir in the marjoram or oregano. Season to taste. Set this sauce aside. Cut the cheese into thin wedge-shaped slices, and drain the anchovy fillets.

When the dough has risen, knead it lightly with the fingertips for 1–2 minutes. Shape it into a circle 12 in (30 cm) across. Put it on a greased and floured baking tray. Cover the dough with the onion and tomato mixture to within 1 in (2½ cm) of the outer edge. Arrange the cheese on top in a fan-like pattern, slightly overlapping the slices. Decorate the cheese with the anchovies and dot with olives.

Bake the pizza near the top of an oven pre-heated to 425°F (220°C, mark 7) for 20–25 minutes or until the cheese has melted and browned slightly, and the dough is well risen.

Pizza is best served straight from the oven, but it can also be served cold, or re-heated in the oven, at low heat. A crisp sald tossed in a well-seasoned dressing would be ideal with the pizza for a main course.

CANNELLONI STUFFED WITH SPINACH

Literally 'big pipes', cannelloni are pasta tubes, about 3 in (7½ cm) long and 1 in (2½ cm) in diameter.

PREPARATION TIME: *45–60 min*
COOKING TIME: *20–30 min*
INGREDIENTS *(for 4):*
8 cannelloni tubes
1 lb (450 g) fresh spinach
½ lb (225 g) cooked chicken
1 oz (25 g) unsalted butter
1 oz (25 g) plain flour
⅓ pint (200 ml) milk
Salt and black pepper*
¾–1 pint (425–570 ml) tomato sauce (use the pizza topping in the previous recipe)
3–4 oz (75–100 g) grated Parmesan cheese

Wash the spinach and put it in a large saucepan – no water is needed. Cover and cook over low heat for about 10 minutes. Drain through a colander, squeezing with a spoon to remove all the moisture. Chop coarsely and set aside. Dice the chicken flesh finely or put it through a mincer.

Melt the butter in a saucepan and stir in the flour; cook gently for 1 minute, then gradually blend in the milk, stirring continuously to get a smooth sauce. Bring to the boil and season to taste with salt and freshly ground pepper; simmer gently for 2–3 minutes or until the sauce has thickened. Take the pan off the heat and stir the spinach and chicken into the sauce; check seasoning.

Put the cannelloni tubes in a pan of boiling salted water and boil for 15 minutes or until the pasta is just tender. Drain and cool for a few minutes before stuffing the tubes with the spinach and chicken. Using a piping bag, with a plain nozzle, pipe the stuffing into the tubes.

Arrange the cannelloni in a buttered ovenproof dish, pour the tomato sauce over them and sprinkle with half the grated cheese. Place the casserole above centre in a pre-heated oven and cook at 350°F (180°C, mark 4) for 20–30 minutes or until bubbling hot and brown. Serve the cannelloni at once, with the remaining cheese in a bowl.

GNOCCHI ALLA ROMANA

Gnocchi are small dumplings made from a flour, semolina or potato paste. The Roman gnocchi are made from semolina and the paste should be left for several hours to rest. They are served with melted butter and plenty of Parmesan cheese.

PREPARATION TIME: *30 min*
COOKING TIME: *50 min*
INGREDIENTS *(for 6):*
1½ pints (900 ml) milk
8 oz (225 g) semolina
4 oz (100 g) unsalted butter
6 oz (175 g) grated Parmesan cheese
Salt and black pepper*
Grated nutmeg
3 large eggs

Heat the milk to just below boiling point, then take the pan off the heat and sprinkle the semolina over the milk, stirring continuously. Return the pan to the heat and bring the mixture slowly to the boil, still stirring. Cook for 2 minutes; remove from the heat and stir in 2½ oz (65 g) of butter and 4½ oz (125 g) of the grated cheese; season to taste with salt, pepper and nutmeg.

Lightly beat the eggs and gradually whisk them into the semolina mixture. Pour this paste into a buttered swiss-roll tin and spread it evenly until ½ in (1 cm) thick. Set aside for several hours until it is firm and cold.

Cut the paste into 1½ in (4 cm) wide pieces with a cold, wet knife. Roll the pieces to the size and shape of walnuts (if necessary, roll them in a little semolina to ease shaping). Place them in a buttered oven-proof dish. Sprinkle with salt and pepper. Melt the remaining butter in a saucepan and pour it over the gnocchi; sprinkle with the remaining cheese and cook for 40 minutes or until pale golden, in the centre of the oven pre-heated to 350°F (180°C, mark 4). Serve the gnocchi at once.

POTATO GNOCCHI

Served with a tomato sauce, these Italian gnocchi or potato dumplings would make a light supper dish on their own.

PREPARATION TIME: *30 min*
COOKING TIME: *12–15 min*
INGREDIENTS *(for 4):*
1 lb (450 g) potatoes
Salt and black pepper*
¼ level teaspoon ground nutmeg
4 oz (100 g) plain flour
1 egg
2 oz (50 g) butter
2 oz (50 g) Parmesan cheese

Peel the potatoes and cut them into 1 in (2½ cm) pieces. Put in a saucepan, cover with cold salted water and bring to the boil. Cook for 15–20 minutes or until tender; drain and return the pan to the heat for a few minutes to dry the potatoes thoroughly.

Rub the potatoes through a coarse sieve into a large bowl. Season to taste with salt and freshly ground pepper, before mixing in the nutmeg and the flour. Beat the egg and stir it into the potatoes, using a wooden spoon; blend thoroughly until smooth. Turn the mixture out on to a floured working surface and knead lightly. Shape the mixture into a roll, cut it into 24 even pieces and shape them into balls.

Bring a large pan of water to the boil. Drop in the gnocchi, a few at a time, and simmer for 5 minutes. When cooked, the gnocchi will rise to the surface; lift them out carefully with a slotted spoon and put in a warm, buttered serving dish.

Sprinkle with the melted butter and grated cheese before serving.

GNOCCHI ALLA ROMANA

SALT SUGAR FAT CHOL FIBRE

WHOLEFOOD VEGETARIAN
TOTAL CALORIES: ABOUT 3100

The **salt** level comes mainly from the cheese, and using only 3 oz (75 g) will reduce the level to low.
For low **fat** and **cholesterol** levels, use only 1 oz (25 g) of butter with the semolina and 1 or 2 eggs. The mixture will in fact work without any eggs, although it will obviously taste less interesting.
Instead of serving with more butter and cheese, provide a well-flavoured mushroom-and-smetana or low-fat yogurt sauce, with cumin or fresh herbs such as tarragon chopped in. (Calories lost: up to 1002.)
Gluten-free millet can be used in place of semolina.

POTATO GNOCCHI

SALT SUGAR FAT CHOL FIBRE

GLUTEN-FREE* WHOLEFOOD* VEGETARIAN
TOTAL CALORIES: ABOUT 1400

The **fat** and **cholesterol** levels can be reduced to low by serving the dish with only 1 oz (25 g) each of butter and cheese If wished, these can be mixed with a few spoonfuls of quark, as the flavours combine well. (Calories lost: up to 287.)

Freezing: ☑ up to 3 months.

SPINACH GNOCCHI

SALT SUGAR FAT CHOL FIBRE

GLUTEN-FREE* WHOLEFOOD* VEGETARIAN
OTAL CALORIES: ABOUT 2400

The **salt** level comes mainly rom the cheese, and can be educed to low by using unsalted quark instead of the cottage cheese or cream cheese, nd only half the Parmesan. The **fat** and **cholesterol** levels can be low if the spinach is fried off in only 1 teaspoon of butter and oil, cottage cheese used rather than cream cheese, nd the remaining butter educed to 2 teaspoonfuls. The ream can be replaced with metana or more quark. Calories lost: up to 1445.)

Microwave: ☑ for the pinach.

SPINACH GNOCCHI

The Italians take infinite trouble over their pasta dishes, and these small spinach dumplings require both patience and practice. They are, however, so light and tasty that they are worth mastering. The quantities are sufficient for a light main course for four or for a first course for six.

PREPARATION TIME: *20 min*
CHILLING TIME: *2 hours*
COOKING TIME: *15–20 min*
INGREDIENTS *(for 4–6):*
1 lb (450 g) fresh spinach
4 oz (100 g) butter
6 oz (175 g) cottage or cream cheese
2 eggs
2 tablespoons double cream
3 level tablespoons plain flour
3 oz (75 g) grated Parmesan cheese
Salt and black pepper*
Nutmeg

Wash the spinach thoroughly in several lots of cold water. Put the spinach in a large pan with a closely fitting lid. Cook, without extra water, over moderate heat for about 5 minutes or until the spinach is just soft. Drain in a sieve, pressing out all moisture. Chop the spinach finely.

Melt half the butter in a pan, add the spinach and cook, stirring constantly, for about 2 minutes or until all moisture has evaporated; if necessary squeeze the spinach in a sieve again. Rub the cottage cheese through a sieve, add to the spinach and cook for a further 3–4 minutes, stirring all the time. Remove the pan from the heat. Fold the lightly beaten eggs into the spinach. Stir in the cream, flour and 1 oz (25 g) of Parmesan cheese. Season to taste with salt, freshly ground pepper and grated nutmeg. Turn the gnocchi into a flat dish and chill for 2 hours or until firm.

Bring a large pan of lightly salted water to simmering point. Shape the gnocchi into small balls no more than ¾ in (2 cm) wide, between floured hands. Drop the balls into the simmering water, a few at a time. As soon as they puff up and rise to the surface, remove them with a slotted spoon.

Arrange the gnocchi in a buttered flameproof dish, melt the remaining butter and pour over them. Sprinkle with the remaining cheese and put the dish under a hot grill until the cheese has melted and browned.

Vegetables

Ideally, vegetables should come straight from the field or the garden to the kitchen. Though this is seldom possible, there are many clues to the freshness or age of vegetables in the shops. Choose crisp and firm vegetables rather than hard ones, and avoid small vegetables which are probably immature and therefore lacking in flavour. Over-large vegetables, on the other hand, are usually coarse.

Vegetables in the shops are displayed to appear as attractive as possible. To achieve this they will have been sprayed, fed with fertiliser and sometimes washed with detergent before being packaged. You may prefer to buy organically grown vegetables which have not had the benefit of such chemical treatment. If so, be prepared for them to look misshapen, often a little dirty and in general quite unlike the glossy, brightly coloured, uniformly sized and neatly packaged produce in the average greengrocer or supermarket. They will also be more expensive, since growing crops organically is labour-intensive and relatively inefficient.

Usually vegetables are at their best in quality and lowest in price at the peak of their seasons. They are packed with vitamins and minerals and will be more nutritious, tastier, and retain their crisp texture if they are cooked only long enough to make them tender.

ROOTS AND TUBERS

Artichokes, Jerusalem

The potato-like tubers of Jerusalem artichokes have a sweet, delicate flavour, slightly reminiscent of the globe artichoke.

The vegetable is thought to have been brought to Europe from Massachusetts early in the 17th century, and certainly has nothing to do with the city of Jerusalem. It is a member of the sunflower family, and the name probably derives from the Italian name for that plant–girasole.

These tubers grow in a mass of twisted knobs and are covered with a thin white or purple skin. The crisp sweet flesh is white. Prime tubers are fairly regular in shape, and measure up to 4 in (10 cm) in length and 2 in (5 cm) across. Avoid artichokes which are misshapen, small or dirty.

Beetroot

Two types are available: long beetroot and globe-shaped. Small globe-shaped beetroot are sold in bunches from early summer onwards, but maincrop beetroot is sold by weight either cooked or raw. Buy cooked beetroot with fresh skin which looks slightly moist, and avoid shrivelled beetroot, which is usually tough and woody. Uncooked beetroot bleeds easily, and care must be taken not to tear the skin when preparing beetroot for cooking.

Carrots

These orange-red root vegetables are among the most nourishing and inexpensive vegetables and a rich source of vitamin A. Young and slender carrots are usually sold in bunches with the foliage intact; they are tender and need only washing before cooking. Maincrop carrots are larger and coarser; they are sold without the leaves and by weight. Available washed and unwashed, but require scraping or peeling. Early carrots showing green in the crown should be avoided, as they are not fully mature; and maincrop carrots should have no woody cores. Avoid pitted and broken carrots.

Celeriac

This is the edible root of a variety of celery. Celeriac, which varies in size from an apple to a coconut, has a brown fibrous skin and creamy-white flesh with a celery flavour. Look for firm roots showing no signs of mushy flesh.

Celery

Celery grows wild in damp places in Europe, Asia, North and South Africa and South America. The Greeks cultivated it for the medicinal value of the seeds. Today, however, special forms are grown for their thick, crisp, juicy stalks, which may be eaten raw, mixed in salads, cooked as a vegetable or used to flavour soups and stews.

The common varieties are white or pink, but pale green celery is also available, blanched, self-blanched or all green. Choose thick crisp celery, plump at the base and with smooth sticks. The leaves indicate freshness: on prime celery the leaves are pale fresh green and straight.

Horseradish

Originally a native of south-east Europe, this hardy herb is now established along roadsides in many parts of the world.

Whether or not it occurs naturally in your area, it is a good idea to grow a few plants in a corner of the garden. As an accompaniment to roast beef and to some fish dishes, a sauce made from freshly grated horseradish root has no equal.

The fact that horseradish is easy to grow has its drawbacks, since if it begins to spread it is difficult to get rid of. The roots are deep and tough; if even a small piece is left in the ground a new plant will grow. Horseradish at its best has straight roots, 1–2 in (3–5 cm) thick at the top.

Kohl rabi

This has a swollen stem, with a mild turnip-like flavour.

The white or purple-skinned vegetables should be bought young, when they are the size of an orange. Avoid large kohl rabi, which may be tough, and any with decayed leaves.

Parsnips

These vegetables are sold both washed and unwashed. The flavour is improved by a touch of frost. They are best from late autumn onwards before the central cores become woody. Buy parsnips with a crisp clean look; avoid any with a split or dried-up root, or with soft brown patches on the crown.

Potatoes

Despite the legends, it seems unlikely that Sir Walter Raleigh had much to do with the introduction of the potato to England, though he may well have planted some on his Cork estates in 1588, the year of the Armada.

There is some evidence, although it is not conclusive, that the potato was brought to England some two years earlier in the holds of Sir Francis Drake's ships, fresh from their profitable raids on South America, where the vegetable originated.

Surprisingly, more than 150 years were to pass before the British regarded the potato as anything more than a novelty or as cattle food. Only since the Irish and Scottish farmers of the 18th century, when its true value was realised, has it become a vitally important food crop in Britain and throughout the world.

Both maincrop and early potatoes are available throughout the year.

Early potatoes should be purchased in small quantities as they quickly lose their earthy crisp flavour. Varieties include *Arran Pilot*, *Home Guard*, *Red Craig's Royal* and *Maris Peer*.

Maincrop potatoes may be bought in larger quantities than early potatoes. After long storage, the red-skinned varieties tend to lose their colour. Maincrop varieties include *Desirée*, *Kerr's Pink*, *King Edward*, *Red King*, *Golden Wonder*, *Majestic*, *Maris Piper*, *Pentland Crown*, *Pentland Dell* and *Redskin*. Different varieties are suitable for different cooking methods.

When buying any kind of potatoes, they should be firm, fairly smooth, well shaped and free from cuts, blemishes and decay. Avoid any that have green areas from light burn or that have sprouted or shrivelled.

Radishes

Small, pungent vegetables, used fresh in salads and for garnishing. Radishes may be round and bright red, tapering and pure white, bright red with white tips or black skinned with white flesh. Choose young, not too large radishes with a crisp look.

Salsify

This little-known root vegetable has soft white flesh. Look for young salsify roots with fresh grey-green leaves, which can be used in salads, and regular tapered roots.

Salsify is also known as the vegetable oyster, or the oyster plant, because of the flavour of its fleshy roots. This makes it a distinctive vegetable for use in late autumn and winter.

Scorzonera, black salsify

This long slender root vegetable, similar to salsify, has black skin and white flesh. Avoid small roots and any that have shrivelled dry skins.

Swedes, Swedish turnips

These winter vegetables are similar to turnips, but the yellow flesh is milder in flavour. Avoid roots which are forked.

Sweet potatoes

These are not related to ordinary potatoes, the only resemblance being that they are both tubers. Sweet potatoes are globular or elongated and may be white, pink, red or purple. The white to yellow flesh is firm and sweet. They are sometimes incorrectly called yams – the true yam is the fruit of a tropical vine. Look for smooth-skinned firm potatoes; avoid any with shrivelled, sunken or discoloured areas.

Turnips

Although the turnip has been a favourite since Roman times, its popularity has little to do with its nutritional value. The root consists of about 90 per cent water, with some sugar and pectin – a jelly-like substance which helps jams to set. Nevertheless, it adds a fresh flavour to a dish of vegetables, particularly when accompanied by the season's first peas and carrots.

There are two types of turnip: early and maincrop. Early turnips have tender mustard-flavoured flesh, which may be eaten both raw and cooked. Maincrop turnips have a somewhat coarser flesh, but are excellent boiled and in soups and stews. Avoid turnips with brown spots and holes, and any with spongy patches. Look for firm, small to medium, round turnips.

GREEN VEGETABLES

Beans

Most beans are eaten in the pod, but some are shelled.

Broad beans These can be long, slender pods, up to 12 in (30 cm) long with kidney-shaped green-white or dark green seeds, or shorter pods, about 6 in (15 cm) long, with round seeds.

All pods should have a uniform bright green colour, free from black markings. Avoid shrivelled, dry-looking pods in favour of soft and tender pods. These beans are excellent for home-freezing; they must be shelled before cooking, although young broad beans are a delicacy cooked complete with pods.

French beans These include a number of types, varying from almost flat pods, up to 5 in (13 cm) long, to shorter and plumper

beans; their colour varies from pale to mid-green. Most are stringless when young. Yellow French beans are also available in small quantities. Buy young, crisp beans.

Kidney beans These are a type of French bean, usually heavier-podded, with the kidney-shaped beans showing through. The most popular is the purple variety, which turns green when cooked. Choose beans with a distinct bloom.

Pea beans Not often available in the shops, pea beans have short, bright green pods, about the size of peas, and round seeds. Cooked and eaten in their pods.

Runner beans Larger, coarser and with more flavour than French beans, runner beans at their best have bright green, succulent pods which need stringing before cooking. A runner bean should snap between the fingers. Avoid beans which are tough, limp, misshapen, dirty, or pitted with brown or black.

Broccoli

While cauliflower has one fused head of curds, broccoli develops into numerous shoots, each terminating in a small floret. There are white or green sprouted, as well as purple broccoli. Choose broccoli with small, fresh-looking heads and brittle stalks which snap easily in the fingers. None of the buds should have opened enough to show the yellow flowers (a sign of age).

Calabrese Type of broccoli from Italy, calabrese has a compact head of white, green or purple firm curds. Buy only well-coloured heads, avoiding any with limp leaves.

Brussels sprouts

These are popular in autumn and winter. The flavour is improved by frost. Look for firm, green sprouts and avoid those with loose leaves and any which show signs of yellowing and wilting.

Cabbages

The cabbage is generally regarded as the most boring of vegetables and has even lent its name as a term of contempt for a solid, unadventurous person. But if grown and cooked properly, it is a tasty food and one rich in nourishment.

There are green, white and red varieties, which may be conical or round, loose leaved or tightly packed.

Chinese cabbage Sometimes also known as **celery cabbage** or **pak choi**, this has some of the characteristics of both cabbage and cos lettuce. It is usually eaten in salads but can be cooked like cabbage.

Red cabbages These cabbages are used for braising, marinating or for pickling. Fresh red cabbages have a good bloom. When red cabbage is cooked, an acid, such as vinegar, red wine, or apples, should always be added to retain the cabbage's colour.

Savoy cabbages Look for firm green heads with crisp and curling outer leaves. Pale green savoys are almost certainly not fresh.

Spring cabbages Choose those with bright green and crisp leaves.

Spring greens Young, mid-green cabbages sold before the hearts have developed. Use on the day of purchase, as they wilt quickly.

Summer and autumn cabbages These follow spring cabbages, but have larger, more solid heads. Choose only firm, crisp-looking cabbages and check that the base of the stalk is clean. Avoid cabbages with slimy stalk ends and leaves pitted with holes.

Winter cabbages

Popular winter vegetables, particularly the round drumhead types. They may be stored for 2–3 days. See that the heads are firm, and avoid any with wilting outer leaves.

White cabbages Excellent both for cooking and in salads. Choose firm, compact heads, and avoid any with loose curling leaves or those with brown smudges.

Cauliflower

Both summer and winter varieties are available; on winter cauliflowers (sometimes wrongly called broccoli) the dark green leaves are folded over the white

curds; on summer cauliflowers the leaves are opened out. Choose cauliflowers with the creamy-white heads not fully developed and with clean white stalks. Avoid any with limp leaves and loose, brown, grey or damaged curds.

Chicory

A salad vegetable with a conical white or pale yellow head of crisp leaves packed firmly together. Choose heads that are firmly packed and avoid any which show yellow, curling leaves. The taste is slightly bitter. Although mainly used for salads it is also delicious cooked.

Endive and Escarole

The curly, narrow, ragged-edged leaves of endive resemble dandelion leaves. The centre of the head has yellowish leaves that have a milder flavour than the dark green outer leaves. Escarole has long wavy leaves that are broader and less crinkly than endive leaves.

Look for crisp, fresh leaves with vivid green outer leaves. Avoid wilted leaves and any yellow or brown discolorations. Season: all year.

Kale

The broad leaves vary in colour from dark green to purple. They are heavily crimped and have prominent pale green or white mid-ribs. Avoid kale with yellow, drooping or damaged leaves.

Lettuces

Although lettuces were popular with the Romans and Greeks – the philosopher Theophrastus identifed three sorts in the 4th century BC – they are believed to have a much longer history, and may have been grown thousands of years earlier in the Far East. In Britain, the lettuce was already popular by the 16th century, and today it is the most widely grown salad vegetable.

Two main types are available: cabbage (or butter-head) and cos. Cabbage lettuce is divided into soft-leaved and curly-leaved lettuces, the Webb strain being the most popular. This is round and crisp with crimped leaves. Cos lettuces are oblong with crisp leaves, and sweeter than cabbage lettuces. Choose lettuce with fresh and bright leaves and avoid any with brown or slimy patches on the hearts.

Okra

These vegetables are curved, generally ribbed seed pods. Select only the small, bright green, tender pods between 2 and 4 in (5 and 10 cm) long. The tips should bend with a slight pressure. Large pods will be tough. Avoid any shrivelled pods.

Peas

The earliest are the flat mangetout or sugar peas which are cooked and served in the pods. Early peas have round seeds, while main-crop and late varieties usually have wrinkled seeds. Buy peas with bright crisp pods and avoid any which are so large that they show through the pods. Test for freshness by eating the peas raw, when they should be sweet and tender.

Spinach

There are two types of true spinach, the round-leaved summer variety and the prickly leaved

winter spinach. Both have tender dark green leaves which must be handled carefully as they easily bruise. Spinach wilts quickly, and should be crisp to the touch. Look for dark green, unblemished leaves, avoiding any that are yellow, wilted, crushed or decayed.

In addition there are three other vegetables that resemble spinach, and are cooked in the same way:

New Zealand spinach is similar to other leaf spinach, but with smaller, drier and tougher leaves.

Spinach beet is grown all-year round and is an excellent source of vitamin A. This is the easiest spinach crop to grow.

Swiss chard, also called sea kale beet, has spinach-like dark green crisp and crinkled leaves with prominent white mid-ribs like celery stalks. The stalks as well as the leaves are used: the leaves should be cooked like spinach and the stalks like celery.

Watercress

This small-leaved peppery plant is mainly used in salads, soups and for garnishing. Avoid any in flower or with a high proportion of yellow or wilting leaves. Use within 24 hours of purchase.

OTHER VEGETABLES

Artichokes, globe

The artichoke is the leafy flower head of the plant. The grey-green, stiff leaves overlap each other, and the edible parts of the leaves are the fleshy bases of each leaf. Below the leaves is the fond (bottom), which has the finest flavour. Buy artichokes with stiff leaves which have a slight bloom.

Asparagus

Asparagus is a choice, but expensive, vegetable. It is sold loose or in bundles, and graded according to thickness of stem and plumpness of buds. Look for asparagus with tight, well-formed heads and avoid any with thin, woody, dry and dirty stems.

Aubergine, egg plant

Oblong and near-round types of these distinctive, purple or white vegetables are available. Prime aubergines should be firm and heavy, with a satiny bloom to the shiny tough skin; the mealy flesh is yellow-green.

Avocados

These pear-shaped fruits are used as a vegetable rather than a dessert fruit. They have green to purple skins. The oily, pale green, soft flesh surrounds a large stone. As avocados are imported they are not always ripe when bought: test for ripeness by pressing the flesh gently at the rounded end – it should yield slightly. Avoid avocados with blotched dry skins.

Corn on the cob, sweet corn

Best cobs should be creamy and shiny within the bright green stiff leaves; they should exude a milky liquid when punctured. Nutritional value and flavour are rapidly lost once the husks have been removed. The tassels at the top should be black and withered.

Cucumbers

Hothouse cucumbers are the ones usually seen in te shops, although small amounts of ridge or outdoor cucumbers also appear. Choose straight firm cucumbers no more than 2 in (5 cm) wide; the skin should have a bloom to it.

Fennel, Florence fennel

This vegetable, which looks like a root, is the swollen stem base. The leaves are bright green and feathery. It has a distinct aniseed flavour. Choose well-rounded roots, of pale green to white colour, avoiding any which are deep green.

Leeks

These thick-stem vegetables are composed of tightly packed skin layers which branch at the top into dark green leaves. The stems are white with a faint onion taste. Look for well-shaped, straight leeks, trimmed at the top and avoid those with yellow, discoloured and slimy leaves.

Mushrooms

These are sold either as buttons, cups or flats according to age. White and brown types are available with no difference in taste. Large flat mushrooms have more flavour than the young buttons. Choose mushrooms carefully as they turn limp quickly and lose their flavour; use on the day of purchase. Avoid limp, broken mushrooms with a sweaty look to them.

Mustard and cress

Pungent, spicy mustard and cress are quick-growing plants that are cut as seedlings for sandwiches and salads. Commercially much of the crop sold is, in fact, rape, but mustard and cress is easy to grow at home.

Most seedsmen stock only one variety of mustard, white, and one of cress, curled. The cress seedlings add a peppery tang to the mixture that is not to everyone's taste. If cress is to be sown, therefore, a much smaller quantity is needed than of the mustard – say, not more than a quarter of the total. A 1 oz (25 g) packet of mustard and a quarter of a 1 oz (25 g) packet of cress will be enough to sow four seed pans or plastic containers, each measuring about 6 × 4 in (15 × 100 cm). A pan of this size will produce enough for two salads or a substantial number of sandwiches. Stagger the sowing so that there is a constant supply.

Place a layer of cottonwool, flannel or sacking on a seed tray of plastic container. Sow the cress first and the mustard three or four days later – either with the cress or in a separate tray – so that the crops mature at the same time.

Spread the seeds thickly and evenly on top of the material and press them down lightly. Sprinkle thoroughly with lukewarm water and cover the tray with brown paper or black polythene. In winter, place the tray in a warm position in the house or in a heated greenhouse. A temperature of 50–61°F (10–16°C) is ideal. From spring to autumn, the tray can be placed under a cloche or in a cold frame. Remove the cover when the seedlings are about $1\frac{1}{2}$ in (4 cm) high, and allow a few days for them to green up an expand fully before cutting. Keep moist.

Onions

Onions vary in shape and colour from flattish bulbs with brown skins to round bulbs with red-brown or pale straw-coloured skins. There is hardly any difference in the sharp taste. They store well, especially during autumn and winter, if they are kept in a cool larder. Choose onions which are firm and regular in shape, with feathery skins. Onions with shrivelled skins and softness around the neck are almost certainly bad.

Small pickling onions, also called button onions, appear in late summer and autumn.

Spanish onions Originally from Spain, the name is now applied to any large mild-flavoured onions.

Spring onions, salad onions The term spring onion is a misnomer, as this vegetable is in season throughout the year. Spring onions are used to flavour other vegetables, but are essentially salad vegetables. The mild-flavoured bulbs have a thin skin, which peels off easily. Choose spring onions with small bulbs and fresh green foliage, and avoid any with traces of worms or wilting leaves.

Parsley
This is the most versatile and useful of all garnishes, in sprigs or chopped. Wash freshly picked parsley as soon as possible, shake well and remove long stems. Place the parsley in a jar of water reaching to the base of the leaves, or put the parsley stems in a polythene bag, tied at the neck. Parsley will then stay crisp and green for several days. Change the water in the container daily.

Chopped parsley can be used as a garnish arranged in neat lines or at random; scissors can be used for chopping, but the result is coarser than when chopped with a knife. Gather the parsley into a tight bunch and with kitchen scissors snip off as much as is required straight on to the dish to be garnished.

To chop large quantities of parsley, place the stripped leaves on a chopping board. Using a sharp straight-bladed knife, hold the handle firmly with one hand and the tip of the knife blade with the other; lift the handle in a see-saw action, gradually chopping the parsley finely or coarsely as required. Alternatively, bunch the parsley leaves in one hand on the chopping board and, using the knife, gradually shred the parsley, moving the fingers back to reveal more parsley. Small wooden chopping bowls equipped with curved-bladed knives are available for chopping parsley, herbs, shallots and garlic. To preserve the vivid green, put choppefdparsley in a piece of muslin, tie loosely and hold the bag under cold water for a few minutes to rinse thoroughly. Squeeze dry, then shake the parsley out into a bowl. Chopped parsley will keep for a day or two in a lidded container in the refrigerator.

Peppers, pimentos
These tropical vegetable fruits have green, yellow or red skins. They are sold with the stalk ends attached, and before use these must be cut off and the inner white mid-ribs and seeds removed. Excellent for stuffing. Choose firm shiny peppers and avoid any which are misshapen and dull-looking.

Shallots

These small onions are chiefly used to flavour sauces. The smooth and firm bulbs have a slight garlic flavour. Choose hard, rounded bulbs, avoiding any with shrivelled skins or thick necks.

Squashes
Courgettes

Courgettes are small marrows; special varieties have been developed that produce several fruits on each plant. They are straight and cylindrical but slightly larger at the base. Large courgettes can be as long as 12 in (30 cm) but will then be very watery inside. The skin is dark green over a light yellow ground with a greenish-black lacy pattern and dark green stripes. Young courgettes, no more than 6 in (15 cm) long, are considered the best.

Marrows

Large marrows have coarse, insipid flesh and tough skin. They should be avoided in favour of young marrows, no more than 12 in (30 cm) long. The skin should be soft, with a dull bloom to it. Avoid awkwardly shaped and flabby marrows.

Pumpkins
Members of the gourd family, these vary greatly in size, from very small, about the size of a cantaloupe, to 100 pounds. Choose firm, bright-coloured pumpkins, heavy for their size and free from excessive scarring. If the pumpkin has already been cut in half by the greengrocer, check that the flesh is close-textured and non-stringy. Do not discard the pumpkin seeds; they can be roasted in the oven.

Tomatoes

Tomatoes are available throughout the year, but the best tomatoes are home grown, in hothouses or in the open under cloches, and allowed to ripen completely before being picked. Tomatoes can also be grown on patios and balconies, in bags of specially prepared peat.

In the autuon, green tomatoes for pickles and chutneys are often available. Pick firm and perfect fruit – yellow or soft areas on the skin indicate bad fruit.

The small Canary Island tomatoes used to be sweet and juicy, and often cheap. They tend nowadays to be of the tasteless Moneymaker variety. Large squat Mediterranean tomatoes are much better flavoured, and are excellent for stuffing and for soups and purées.

Tomatoes should be firm and regular in shape and bright in colour. The skin should have a matt texture; avoid any with blotched or cracked skins.

Pasta and rice

Dried foods such as pasta and rice are valuable in the store cupboard because they keep well and can be used for quick, filling, economical meals. Pasta, made mostly from wheat but sometimes from buckwheat, comes from Italy, with similar products being found in China and Japan. Rice is grown mainly in America, the Far East and the Mediterranean countries. Both can be rather bland in themselves but for this reason they combine well with many other types of food and with herbs, spices and other strong flavourings.

PASTA

In its simplest form pasta is a dough made from flour and water. The flour comes from durum wheat, or hard wheat, which is very high in gluten and grows particularly well in Italy. Ordinary or soft wheat can be used, but if you have ever tried making your own pasta you will see the difference at once between pasta made with strong (hard) flour and pasta made with ordinary flour. Eggs are often added to enrich it, and puréed spinach to colour it green (*pasta verde*). A combination of yellow egg pasta and green spinach pasta is sold as *paglia e fieno* (straw and hay).

Dried pasta keeps indefinitely in a cool cupboard, but fresh pasta should be used within two or three days and preferably on the day it is made.

RICE

Most rice consists of polished white grains with the husks and brown cuticles removed. The two main types are long grain and short grain (or round grain) rice.

Long grain rice is used for curries and pilafs. The best is generally considered to be Basmati rice.

Patna rice is cheaper and also good. Short grain rice is much grown around the Mediterranean and is the kind used for risottos and paella, as well as for sweet puddings.

Brown or unpolished rice retains many valuable nutrients. It is now widely available, although less so in the rice-producing countries themselves. Both white and brown rice can be ground into flour: it has a pleasant nutty taste and is useful to those on gluten-free diets.

Wild rice is not related to rice at all: it is the seeds of a grass which grows wild in the northern United States.

PASTA, IN ALL SHAPES AND SIZES Pasta can be divided into four main types: solid strings, which include vermicelli, noodles, spaghetti; hollow pasta tubes, such as macaroni and cannelloni; ribbon pasta, from tagliatelle to lasagne; and stuffed pasta, of which the best known is ravioli. Pasta is also made into a wide variety of small shapes, for garnishing soups.

Other dried foods, including cereals and the various dried beans, peas and lentils known collectively as pulses or legumes, are also valuable nutritionally as well as being useful standbys.

OTHER CEREALS

Barley Pearl barley, which is the polished grain, is used to thicken soups and in pilafs, mixed with meat or fish and spices. Pot barley is the unpolished grain, analogous to brown rice.

Rye Rye flour is used to make bread, usually mixed with wheat flour to help it rise, as gluten in rye is different from that in wheat.

Buckwheat This is gluten-free and is used for pancakes (in northern France) and noodles (in Japan and formerly in the countryside around Venice).

Millet Another gluten-free cereal which is an important crop in Asia and parts of Africa.

Oatmeal The whole grain is dried, husked and ground to make coarse, medium or fine oatmeal, all used for porridge, oatcakes and oatmeal biscuits.

Rolled oats This is the crushed, partly cooked grain, which is sold under various brand names. It is cooked to make quick porridge; mixed with fresh or dried fruit and nuts to make muesli, and used as the basis of cakes such as flapjacks.

Semolina, sago and tapioca Semolina, coarsely milled hard wheat, is also made into gnocchi– savoury dumplings, baked or poached and served as a starter. Sago is made from the pith in the trunk of the sago palm. Tapioca comes from the root of the West Indian cassava plant.

PULSES

Dried peas and beans of various types are known as pulses. The best known are butter, haricot and kidney beans.

Dried peas are a specially grown variety of garden pea, sometimes called blue peas. Lentils, one of the most nutritious pulses, are a type of pea widely grown in the south of Europe. Dried soya beans are sold in health food shops. They are also processed to make textured vegetable protein, which can be used on its own or mixed with fresh meat for hamburgers, mincedmeat dishes and stews.

A SELECTION OF CEREALS AND PULSES These foods tend to be bland on their own, but can easily be varied in flavour with the addition of spices and other ingredients. Wild rice, which is expensive, is the seed of an American grass and is served as an accompaniment to game. Chick peas are grown in the tropics and are used in soups and stews or cold in salads.

Herbs

Many herbs are best used fresh, but only a limited number are easily available unless they are grown at home. Bay leaves, chervil, fennel, parsley, rosemary, sage and thyme are sometimes sold fresh in shops, and are in season all the year round.

These herbs, as well as many less well-known ones, are also sold dried.

DRYING HERBS

Most herbs can be dried during the summer for use in winter. Pick the herbs just before flowering time when the flavour is best. Wash them thoroughly then shake off the excess moisture. Tie the herbs into small bunches and hang them in a cool, airy place or spread them out on a clean cloth and put them to dry in a warm place such as an airing cupboard. Dry different types of herbs separately or the flavours will mingle. When they are dry and brittle, strip off the leaves and store them in air-tight, labelled jars. Use within six months, before their flavour fades.

BASIL
Spicy herb that can be grown in pots or boxes. Does not lose pungency when it is dried.

SAGE
One of the best-known herbs, sage grows well in this country and can be used fresh or dried.

TARRAGON
Usually used dry, but the fresh leaves are particularly good for flavouring egg and tomato salads.

MARJORAM
Spicy, bitter herb which can be used instead of basil, sprinkled on meat. More pungent dried.

FENNEL
The leaves and seeds of the herb are used to counteract the richness of oily fish and in sauces.

CHIVES
Not easily available in the shops, chives are simple to grow and are best when freshly cut.

BAY
The leaves can be used fresh or dried to flavour savoury dishes, particularly sauces and stews.

DILL
The leaves have a delicate, aniseed flavour, which enhances the flavour of grilled fish.

GARLIC
The very pungent cloves should be used sparingly. Garlic keeps for several months in a dry place.

ROSEMARY
The shrub grows well in Britain and the sweet, aromatic leaves are more pungent fresh.

PARSLEY
Mild-flavoured parsley leaves are rich in iron and vitamins. Use them in sauces and as a garnish.

BOUQUET GARNI
Ready-made bouquets garnis are available, in muslin, and include bay leaf, thyme and parsley.

THYME
Widely used herb, fresh or dried. The strongly flavoured leaves go well with most meat dishes.

CAPERS
Flower buds, usually sold pickled, capers are most often used to make sauce for mutton or fish.

OREGANO
Wild marjoram, used in Greek and Italian dishes. Often sold as a dried powder.

MINT
Widely grown, popular herb used in fruit tarts and cocktails as well as with meat and vegetables.

HERBS AND THEIR USES These fresh herbs are widely used in cooking. Many of them, not just the more usual ones, such as mint, parsley and thyme, can be grown in the garden or in pots on a sunny kitchen window-sill. This allows you to use them fresh, or to freeze or dry them at home. Remember that constant picking encourages the plants to grow.

Stocks and Soups

The basis for all soups is good fresh stock usually made from the bones and flesh of fish, meat and poultry, with added vegetables, herbs and spices. The stock ingredients should harmonise with those of the finished soup. Chicken stock is most often used as a basis for vegetable soups, but stock based on a ham bone is very good with some vegetables, especially peas.

There are five basic stocks: brown (or household stock), white, fish, vegetable and game stock. Brown stock can be used for most soups, although fish, vegetables and game soups all gain in flavour when prepared with their own type of stock.

Fresh bones and meat are essential ingredients for brown and white stocks. Use marrow bone and shin of beef for brown stock, and knuckle of veal for a white stock and ask the butcher to chop the bones into manageable pieces. The chopped bones release gelatine while cooking, which gives body to the stock.

Vegetables give additional flavour, but avoid potatoes, which make the stock cloudy. Strong-flavoured vegetables, such as turnips, swedes and parsnips should be used sparingly.

STOCKS

Brown Stock

PREPARATION TIME: *15 min*
COOKING TIME: *5 hours*
INGREDIENTS *(for 6 pints, 3½ litres):*
1 lb (450 g) marrow bones
2–3 lb (1–1½ kg) shin of beef
1½ oz (40 g) butter or dripping
1–2 leeks
1 large onion
1–2 celery sticks
½ lb (225 g) carrots
2 bouquets garnis (page 99)
Salt and black peppercorns*

Blanch the bones for 10 minutes in boiling water, then put them, with the chopped meat and butter or dripping, in a roasting tin. Brown the bones in the centre of the oven for 30–40 minutes, at a temperature of 425°F (220°C, mark 7). Turn them over occasionally to brown them evenly. Put the roasted bones in a large pan, add the cleaned and sliced vegetables, the bouquets garnis and peppercorns. Cover with cold water, to which ½ teaspoon of salt has been added.

Bring the contents slowly to boiling point, remove any scum from the surface and cover the pan with a tight-fitting lid. Simmer the stock over lowest possible heat for about 4 hours to extract all flavour from the bones. Top up with hot water if the level of the liquid should fall below the other ingredients.

Strain the stock through a fine sieve or muslin, into a large bowl. Leave the stock to settle for a few minutes, then remove the fat from the surface by drawing absorbent paper over it. If the stock is not required immediately, leave the fat to settle in a surface layer which can then be easily lifted off.

Once the fat has been removed correct seasoning if necessary.

White Stock

This is made like brown stock, but the blanched veal bones are not browned. Place all the ingredients in a large pan of water and proceed as for brown stock.

Fish Stock

The basis for this stock is bones and trimmings, such as the head and the skin. White fish such as cod, haddock, halibut, whiting and plaice can all be used. Fish stock is less useful than other stocks as a basis for vegetable soups, but could be used for leek or celery soup.

PREPARATION TIME: *5–10 min*
COOKING TIME: *30 min*
INGREDIENTS *(for 1 pint, 570 ml)*
1 lb (450 g) fish trimmings
*Salt**
1 onion
Bouquet garni (page 99) or 1 large leek and 1 celery stick

Wash the trimmings thoroughly in cold water and put them in a large pan, with 1 pint (570 ml) lightly salted water. Bring to the boil over low heat and remove any surface scum. Meanwhile, peel and finely chop the onion and add to the stock with the bouquet garni or the cleaned and chopped leek and celery. Cover the pan with a lid and simmer over low heat for 30 minutes. Strain the stock through a sieve or muslin. Store, covered, in the refrigerator.

Fish stock does not keep well and should preferably be used on the day it is made.

SKIMMING STOCK

Lifting scum from boiling stock

Removing surface fat

Poultry or Game Stock

The ingredients for this stock can be the carcass of a chicken, turkey or game bird, together with the feet of the bird, and the cleaned giblets. Cook as for white stock, simmering for 2–3 hours. Strain and remove the fat.

Vegetable Stock

This inexpensive but quick and tasty stock is made from uncooked vegetables. The ingredients may include the outer leaves of cabbage, lettuce and other greens, cauliflower stalks, and peelings from carrots, leeks and parsnips. Chop these trimmings roughly, put them in a pan and cover with lightly salted water. Put the lid on the pan, and simmer the stock over low heat. A bouquet garni (page 99) and 6–8 peppercorns may be added for extra flavour. Strain the stock through muslin.

Cooking stock in a pressure cooker

Place the stock ingredients, with lightly salted water, in the pressure cooker – it must not be more than two-thirds full. Bring to the boil and remove the scum from the surface before fixing the lid. Lower the heat and bring to 15 pounds (6·7 kg) pressure. Reduce the heat quickly and cook steadily for 1 hour. Strain the stock and remove the fat.

Storing stock

If not required for immediate use, store prepared stocks in the refrigerator. After the fat has been removed, pour the cooled stock into a container and cover with a lid. It will keep for three or four days, but to ensure absolute freshness, boil up the stock every two days. Fish and vegetable stocks spoil quickly and should be made and used on the same day. If refrigerated they will keep for two days.

Freezing stocks

Stocks can be satisfactorily stored in a home freezer, where they will keep for up to two months. Boil the prepared stock over high heat to reduce it by half. Pour the concentrated cooled stock into ice-cube trays, freeze quickly and transfer the stock cubes to polythene bags. Alternatively, pour the stock into freezing containers, leaving a 1 in ($2\frac{1}{2}$ cm) space at the top.

To use frozen stock, leave it to thaw at room temperature, or simply turn it into a saucepan and heat over low heat, stirring occasionally. Add 2 tablespoons water to every cube of concentrated stock.

Ready-made stocks

Many ready-made stock preparations are available, usually in the form of bouillon cubes, meat extracts, and meat-and-vegetable extracts. In an emergency, these preparations are acceptable replacements for home-made stocks, but they have a sameness of flavour and lack body and jellying qualities. As they are highly seasoned, be careful about extra flavourings until the soup has been tasted.

SOUPS

There are an enormous number of classic and international soups which all fall into two distinct categories, according to their consistency: thin soups and thick soups. Thin soups are again divided into consommés and broths; and thick soups into purée and cream soups. Thick soups also include classic velouté soups, which are based on a velouté sauce, but these are seldom made today.

Thin Soups

(consommé and broth)

A consommé is a clear soup made from meat, poultry, fish or vegetables and clarified stock. The basic stock must be accentuated by the main ingredient, so that a beef consommé is made from brown stock and lean beef, a chicken consommé from chicken stock and chicken flesh. Consommés are particularly suitable for party menus and may be served piping hot or chilled as a jellied soup.

Broths

These semi-clear soups consist of uncleared stock with added meat, vegetables, rice or barley. Broths are often a by-product of the main course.

Thick Soups

This group includes purée soups which are thickened with starchy ingredients, such as flour, cereals, pulses and potatoes. Cream soups are thickened with butter, cream and egg yolks.

The thickening agents, known as liaisons, also enrich the texture of a soup and change its colour. Liaisons must be added in correct proportions to the liquid, otherwise the soup may curdle or become too starchy.

Liaison to liquids:

$\frac{1}{4}$–$\frac{1}{2}$ oz (10–15 g) flour	1 pint (570 ml) liquid *(for purées rich in starch)*
$\frac{1}{2}$–1 oz (15–25 g) flour	1 pint (570 ml) liquid *(for purées with little starch)*
1–2 egg yolks	1 pint (570 ml) liquid
5 fl oz (150 ml) cream	1 pint (570 ml) liquid

Purée Soups

For these soups, the main ingredients are rubbed through a sieve or put through a liquidiser. The soup is further thickened with a starchy liaison. Purée soups are usually made from vegetables, but can also be prepared from meat, poultry, game, fish and even fruit.

A purée made from starchy vegetables, such as dried peas, split peas, haricot and butter beans, or potatoes, will produce a thick soup that needs little or no additional starch. It can be adjusted to soup consistency by adding stock or water. A thin purée from spinach or watercress will need thickening with flour. This also prevents the purée from sinking to the bottom. Mix the correct liaison of flour with a little hot soup, then stir it back into the soup, and bring to boiling point over gentle heat.

MAKING PURÉE SOUPS

Sieving cooked vegetables

Scraping purée off the sieve

Potato Soup

PREPARATION TIME: *15–20 min*
COOKING TIME: *20 min*
INGREDIENTS *(for 4–6):*
2 leeks
1 lb (450 g) potatoes
$1\frac{1}{2}$ oz (40 g) butter
2 pints (1 litre) white stock
Salt★ and black pepper

Wash and finely chop the leeks and peel and roughly chop the potatoes. Cook the leeks in 1 oz (25 g) of butter in a large pan until soft, but not coloured. Add the potatoes, and pour over the stock; season lightly with salt and freshly ground pepper. Bring the ingredients to the boil, cover with a lid and simmer until the potatoes are quite tender.

Remove the soup from the heat and leave it to cool slightly. Rub the soup through a sieve or put it through a liquidiser, a little at a time. Re-heat the purée soup over low heat, adjust seasoning and stir in the remaining butter.

Cream Soups

These thick soups are a combination of a purée soup and béchamel sauce (page 84). They are thickened and enriched with cream, egg yolks or both. Cream soups take little time to prepare and are excellent for storing in a home freezer.

Care is required when thickening with cream or egg yolks to prevent the soup curdling. Put the cream or yolks in a small bowl and beat in a little hot soup until the liaison has the same temperature as the soup. Blend the liaison slowly into the hot soup, stirring continuously, but do not let the soup reach boiling point. The soup can also be re-heated in the top of a double saucepan.

Cream of Vegetable Soup

PREPARATION TIME: *20 min*
COOKING TIME: *15–20 min*
INGREDIENTS *(for 4):*
1 lb (450 g) mixed vegetables (carrots, celery, leeks, cabbage)
2 oz (50 g) butter
1 pint (570 ml) béchamel sauce (page 84)
Salt and black pepper*
$\frac{1}{2}$–$\frac{3}{4}$ *pint (300–450 ml) milk*
$\frac{1}{4}$ *pint (150 ml) fresh cream*

Peel or scrape and wash the vegetables before chopping them finely. Blanch the vegetables for 2 minutes in boiling water, then drain thoroughly.

Melt the butter in a heavy-based pan over low heat, and cook the vegetables, covered, for 5–10 minutes, until soft. Blend in the béchamel sauce and simmer gently for 15 minutes or until the vegetables are tender.

Rub the thick mixture through a sieve or put it through a liquidiser. Re-heat the soup without boiling, over low heat, thinning with milk to the desired consistency. Correct seasoning, and blend in the cream just prior to serving.

SOUP GARNISHES

Garnishes are added to soups either as an embellishment to improve the flavour or to provide a contrasting texture.

Consommé julienne, for example, is garnished with julienne (narrow) strips of carrot, celery, leek and turnip. These strips are boiled until soft in lightly salted water, then rinsed in cold water and added to hot consommé just before serving.

Consommé royale is a garnish of firm savoury egg custard cut into tiny fancy shapes. Beat one egg with one tablespoon of cleared stock and pour into a small bowl or dariole moulds. Bake the moulds in a pan of water for 20 minutes or until firm, in the centre of a pre-heated oven at 350°F (180°C, mark 4).

Pasta is used to garnish many thin soups. Macaroni, tagliatelli and spaghetti can be broken into short pieces and added to purée soups for the last 20 minutes of cooking. For hot consommés, cook the pasta separately so that the starch will not cloud the soup.

Cheese makes a pleasant accompaniment to most vegetable soups. Choose a well-flavoured hard cheese, and serve it finely grated in a separate dish.

Bread croûtons are a classic garnish with thick soups. Remove the crusts from $\frac{1}{2}$ in (1 cm) thick slices of white bread; cut into cubes and toast or fry in a little butter until crisp and golden. Serve in a separate dish or sprinkled over the soup.

Dumplings are ideal for turning a meat or vegetable soup into a substantial family meal. Mix 4 oz (100 g) self-raising flour with 2 oz (50 g) shredded suet and a sprinkling of salt and pepper. Bind the mixture with sufficient cold water to make a soft dough. Shape the dough into 16 balls and drop them into the soup for the last 15–20 minutes of cooking.

Melba toast is made by toasting thin slices of white bread, splitting them through the middle, and toasting the uncooked surfaces under a hot grill. Alternatively, cut stale bread into very thin slices, place them on a baking tray and dry them off in the bottom of the oven until crisp and curling at the edges.

Vegetable and fruit garnishes add colour to plain cream soups. Trim and wash celery leaves, watercress or parsley before floating them on the soup.

Cucumber may be cut into julienne strips as a garnish for chilled soups. For hot soups, sauté cucumber strips or thin rounds of leeks in a little butter.

Thin slices of lemon or orange make an attractive garnish for clear soups and tomato soup.

A mushroom garnish adds texture and flavour to cream soups. Fry the sliced mushrooms in a little butter until soft. Drain thoroughly before spooning them over the soup.

Thin onion rings add more flavour to soups. They can be sautéed like cucumber strips and leek rounds; alternatively, coat them in milk and flour, and deep fry them until crisp and golden.

SOUP GARNISHES

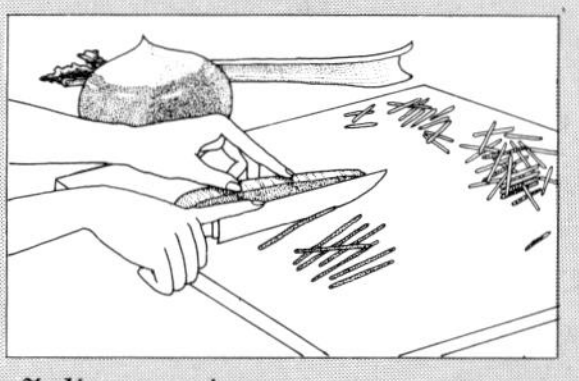

Julienne strips

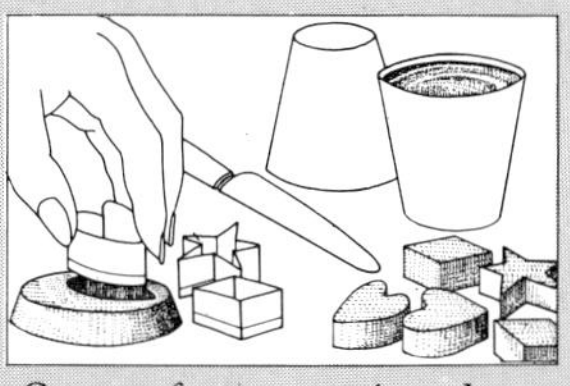

Cut-outs for consommé royale

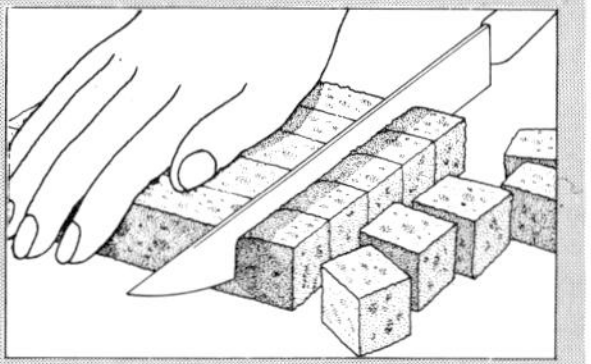

Cutting bread croûtons

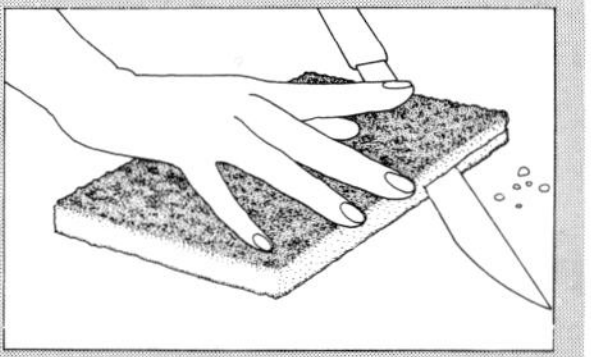

Slicing Melba toast

Sauces and Dressings

Sauces first came into widespread use in the Middle Ages, to disguise the flavour of long-stored meat that had been inadequately cured. Today, they are used to add flavour to bland food, colour to simple meals and moisture to otherwise dry foods.

BASIC WHITE SAUCE

This is prepared either by the roux or the blending method:

Roux method

A roux is usually composed of equal amounts of butter and flour which are then combined with liquid (usually milk) to the required consistency. Melt the butter in a heavy-based pan, blend in the flour, and cook over low heat for 2–3 minutes, stirring constantly with a wooden spoon.

Gradually add the warm or cold liquid to the roux, which will at first thicken to a near solid mass. Beat vigorously until the mixture leaves the sides of the pan clean, then add a little more milk. Allow the mixture to thicken and boil between each addition of milk. Continuous beating is essential to obtain a smooth sauce. When all the milk has been added, bring the sauce to the boil; let it simmer for about 5 minutes and add the seasoning.

A basic white sauce can also be made by the one-stage method. This consists of putting the basic ingredients (fat, flour and liquid) into a pan at the same time. Cook over low heat, beating until the sauce has thickened. Boil for 3 minutes and season.

MAKING A WHITE SAUCE

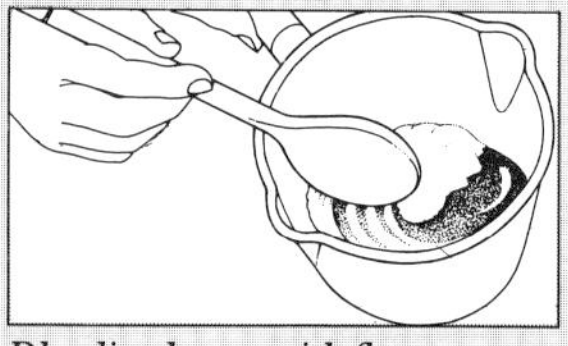

Blending butter with flour

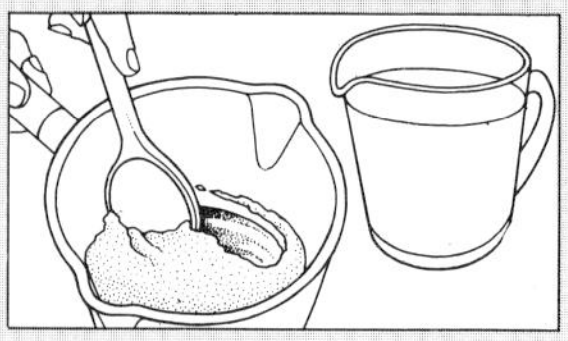

Thickening the roux

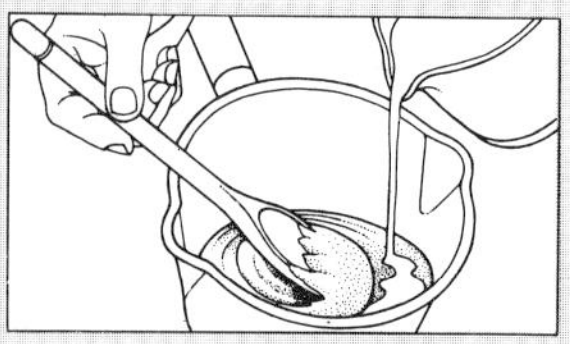

Adding the remaining milk

Blending method

For this method the thickening agent is mixed to a paste with a little cold milk. Mix 1 oz (25 g) plain flour with a few tablespoons taken from ½ pint (300 ml) of cold milk. Blend to a smooth paste in a bowl, and bring the remaining milk to the boil.

Pour the hot milk over the paste and return the mixture to the pan. Bring to the boil over low heat, stirring continuously with a wooden spoon. Simmer the sauce for 2–3 minutes, until thick. Add a knob of butter and seasoning and cook for 5 minutes.

A basic white sauce can be made into other savoury sauces, such as béchamel and velouté.

Béchamel Sauce

PREPARATION TIME: *20 min*
COOKING TIME: *5–10 min*
INGREDIENTS *(½ pint, 300 ml):*
½ pint (300 ml) milk
½ small bay leaf
Sprig of thyme
½ small onion
¼ level teaspoon grated nutmeg
1 oz (25 g) butter
1 oz (25 g) plain flour
Salt and black pepper*

Put the milk with the bay leaf, thyme, onion and nutmeg in a pan, and bring slowly to the boil. Remove from the heat, cover with a lid and leave the milk to infuse for 15 minutes.

In a clean heavy-based pan, melt the butter, stir in the flour and cook the roux for 3 minutes.

Strain the milk through a fine sieve and gradually blend it into the roux. Bring to the boil, stirring continuously, then simmer for 2–3 minutes. Adjust the seasoning.

Velouté Sauce

PREPARATION TIME: *5–10 min*
COOKING TIME: *1 hour*
INGREDIENTS *(½ pint, 300 ml):*
1 oz (25 g) butter
1 oz (25 g) plain flour
1 pint (300 ml) white stock
Salt and black pepper*

Make the roux with the butter and flour. Gradually stir in the hot stock until the sauce is quite smooth. Bring to boiling point, lower the heat, and let the sauce simmer for about 1 hour until reduced by half. Stir occasionally. Strain through a sieve.

Thickening agents for sauces

Basic white and brown sauces can be thickened or enriched with various other liaisons: cornflour or arrowroot with water; beurre manié (kneaded butter and flour); egg yolks and cream.

Cornflour and arrowroot

To thicken ½ pint (300 ml) of liquid to a sauce of coating consistency, stir 1 level tablespoon cornflour with 1½ tablespoons cold water, and mix into a smooth paste. Blend a little of the hot liquid into the liaison, then return this to the sauce. Bring the sauce to the boil, stirring constantly for 2–3 minutes to allow the starch to cook through.

Arrowroot is best used to thicken clear sauces that are to be served at once. To thicken ½ pint (300 ml) sauce use 2¼ level teaspoons arrowroot mixed to a paste with water.

The sauce cannot be reheated and quickly loses its thickening qualities.

Beurre manié

This liaison is ideal for thickening sauces, casseroles and stews at the end of cooking. Knead an equal amount of butter and flour, about 1 oz (25 g) each, into a paste with a fork or the fingers. Add small pieces of the beurre manié to the hot liquid. Stir or whisk continuously to dissolve the butter and disperse the flour. Simmer the sauce until it is thick and smooth and has lost the starchy taste of raw flour. Do not let the sauce boil or the beurre manié will separate out.

EGG-BASED SAUCES

These rich sauces require care and practice to prevent them curdling. They are made from egg yolks and a high proportion of butter. Through continuous whisking, these two main ingredients are emulsified to the stage where they form a thick and creamy consistency.

Hollandaise Sauce

PREPARATION AND COOKING TIME: *20 min*
INGREDIENTS (*½ pint, 300 ml*):
3 tablespoons white wine vinegar
1 tablespoon water
6 black peppercorns
1 bay leaf
3 egg yolks
6 oz (175 g) soft butter, preferably unsalted
Salt and black pepper*

Boil the vinegar and water with the peppercorns and the bay leaf in a small pan, until reduced to 1 tablespoon. Leave to cool. Cream the egg yolks with ½ oz (10 g) butter and a pinch of salt. Strain the vinegar into the eggs, and set the bowl over a pan of boiling water. Turn off the heat. Whisk in the remaining butter, ¼ oz (5–10 g) at a time, until the sauce is shiny and has the consistency of thick cream. Season with salt and freshly ground pepper.

Until the technique of egg-based sauces has been mastered, a Hollandaise sauce may sometimes curdle during preparation. This is generally because the heat is too sudden or too high, or because the butter has been added too quickly.

If the finished sauce separates, it can often be saved by taking it off the heat immediately and beating in 1 tablespoon of cold water.

Whisking in pieces of butter to thicken Hollandaise sauce

Béarnaise Sauce

This sauce is similar to Hollandaise sauce, but has a sharper flavour. It is served with grilled meat and fish.

PREPARATION AND COOKING TIME: *20 min*
INGREDIENTS (*½ pint, 300 ml*):
2 tablespoons tarragon vinegar
2 tablespoons white wine vinegar
½ small onion
2 egg yolks
3–4 oz (75–100 g) butter, preferably unsalted
Salt and black pepper*

Put the vinegars and finely chopped onion in a small saucepan; boil steadily until reduced to 1 tablespoon. Strain and set aside to cool. Follow the method used for making Hollandaise sauce.

Mayonnaise

Mayonnaise and its variations are the most widely used of savoury cold sauces. They are served with hors d'oeuvre, salads, cold meat, poultry and vegetable dishes. Mayonnaise, like Hollandaise and Béarnaise sauce, is based on eggs and fat, but oil is used instead of butter.

It is essential that all the ingredients and equipment are at room temperature. Assemble the bowl, egg and oil at least 1 hour before making a mayonnaise.

PREPARATION TIME: *20 min*
INGREDIENTS (*¼ pint, 150 ml*):
1 egg yolk
¼ level teaspoon salt
½ level teaspoon dry mustard
Pinch caster sugar
Black pepper
¼ pint (150 ml) olive oil
1 tablespoon white wine vinegar or lemon juice

Beat the egg yolk in a bowl until thick. Beat in the salt, mustard, sugar and a few twists of freshly ground pepper. Add the oil, drop by drop, whisking vigorously between each addition of oil so that it is absorbed completely before the next drop. As the mayonnaise thickens and becomes shiny, the oil may be added in a thin stream. Finally, blend in the vinegar.

A mayonnaise may curdle if the oil was cold or was added too quickly, or if the egg yolk was stale. To save a curdled mayonnaise, whisk a fresh yolk in a clean bowl, and gradually whisk in the curdled mayonnaise. Alternatively, whisk in a teaspoon of tepid water until the mayonnaise is thick and shiny.

SALAD DRESSINGS

A good dressing is essential to a salad, but it must be varied to accord with the salad ingredients. A sharp vinaigrette sauce is probably best for a green salad, but more substantial salads might need additional flavours.

Sauce Vinaigrette

PREPARATION TIME: *3 min*
INGREDIENTS (*¼ pint, 150 ml*):
6 tablespoons oil
2 tablespoons vinegar
2 teaspoons finely chopped herbs
Salt and black pepper*

Put the oil and vinegar in a bowl or in a screw-top jar. Whisk with a fork or shake vigorously before seasoning to taste with herbs, salt and freshly ground pepper.

French Dressing

PREPARATION TIME: *3 min*
INGREDIENTS (*⅓ pint, 200 ml*):
8 tablespoons oil
4 tablespoons vinegar
2 level teaspoons French mustard
½ level teaspoon each salt and black pepper*
Caster sugar (optional)

Whisk or shake all the dressing ingredients together, seasoning with sugar (optional). Either of the following ingredients can be added to a basic French dressing: 1–2 crushed garlic cloves; 2 tablespoons chopped tarragon or chives; 1 tablespoon tomato paste and a pinch of paprika; 2 tablespoons each finely chopped parsley and onion; 1 teaspoon anchovy essence (for cold fish).

Vegetables

Vegetables are at their best for food value and flavour when fresh. But if they have to be stored, keep them in a cool airy place, such as a larder or in the vegetable compartment of the refrigerator. However, certain fruits and vegetables should not be stored together. Carrots stored next to apples will take on a bitter taste; and potatoes will quickly spoil if they are stored with onions. Cut the leaves from root vegetables before storing, to prevent the sap rising from the roots.

Choose vegetables that are crisp and firm rather than hard. The size is sometimes an indication of age and quality. For example, very small vegetables may be flavourless because they are immature, whereas over-large vegetables may be old, and therefore coarse.

Prepare vegetables immediately before cooking by thorough washing and, if necessary, scrubbing with a brush. But do not soak vegetables at any stage during preparation because their mineral salts and vitamins are soluble in water. Because the most nutritious part of root vegetables and onions lies just under the skin, only a thin outer layer should be peeled away with a knife. If the vegetables are young; just scrape them lightly.

Vegetables can be used whole or can be cut up for quicker cooking. To cut vegetables, use a sharp kitchen knife. When slicing, do not lift the point of the knife from the chopping board but use it as a pivot. Keep the wrist flexible and raise the knife just above the vegetable before chopping down again. Guide the knife with a forefinger down the back of the blade.

Some vegetables – cabbages, for example – may be merely halved and quartered before cooking; but most can be prepared by the following methods:

Slicing
Cut the vegetables into narrow rounds or slices, and divide these into strips. Fine match-like sticks, known as julienne strips, are used to garnish soups.

Dicing
Slice the vegetables lengthways into sticks; then cut these across into small cubes.

Shredding
Cut thin slivers from the sides of a vegetable, such as cabbage, which has been quartered. Slice evenly and rhythmically, always bringing the knife just above the vegetable before pressing down.

Rounds
Cut the vegetable crossways to get thick, round slices.

Chopping
Cut the vegetables finely or roughly as required.

COOKING METHODS

After preparing vegetables, do not soak them. Only peeled potatoes need to be kept in water; otherwise they turn brown. Dried peas and beans are quicker to cook if soaked.

PREPARING VEGETABLES

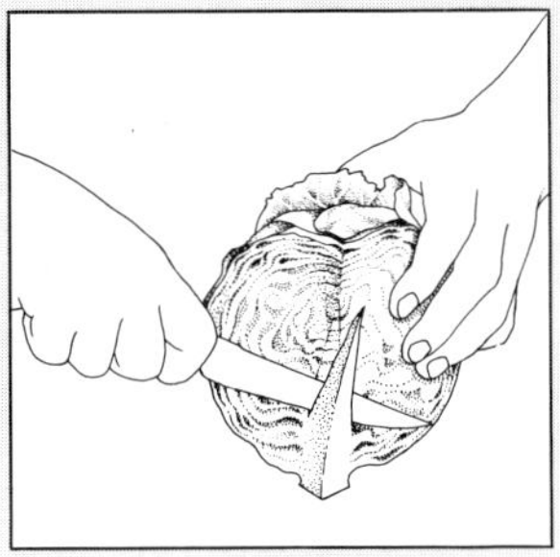

Removing stalk from cabbage

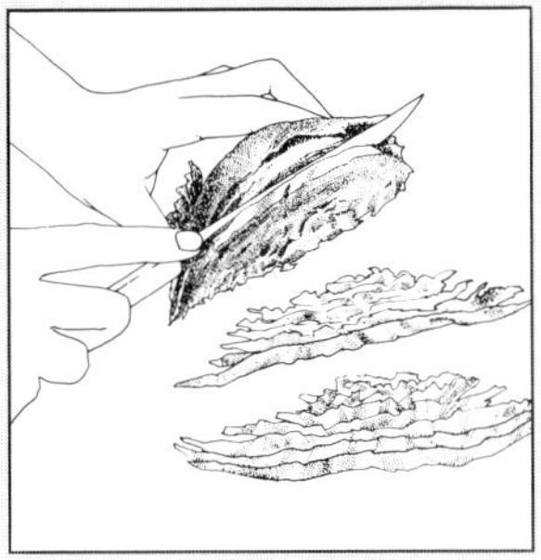

Shredding quartered cabbage

SLICING AND DICING

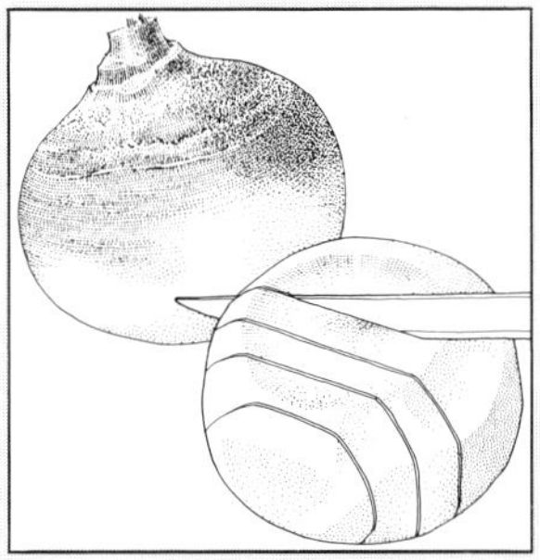

Slicing turnips into rounds

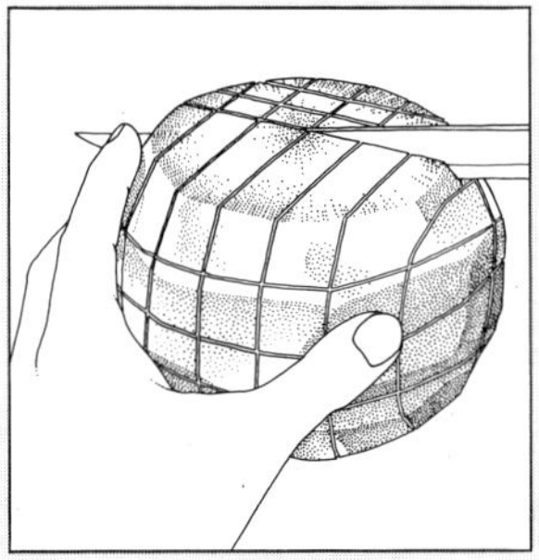

Cutting slices into dice

Boiling
Perhaps the most common mistake in British cooking is to overboil vegetables.

Use only a minimum of salted water, and for each $\frac{1}{2}$ pint (300 ml) of water, add $\frac{1}{2}$ teaspoon of salt. Root vegetables are put into cold salted water, and all other vegetables into boiling water.

Bring the water to the boil. Add the prepared vegetables, cover the pan and quickly return to the boil. Reduce the heat and boil at moderate heat until the vegetables are tender but firm. The vegetable liquid can be used to make stock, sauce or gravy.

Steaming
Method 1 – Place the prepared vegetables in a steamer above rapidly boiling water. Sprinkle with salt, allowing 1 teaspoon to each pound of prepared vegetables. Cover the steamer with a tightly fitting lid, and steam until just tender, usually 3–5 minutes longer than the vegetables would take to boil.

Method 2 – Use a wide shallow pan. Melt 1–2 oz (25–50 g) butter in the pan, and add the prepared vegetables. Cover the pan with a tightly fitting lid, and heat over moderate heat until steam forms. Reduce the heat and cook until the vegetables are tender, shaking the pan occasionally.

Pressure cooking
Pressure cook older root vegetables and dried peas and beans. Follow the manufacturer's instructions, and time the cooking with care. Vegetables will quickly over-cook by this method.

Shallow frying (sauté)
This method is suitable for very

tender vegetables such as aubergines, courgettes and tomatoes, or for onion slices. Cook these vegetables in butter in an uncovered pan.

Most other vegetables must be pre-cooked or par-boiled before frying. Heat butter, oil or other fat in a heavy-based pan, add the prepared and thoroughly drained pre-cooked vegetables, and fry until tender and golden brown.

Braising

This method is suitable for root vegetables and onions. After preparing the vegetables, blanch them by plunging them into a pan of boiling water for 2–3 minutes.

Lightly fry the drained vegetables in butter in a pan. Then add $\frac{1}{4}$–$\frac{1}{2}$ pint (150–300 ml) of stock to each pound of prepared vegetables. Season lightly, add a knob of butter, and cover with a tightly fitting lid. Cook until tender.

Lift the vegetables out of the pan and reduce the juices by rapid boiling, or thicken with cornflour (see page 84).

Baking

Brush the prepared vegetables (cucumber, courgette, marrow) with melted butter or oil and cook in an oven set at 400°F (200°C, mark 6) until tender.

Roasting

This method is applied to roots and tubers, usually cooked around a meat joint. Place the prepared vegetables in the hot fat and cook at 425°F (220°C, mark 7) for $\frac{3}{4}$–1 hour. Or par-boil the vegetables for 10 minutes, drain and then add to the hot fat. Roast for 20–30 minutes.

POTATOES

Potatoes fall into two main categories: early and maincrop.

Early potatoes are best boiled, chipped, roasted or used in salads. When buying early potatoes, check that any soil on them is damp and that the skin rubs off; these are signs of freshness.

Maincrop potatoes can be jacket-baked, roasted, chipped and used in potato salads.

PREPARATION OF POTATOES

New potatoes need only be washed, scraped lightly, and washed again. They may also be boiled in their skins and peeled before serving, to save scraping time. Old potatoes should be washed well, peeled thinly, and then cut into even-sized pieces, and cooked as soon as possible.

A pound (450 g) of old potatoes gives about 3 portions; a pound (450 g) of new ones about 4 portions.

COOKING METHODS

Boiled

Cut the potatoes into even-sized pieces and put into cold salted water; bring to the boil and simmer under lid about 15–20 minutes for new potatoes and about 20 minutes for old potatoes.

Mashed

Boil old potatoes. Drain well, and dry the potatoes in the pan over low heat. Using a potato masher or a fork, mash the potatoes in the pan until free of lumps. Alternatively, rub the potatoes through a sieve on to a dish.

Creamed

Put mashed potatoes in a clean pan. To each pound of potatoes add 1 oz (25 g) of butter, a little milk and seasoning, and put the pan over gentle heat; beat the mixture until light and fluffy. For a smoother mixture beat in 1 egg.

Duchesse potatoes

Prepare a portion of creamed potatoes with an egg and put the mixture in a piping bag. Pipe into mounds, about 2 in (5 cm) high, on a lightly greased baking tray, or into a border round a shallow ovenproof dish. Bake near the top of the oven at 400°F (200°C, mark 6) for about 25 minutes, or until golden.

Potato croquettes

Prepare creamed potatoes. Roll the mixture into cork shapes, and coat thickly with egg and breadcrumbs. In a frying pan heat the fat to 375°F (190°C) – at this temperature a cube of bread dropped into the fat should brown in 40–50 seconds. Fry the croquettes for 2–3 minutes, drain thoroughly and fry again, at the same temperature, for 2–3 minutes.

Fried (or sautéed)

Boil potatoes until they are almost cooked, and cut them into slices about $\frac{1}{4}$ in ($\frac{1}{2}$ cm) thick. Fry in hot fat, turning them until crisp and golden brown on both sides.

Chips

Peel old potatoes and cut them into $\frac{1}{4}$–$\frac{1}{2}$ in ($\frac{1}{2}$–1 cm) slices. Cut these slices into strips $\frac{1}{4}$–$\frac{1}{2}$ in ($\frac{1}{2}$–1 cm) wide. Soak in cold water. Drain well and dry thoroughly before using. Put some fat into a fryer (or a deep saucepan) and heat to 385°F (195°C). When a chip dropped in the fat rises to the surface, surrounded by bubbles, the fat is hot enough for frying. Place a layer of chips in a wire basket and lower into the fryer; cook for 4–6 minutes, or until golden. Drain well on absorbent paper. Just before serving, fry all the chips again for 1–2 minutes. Drain, sprinkle with a little salt, and serve.

Matchstick chips

Peel old potatoes and cut them into very small chips, about the size of matchsticks. Cook in the same way as chips, allowing a shorter cooking time – about 3 minutes for the first frying.

Crisps (game chips)

Peel and wash the potatoes. Cut into thin rounds. Soak in cold water, dry, and fry once only in hot fat for about 3 minutes.

Jacket-baked

Select good-sized old potatoes, allowing one per person. Scrub, wash, dry and prick all over with a fork. Cut a small cross through the skin on the upper side of the potato. Bake near the top of an oven set at 400°F (200°C, mark 6) until tender in the centre. Cut through the cross and open up the potato. Top with butter.

Roasted

Select old potatoes. Peel and cut them into even-sized pieces. Parboil for 5 minutes, then drain well. Place in a roasting tin with melted lard or dripping, and roast near the top of the oven at 425°F (220°C, mark 7) for 40 minutes, turning once; or put the cut potatoes around a meat joint to roast for the last 50–60 minutes.

ARTICHOKES, GLOBE

PREPARATION:
Cut off stalk and, using scissors, trim off point from each outer leaf; rinse and drain. Rub cut surfaces with lemon. Chokes can be removed before or after cooking. Spread top leaves apart and pull inside leaves out to reveal hairy choke. Using a teaspoon, scrape away hairs to expose the heart or fond. Remaining leaves around the base can also be stripped away

COOKING METHODS:
Boiling Whole artichokes: 40–45 min, in salted water. Without chokes: for 15–20 min. Drain upside-down.
Braising Blanch for 5 min. Refresh in cold water. Place on a bed of sautéed vegetables, moistened with wine or stock and add a bouquet garni (page 99). Cover and cook for 1 hour.
Steaming Whole artichokes: Method 1, for 50–55 min. Without chokes: Method 1, for 20–25 min. Stuffed artichokes: Method 1, for 30–35 min.

SERVING SUGGESTIONS:
Hot: with melted butter or Hollandaise sauce (page 85). To eat, pull out one leaf at a time and dip edible base of leaf in sauce. Scrape off fleshy base of leaf between the teeth. When leaves are removed, eat heart with knife and fork. Cold: with mayonnaise, French dressing or tartare sauce (page 85).

ARTICHOKES, JERUSALEM

PREPARATION:
Scrub and thinly peel under running water; place in acidulated water.

COOKING METHODS:
Boiling For 25–30 min in acidulated salted water. Drain. Artichokes can be boiled in their skins and then peeled.
Steaming Whole artichokes: Method 1, for 35–40 min. Quartered: Method 2, for 30 min.

SERVING SUGGESTIONS:
Boiled or steamed with melted butter, Hollandaise or béchamel (pages 84 and 85) or cheese sauce.

ASPARAGUS

PREPARATION:
Cut off woody parts from base of stems. Using knife, scrape white part of stems downwards. Tie asparagus in bundles, all heads together.

COOKING METHOD:
Boiling For 11–14 min, in salted water to just below the heads.

SERVING SUGGESTIONS:
Serve 8–10 stems per portion: an average bundle gives 3–4 portions.
Hot: with melted butter or Hollandaise sauce (page 85). Cold: with French dressing or mayonnaise (page 85).

AUBERGINES

PREPARATION:
Wipe, trim both ends and peel if necessary. Slice, dice or halve. Sprinkle cut surfaces with salt and leave for 30 min. Rinse and dry.

COOKING METHODS:
Frying Coat prepared slices in seasoned flour or leave plain. Fry in butter.
Grilling or baking Brush aubergine slices with melted butter or oil.
Stuffing and baking Cut aubergine in half lengthways. Scoop out the pulp, leaving a shell. A savoury mixture, including the pulp and other ingredients, is piled back into the shells then baked at 325°F (170°C, mark 3) for 20–30 min.

SERVING SUGGESTIONS:
Fried or grilled with meat; stuffed with Parmesan cheese topping, tomato or cheese sauce.

AVOCADOS

PREPARATION:
Just before serving, slice in half lengthways, round the stone, using a stainless steel or silver knife to prevent discoloration of the flesh. Leave the skins on if avocados are to be served as a first course with a filling or dressing. The flesh can also be carefully scooped out and mixed with salad vegetables or sea food.

If avocados are to be left for any length of time, toss the flesh in lemon juice to prevent discoloration.

COOKING METHODS:
Baking Peel off skin from halved avocados, slice thinly, place in buttered ovenproof dish, sprinkle with lemon juice and seasoning; cover with slices of chicken breast, white sauce, crumbs and butter. Bake at 375°F (190°C, mark 5) for 45 min.

SERVING SUGGESTIONS:
Usually served fresh with sauce vinaigrette (page 85), as a dip or a mousse.

BEANS, BROAD

PREPARATION:
Young and tender beans: wash, top and tail, and cook in their pods. Mature beans: remove from pods. Large beans: remove from their skin after cooking and make into a purée.

COOKING METHODS:
Boiling For 15–20 min, both in and out of their pods. Mature beans, up to 30 min.
Steaming Method 1, for 10–15 min.

SERVING SUGGESTIONS:
Serve small beans shelled or in their pods, tossed in butter, and sprinkled with finely chopped parsley or savory. Serve more mature beans with a white, parsley or cream sauce.

BEANS, FRENCH

PREPARATION:
Young beans: wash, top and tail; leave whole or cut into 1½–2 in (4–5 cm) lengths. Mature beans: top, tail and string before slicing.

COOKING METHODS:
Boiling For 5–10 min in salted water. Refresh with cold water. Drain well, then re-heat with butter and herbs.
Steaming Method 1, for 10–15 min.

SERVING SUGGESTIONS:
Dress with garlic, anchovy or herb butters.

BEANS, RUNNER

PREPARATION:
Wash, top, tail and string. Cut into oblique slices 1½–2 in (4–5 cm) long.

COOKING METHODS:
Boiling For 10 min in salted water.
Braising Par-boil mature runner beans in salted water for 5 min, then drain. Finish cooking in a tightly covered casserole with butter, savory and sliced onion, with enough stock to cover. Cook for 1 hour at 350–375°F (180–190°C, mark 4–5).
Steaming Method 1, for 20 min.

SERVING SUGGESTIONS:
As for French beans.

BEETROOT

PREPARATION:
Cut off leaf stalks 1–2 in (3–5 cm) above the root, but do not trim off tapering root. Wash carefully to prevent the beetroot 'bleeding'.

COOKING METHODS:
Boiling Depending on the size, for 1–2 hours, in salted water. Slide off the skin when cooked.
Steaming Method 1, for about 2 hours.
Baking Wrap in buttered paper. Bake at 325°F (170°C, mark 3) for ½–1 hour.

SERVING SUGGESTIONS:
Cooked beetroot can be sliced or diced, and served cold in salads.

BROCCOLI

PREPARATION:
Wash thoroughly in cold water; drain well. Remove any coarse outer leaves and tough part of the stalk.

COOKING METHODS:
Boiling For 15–20 min in salted water.
Steaming Method 1, for 20–25 min

SERVING SUGGESTIONS:
With butter or Béarnaise sauce (page 85).

BRUSSELS SPROUTS

PREPARATION:
Wash, trim off damaged outer leaves.

Make an 'X' cut in base of stems.
COOKING METHODS:
Boiling For about 10 min in minimum of salted water.
Braising Par-boil in salted water for 5 min. Drain and keep warm. Sauté thinly sliced onion rings. Add a little stock and seasoning. Simmer 5 min. Add sprouts; simmer for further 5 min, and baste occasionally.
Steaming Method 1, for about 15 min.
SERVING SUGGESTIONS:
Tossed with butter, soured cream and seasoning.

CABBAGES
PREPARATION:
Remove the coarse outer leaves; cut cabbage into quarters and remove hard centre core. Wash thoroughly, drain and cook either in wedges or finely shredded.
COOKING METHODS:
Boiling Shredded cabbage: cook in salted water for 5–8 min. Cabbage wedges: for 10–15 min.
Braising Par-boil cabbage wedges in salted water for 10 min. Refresh in cold water. Place on a bed of sautéed vegetables. Add bouquet garni (page 99) and enough stock to cover. Bake for 1 hour at 350–375°F (180–190°C, mark 4–5). Red cabbage: braise shredded cabbage in butter, add chopped apples, vinegar and sugar to taste. Simmer covered for 1 hour.
Steaming Shredded cabbage: Method 1, for 10 min. Cabbage wedges: Method 1, for 20 min.
SERVING SUGGESTIONS:
Toss boiled white and green cabbage with butter and seasoning.

CARROTS
PREPARATION:
Trim away root end and tip; remove any damaged areas and green patches. Scrub in cold water. Scrape young carrots; peel old ones with a potato peeler. Small carrots can be left whole; large ones can be cut into quarters, rings, sticks or cubes.
COOKING METHODS:
Boiling For 10–30 min in salted water or stock.
Steaming Method 1, for 15–40 min, depending on age and size.
SERVING SUGGESTIONS:
Toss boiled carrots with butter, chopped parsley or mint, or serve with a béchamel sauce (page 84).

CAULIFLOWERS
PREPARATION:
Cut off damaged outer leaves. If cauliflower is to be cooked whole, cut an 'X' in base of stalk. Alternatively, separate cauliflower into individual florets. Wash well in cold water.
COOKING METHODS:
Boiling For 12–15 min, in salted acidulated water, partially covered with saucepan lid.
Steaming Method 1, for 15–25 min.
SERVING SUGGESTIONS:
Serve the florets or whole cauliflower with white, cheese or parsley sauce.

CELERIAC
PREPARATION:
Wash, slice, then peel, dice or cut into matchstick strips.
COOKING METHODS:
Boiling For 25–30 min in salted, acidulated water with lid on. Drain.
Steaming Method 1, for 35 min.
Frying Sauté matchstick celeriac strips in butter for 30 min.
SERVING SUGGESTIONS:
Boiled celeriac with béchamel or Hollandaise sauce (page 85). Celeriac can also be puréed, or grated fresh as a salad vegetable.

CELERY
PREPARATION:
Trim away root end and remove damaged outer stalks and green tops. Separate stalks and scrub clean in cold water. Remove any coarse fibres and cut stalks into even lengths: $2–2\frac{1}{2}$ in (5–6 cm) for boiling; 3–4 in (8–10 cm) for braising or steaming.
COOKING METHODS:
Boiling For 15–20 min in salted water, covered with a lid.
Braising Blanch halved or whole heads of celery for 10 min. Sauté diced bacon, sliced onions and carrots in buttered casserole. Add celery and enough stock to cover. Bring to boil, cover and simmer $1\frac{1}{2}–1\frac{3}{4}$ hours.
Steaming Method 1, for 20–30 min.
Au gratin Sprinkle with grated cheese or breadcrumbs, and bake or grill.
SERVING SUGGESTIONS:
Boiled and steamed with cheese or parsley sauce, made from half the cooking liquid and the same quantity of milk. Fresh as a salad vegetable.

CHICORY
PREPARATION:
Trim away outside leaves. Separate into spears or slice across. If chicory is green, it should be blanched before cooking to reduce its bitterness.
COOKING METHODS:
Boiling For 15–20 min in salted, acidulated water.
Braising Scoop out the hard core at the base and leave chicory whole. Blanch, if necessary, and drain. Butter casserole, arrange chicory in base and dot with more butter. Add 2–3 tablespoons water and a little lemon juice and salt. Cover and bake for $1–1\frac{1}{4}$ hours at 350°F (180°C, mark 4).
SERVING SUGGESTIONS:
Serve boiled chicory with cheese, béchamel (page 84) or tomato sauce.

CORN
PREPARATION:
Strip the husks off the cobs and remove the silky threads.
COOKING METHODS:
Boiling Cook whole corn cobs in water for 5–10 min. Add salt halfway through cooking time.
Steaming Method 1, for 10–15 min.
SERVING SUGGESTIONS:
With butter, salt and pepper.

COURGETTTES
PREPARATION:
Wash the courgettes and trim both ends; cook without peeling, either whole, sliced in rounds, or halved with the centres scooped out, before filling with a savoury mixture.
COOKING METHODS:
Boiling For 10–15 min in salted water.
Steaming Whole courgettes: Method 1, for 15–20 min. Sliced: Method 2, for about 10 min.
Baking Par-boil hollowed-out courgettes for 5 min. Drain, brush with butter and season. Bake at 375°F (190°C, mark 5) for 25 min.
SERVING SUGGESTIONS:
Sprinkled with tarragon or chopped parsley.

CUCUMBERS
PREPARATION:
Peel cucumber, cut into strips, slice or dice. If cucumber is to be stuffed, cut in half lengthways and scoop out seeds.
COOKING METHODS:
Boiling For about 10 min in salted water.
Steaming Method 1, for 20 min. Method 2, for 10–20 min.
Baking Peel, slice thickly, dot with butter and freshly chopped herbs. Bake at 375°F (190°C, mark 5) for 30 min.
SERVING SUGGESTIONS:
Boiled cucumber with a white or cream sauce flavoured with dill, tarragon or celery seeds. Cucumber is also used as a raw salad vegetable or garnish.

ENDIVE
PREPARATION:
Discard damaged outer leaves. For salads, separate remaining leaves and wash thoroughly in cold water. Leave vegetable whole for braising.
COOKING METHOD:
Braising As for lettuce.
SERVING SUGGESTIONS:
Fresh as a salad vegetable, by itself or tossed in a French dressing; braised, with béchamel sauce (page 84).

FENNEL

PREPARATION:
Trim off top stems and slice off base. Scrub well in cold water.
COOKING METHOD:
Braising As for celery.
SERVING SUGGESTIONS:
Thinly sliced as a salad vegetable or as a garnish. Also used to flavour sauces and fish dishes.

KALE

PREPARATION:
Separate leaves from stems, remove mid-rib from leaves. Wash thoroughly in cold water. Cut leaves in pieces.
COOKING METHODS:
Braising In minimum salted water and a little butter for 8–10 min. Drain.
Steaming Method 1, for about 15 min.
SERVING SUGGESTIONS:
With butter or béchamel sauce (page 84).

KOHL RABI

PREPARATION:
Cut off leaves around bulb and trim off tapering roots. Scrub in cold water, then peel thickly. Small globes can be left whole. Slice or dice large ones.
COOKING METHODS:
Boiling Depending on size, for ½–1 hour in salted water. Drain.
Braising Par-boil in salted water for 5 min. Braise with a little chopped onion and bacon; moisten with white wine or stock. Cook for 1 hour or until tender, depending on size.
SERVING SUGGESTIONS:
Kohl rabi can be mashed, puréed, baked *au gratin* and used for fritters. Toss boiled kohl rabi in melted butter, or served with a white sauce.

LEEKS

PREPARATION:
Cut off roots and green tops; remove coarse outer leaves if necessary. Cut down through the white part and wash carefully to remove dirt from leaves. Leeks can be left whole or halved, sliced into thick rings or 2 in (5 cm) lengths.
COOKING METHODS:
Boiling Boil 2 in (5 cm) pieces of leeks in salted water for 15 min. Sliced into rings, for 10 min. Whole, for 20 min.
Braising Blanch in boiling salted water for 5 min. Drain, sauté in butter for 5 min. Add stock or water to cover and a bouquet garni. Cover and cook for 1 hour.
Steaming Method 1, for about 25 min depending on the size of leeks. Leeks cut in rings: Method 2, for about 10–15 min.
Frying Prepared leeks may be blanched for 5 min, drained and marinated in lemon juice. Dip in a light batter before deep-frying.
SERVING SUGGESTIONS:
Boiled with a béchamel (page 84) or cheese sauce. Use young leeks as a salad vegetable.

LETTUCE

PREPARATION:
Trim off base and remove any damaged outer leaves. Separate the leaves and wash in cold water; drain well. Leave whole if lettuce is to be braised.
COOKING METHODS:
Boiling For 10 min in salted water. Drain thoroughly and chop finely. Heat butter in a pan and add a little chopped onion, garlic and cream. Stir in chopped lettuce and season.
Braising Blanch 5–6 min. Refresh under cold running water, and drain thoroughly. In a casserole, melt butter and fry a little chopped bacon, carrot and onion. Fold in tops of lettuce to make a neat shape and lay on fried vegetables. Add stock to a depth of ½ in (1 cm), cover, bake 40–45 min at 325–350°F (170–180°C, mark 3–4). Pour over reduced pan juices.
SERVING SUGGESTIONS:
Boiled with Hollandaise (page 85) or cheese sauce. Fresh, shredded in green salads, tossed in dressings. Also used for garnish.

MARROWS

PREPARATION:
Marrow may be peeled, seeded and cubed for boiling, or cut into thick rings for stuffing. It may also be halved lengthways and deseeded before filling.
COOKING METHODS:
Boiling For about 10 min in salted water.
Steaming Method 1, for 20–40 min, depending on the age and size of the marrows.
Frying Marrow can be sautéed in butter and herbs for 7–10 min. Shake the pan occasionally.
Baking Whole or halved stuffed marrow can be baked for ¾–1 hour. Serve with a tomato sauce. Marrow rings can be stuffed with a savoury filling and baked in a well-buttered dish covered with foil for 20–30 min.
SERVING SUGGESTIONS:
Toss in butter, or serve with a white or cheese sauce.

MUSHROOMS

PREPARATION:
Cultivated mushrooms: trim the base of the stalks, rinse mushrooms in cold water; dry well. Field mushrooms: peel, and trim stems. Leave whole, quarter or slice thinly.
COOKING METHODS:
Steaming Cover and cook in the top of a double saucepan with a little butter and salt for 20 min, or until tender.
Frying and grilling Field mushrooms and flat cultivated mushrooms are suitable for frying and grilling. Fry sliced mushrooms in butter for 3–5 minutes, serve with juices. Brush whole mushrooms with butter or oil, grill under moderate heat for 6–8 minutes, turning once.
SERVING SUGGESTIONS:
Fried, with pan juices, cream and thyme. Button mushrooms as garnish or fresh in salads.

MUSTARD AND CRESS

PREPARATION:
Snip the cress from its bed into a colander or sieve; rinse thoroughly in cold water and dry well.
SERVING SUGGESTIONS:
Use in salads, sandwiches or as a garnish for savoury dishes.

OKRA

PREPARATION:
Wash thoroughly but do not remove the stems.
COOKING METHODS:
Boiling For 7–15 min in salted water. Alternatively, par-boil for 5 min, then finish cooking in butter.
Braising Par-boil okra in boiling salted water for 5 min; braise for a further 30–45 min.
SERVING SUGGESTIONS:
Toss in melted butter or serve with Hollandaise sauce (page 85).

ONIONS

PREPARATION:
Trim roots and peel away papery skins. Onions can be left whole or chopped, sliced or diced. Spring onions need the root removed and the tops trimmed.
COOKING METHODS:
Boiling Cook in salted water for 20–30 min, depending on size.
Braising Cook button onions in white stock or wine, butter and seasoning for 40 min.
Shallow-frying Cut onions in thin slices and fry gently in hot fat.
SERVING SUGGESTIONS:
Boiled with a white or cheese sauce; glazed button onions on their own, with chopped parsley or in béchamel sauce (page 84).

PARSNIPS

PREPARATION:
Cut off roots and tops, peel. If young, cut in thick slices; if mature, cut in quarters and remove the hard core.
COOKING METHODS:
Boiling For 30–40 min in salted water.
Roasting Par-boil for 5 min. Drain and roast with a joint of meat, or braise in

butter with a little stock.
Steaming Method 1, for about 35 min; this should be applied only to young parsnips.
Purée Parsnips can be boiled with carrots and pumpkin, then puréed with a little butter and nutmeg.
SERVING SUGGESTIONS:
Tossed with butter and parsley.

PEAS

PREPARATION:
Shell fresh peas. (Mange-tout or sugar peas are cooked, pods and all, in the same way as French beans.)
COOKING METHODS:
Boiling Gently for 15–20 min in salted water with a sprig of mint and 1 teaspoon of sugar. A little lemon juice helps to preserve the colour.
Steaming Method 1, for about 25 min.
SERVING SUGGESTIONS:
Tossed with butter and chopped mint and walnuts.

PEPPERS

PREPARATION:
Wash, cut in half lengthways and remove the stalk, seeds and whitish membrane around the sides. Slice or dice as required. If peppers are to be filled with a savoury mixture, cut around the stalk and lift away the core. Scoop out membrane and seeds.
COOKING METHOD:
Baking Par-boil in salted water for 10 min. Drain, fill with a savoury meat or vegetable filling. Add a little stock and bake at 350°F (180°C, mark 4) for 25–30 min.
SERVING SUGGESTIONS:
Hot: with cheese or tomato sauce. Cold: with French dressing.
Diced or sliced fresh pepper is used in salads or as garnish.

PULSES (DRIED PEAS, BEANS, LENTILS)

PREPARATION:
Pick over and wash the pulses under running water. Place in a large bowl and cover with boiling water; soak for 2 hours.
COOKING METHODS:
Boiling Put in a saucepan and add salt – 1 teaspoon for ½ lb (225 g) pulses. Bring to the boil and keep boiling rapidly for not less than 10 min (this is particularly important for dried beans in order to destroy the poisonous chemical lectin). Cover and simmer as follows: butter beans: 2½–3 hours; haricot beans: 2–2½ hours; lentils: ½–¾ hour; peas 1–1½ hours; split peas: ¾–1 hour. Pulses can also be soaked overnight in cold water, drained, placed in a saucepan with fresh water and salt. Bring to the boil and simmer: butter beans 1 hour; haricot beans ¾ hour; peas ½ hour; split peas ½ hour.
SERVING SUGGESTIONS:
Hot: puréed with butter and seasoning. Cold: tossed in garlic-flavoured French dressing. Also used in stews and casseroles. Dried, soaked beans must always be par-boiled for not less than 10 min and drained before being eaten.

PUMPKIN

PREPARATION:
Wash and cut pumpkin into bite-size pieces. Peel off skin, and remove pith and seeds.
COOKING METHODS:
Boiling For 20–30 min in salted water.
Steaming Method 1, for 35–40 min.
Roasting For 45–50 min around a joint of meat.
SERVING SUGGESTIONS:
With a cheese sauce.

RADISHES

PREPARATION:
If served whole cut off the tops, leaving ½ in (1 cm) of stalk, and remove tapering root; wash in cold water.
COOKING METHOD:
Boiling Cook large radishes whole in salted water for about 10 min.
SERVING SUGGESTIONS:
As a raw salad vegetable or as a garnish for savoury dishes. Serve boiled radishes with a well-seasoned parsley sauce.

SALSIFY

PREPARATION:
Scrub well in cold water, cut off top and tapering root end. Scrape off skin, cut into 1–2 in (3–5 cm) lengths. Plunge immediately into cold, acidulated water.
COOKING METHOD:
Boiling For 45 min in salted water.
SERVING SUGGESTIONS:
With a butter, white or Béarnaise sauce (page 85). Use leaves in salads or cooked as a green vegetable.

SHALLOTS

PREPARATION:
Prepare and cook as for onion.
SERVING SUGGESTIONS:
Used to flavour stocks and soups.

SPINACH

PREPARATION:
Wash spinach several times in cold water to remove dirt and grit. Do not dry, but place in a saucepan with no extra water.
COOKING METHOD:
Boiling Sprinkle leaves with a little salt; cover and cook gently, shaking the pan occasionally for about 10 min. Drain thoroughly.
SERVING SUGGESTIONS:
Re-heat with cream and seasoning, chop finely or make into a purée.

SWEDES

PREPARATION:
Trim stalk and root ends, peel thickly and cut in ½–1 in (1–2 cm) cubes.
COOKING METHOD:
Boiling For 30–40 min in salted water. Drain and dry out over gentle heat.
SERVING SUGGESTIONS:
Toss with melted butter and seasoning; or mash with butter, nutmeg and ginger. Use in stews and casseroles.

SWEET POTATOES

PREPARATION:
Scrub well and peel, if necessary.
COOKING METHOD:
Boiling Cook in jackets in salted water, covered, for about 25 min. If peeled, cook uncovered for 15 min.
SERVING SUGGESTIONS:
As potatoes.

TOMATOES

PREPARATION:
Remove stalk if necessary. To skin: see illustrations.
COOKING METHODS:
Grilling Cut tomato in half, top with a small knob of butter and season. Grill under moderate heat for 5–10 min.
Baking Prepare tomatoes as above or leave whole. Arrange in a shallow greased baking dish. Bake at 350°F (180°C, mark 4) for 15 min. Whole tomatoes should be placed stalk end down, cut crossways on top and brushed with oil, before baking.
SERVING SUGGESTIONS:
Hot: as first course or accompaniment to savoury dishes. Cold: sliced or quartered in salads and as garnish.

TURNIPS

PREPARATION:
Wash, trim stalk ends and tapering roots. Peel thickly. Small young turnips can be left whole; large ones should be quartered.
COOKING METHODS:
Boiling For 25–30 min in salted water.
Steaming Method 1, for 30–40 min.
SERVING SUGGESTIONS:
Toss in parsley and butter, or serve with a white sauce.

WATERCRESS

PREPARATION:
Wash thoroughly in cold water and drain well.
SERVING SUGGESTIONS:
Watercress is used in salads or as a garnish for savoury dishes. Chopped watercress can be mixed with salad vegetables or mixed into sauces and mayonnaise.

PREPARING GLOBE ARTICHOKES FOR COOKING

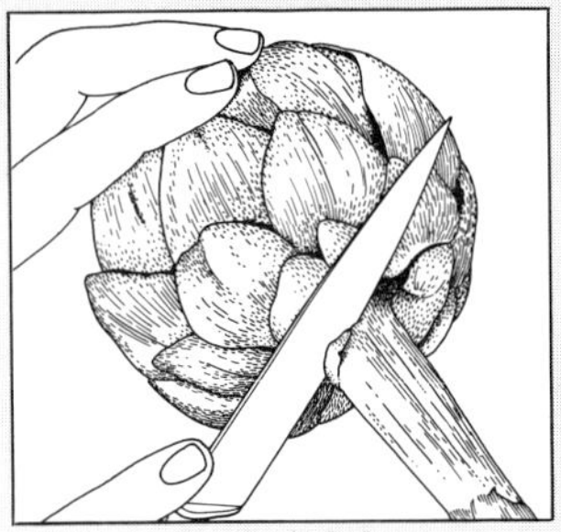

1. *Cut stalk off artichoke*

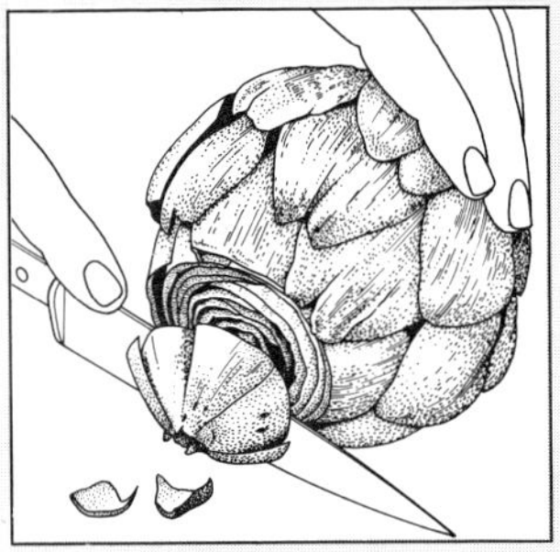

2. *Slice off top leaves*

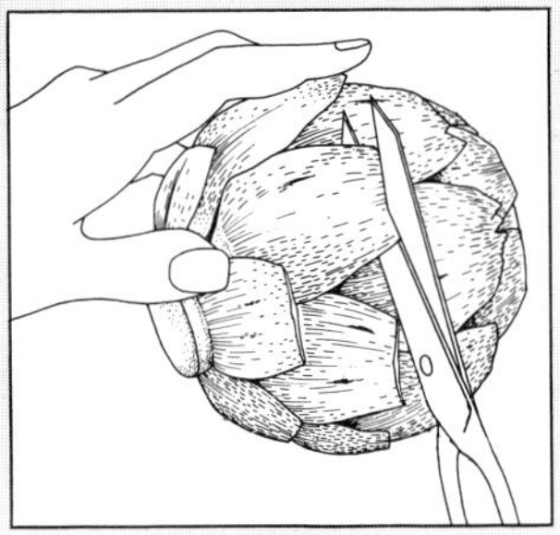

3. *Trim points off leaves*

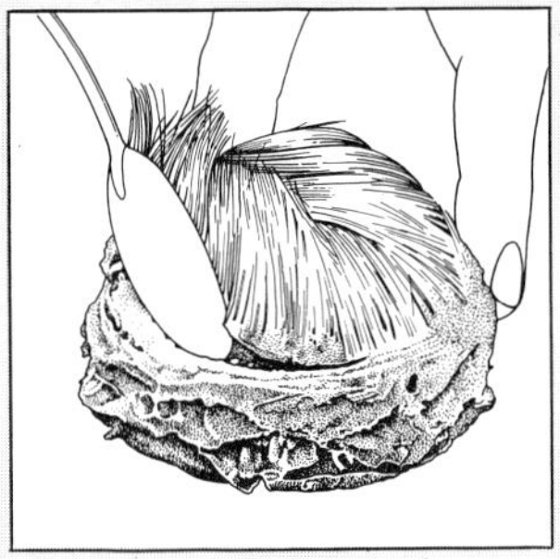

4. *Remove choke from fond*

CHICORY

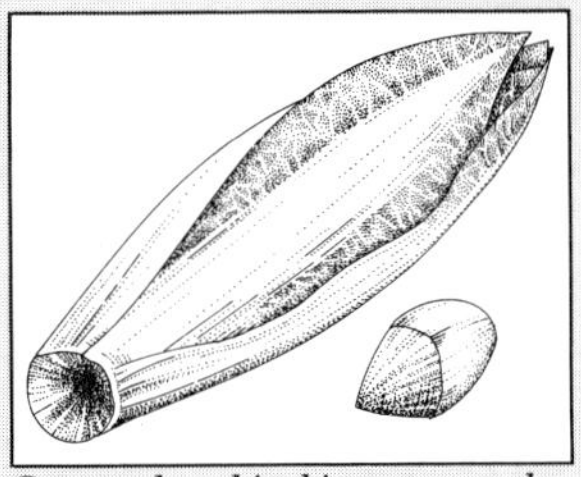

Cut out the white bitter root at the base of blanched chicory

CORN ON THE COB

Strip the green husks and silky threads from corn on the cob

SKINNING FRESH TOMATOES

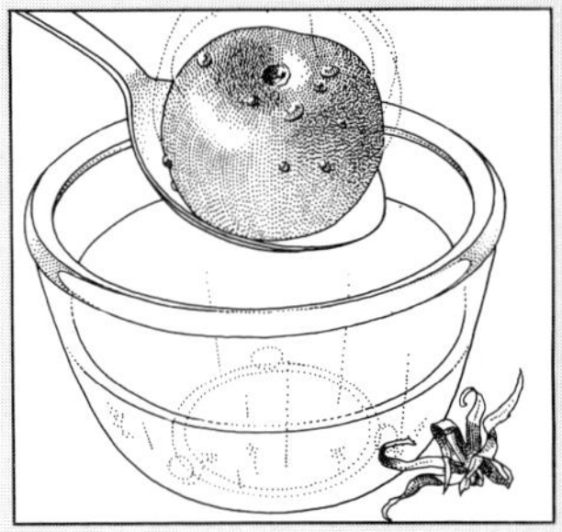

1. *Put in hot water for 1 min*

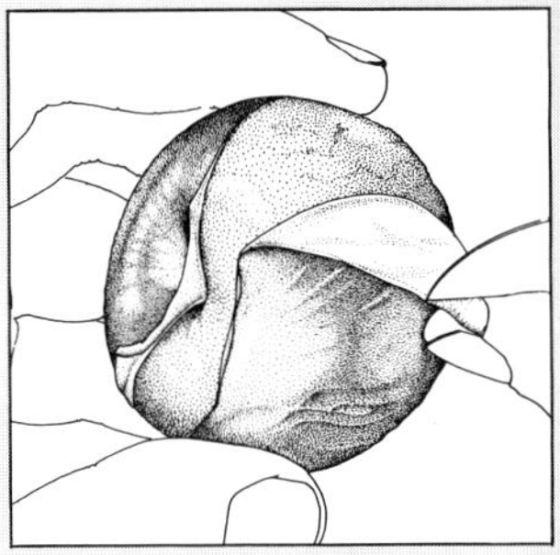

2. *Peel soft skin from wet tomato*

ASPARAGUS

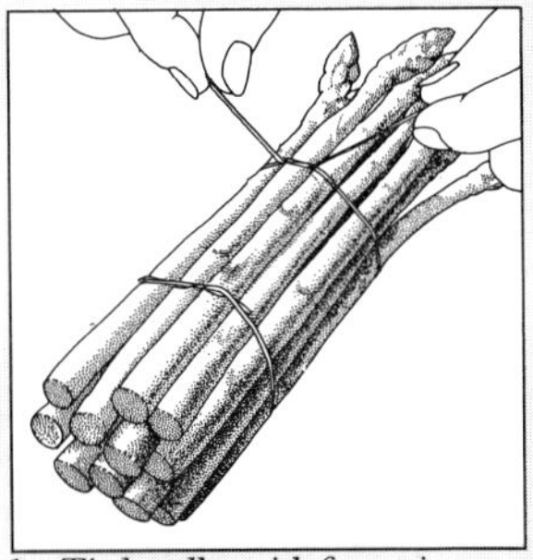

1. *Tie bundles with fine string*

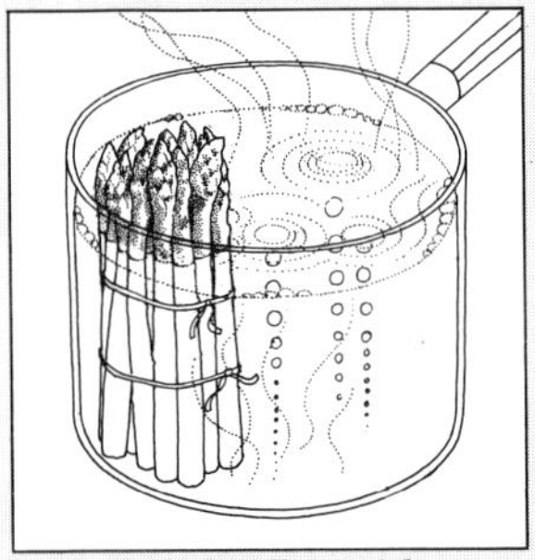

2. *Cook the bundles upright*

MARROW

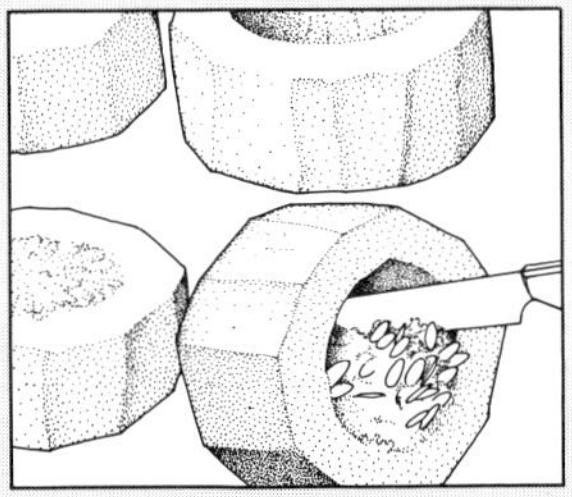

Scrape out the seeds from peeled marrow slices

MUSHROOMS

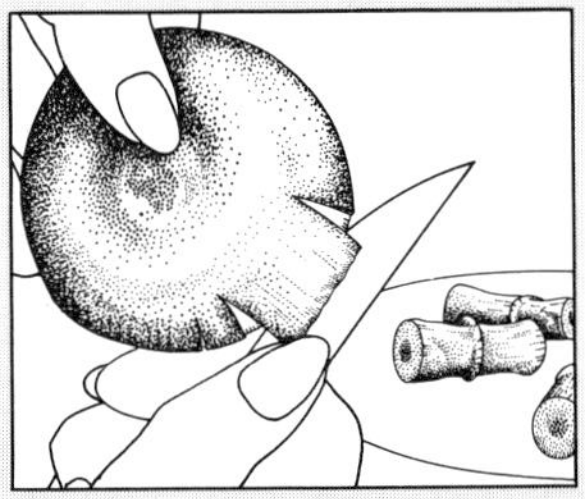

Trim by removing stalks, and peeling ragged skin

PEPPERS

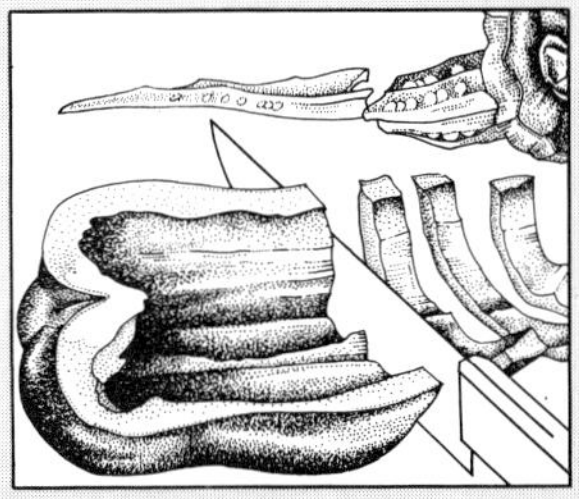

Slice peppers from which stalk and seeds have been removed

PEELING, SLICING AND CHOPPING ONION

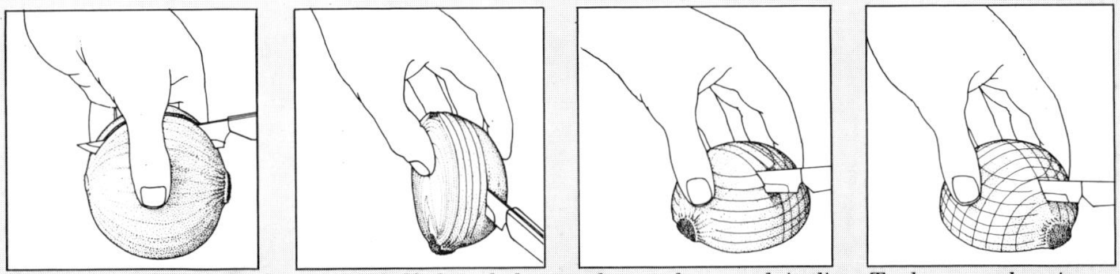

Peel off skin and trim root. Cut onion in half, through the root, then cut downwards in slices. To chop, turn the onion and slice across the first cuts. To dice, chop again across these cuts

Pasta, Rice and Pulses

All pasta is boiled, but cooking times vary according to the shape, size and freshness of the different kinds. Pasta should be cooked until it is just firm to the bite (*al dente*). Too long cooking turns pasta into a soft and soggy mass. Allow 4 oz (100 g) of pasta for each person. Rice, other cereals and dried peas, beans and lentils are also cooked by boiling.

Preparing pasta
Dried pasta swells in cooking, yielding about 3 times its uncooked weight. Cooking times are given below. Fresh pasta scarcely increases in bulk and needs no more than 4–5 minutes.

COOKING TIMES

Cannelloni	20 min
Lasagne	10–15 min
Macaroni	15 min
Ravioli	15–20 min
Spaghetti	10–12 min
Tagliatelle	10 min
Vermicelli	5 min

For every 2 oz (50 g) of pasta, use 1 pint (570 ml) of water, and 1 level teaspoon salt. Bring the salted water to the boil and add the pasta. The long strands of spaghetti should not be broken up. Hold the spaghetti at one end and lower the other into the boiling water; as the spaghetti softens and curls round in the water, push the rest of the spaghetti down.

Keep the pasta at a steady boil, uncovered, until just tender. Stir occasionally to prevent the pasta from sticking to the pan. To test, try a piece between the teeth; it should be just soft. Drain thoroughly in a colander. Return the pasta to the pan with a good knob of butter or a tablespoon of olive oil. Toss thoroughly, season with salt and pepper.

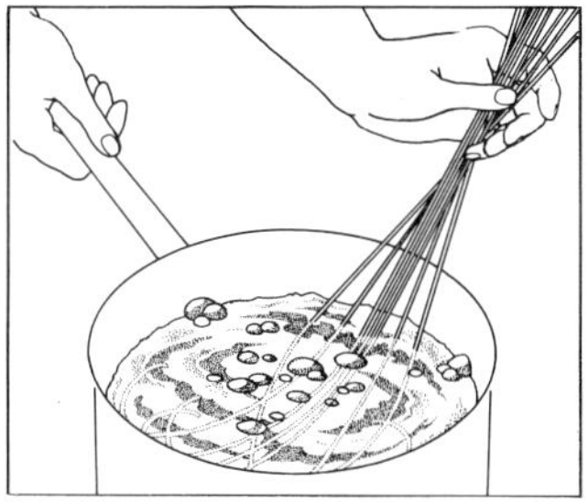

Do not break spaghetti, but curl the strands gradually into boiling water

In Italy pasta is invariably served as a first course; perhaps simply with butter and grated cheese, perhaps with oil and garlic and nothing else, perhaps with a more elaborate sauce. One of the most popular is pesto, a sauce made with basil, pine nuts, garlic and Parmesan. It can be made at home or bought ready to use.

Grated cheese (Parmesan or pecorino) is usually but by no means always served: never, for example, with sauces based on fish or shellfish. In other countries it may be the main dish, perhaps for a light lunch or a family supper, especially if, like spaghetti bolognese, cannelloni or lasagne, it is served with a fairly robust sauce. In France buttered noodles are sometimes served as an accompaniment to meat.

RICE

Preparing white rice
Wash rice before cooking it by putting it in a strainer and rinsing it under cold running water. Allow 2 oz (50 g) uncooked rice per person. During cooking, rice almost trebles in bulk.

After cooking, rice should be dry and slightly fluffy, separated into individual grains. To obtain this result, cook rice by boiling or by absorption methods.

Boiling white rice
Use 1 pint (570 ml) of water and 1 teaspoon salt to each 2 oz (50 g) of rice. Measure the water into a large pan and bring to the boil; add the salt and rice. Boil the rice rapidly for 12–15 minutes, or until soft, but not mushy. To test the rice, squeeze a grain between thumb and forefinger – when cooked, the centre will be just soft.

Drain the rice in a sieve and rinse it under hot water. Return it to the pan, with a knob of butter, and toss the rice.

Cover the pan with a lid and leave for 10 minutes to dry the rice. Shake the pan to prevent the grains sticking together.

Alternatively, put the drained rice in a shallow, buttered baking dish, cover it tightly and dry in the centre of an oven pre-heated to 325°F (170°C, mark 3) for 10 minutes.

Absorption method 1
This is an easy cooking method which ensures tender separate grains. For each cup of rice (enough for three servings), use 2 cups of water or clear stock and ½ level teaspoon salt. Bring the water to the boil in a large pan, then add the salt and rice, stirring for a few minutes.

As soon as the water boils again, cover with a folded tea cloth and the upturned lid. To prevent the steam from escaping, place a weight on the lid.

At the end of 15 minutes, all the water should be absorbed and the rice dry and tender. Remove the pan from the heat and separate the grains with a fork. Serve immediately.

Alternatively, cook the tightly covered rice over low heat for 10 minutes, remove from the heat and leave the rice for 10 minutes before uncovering it.

Absorption method 2
Rice can also be cooked by absorption in the oven. Use the same measurements as in the first method, and put the rice in a casserole dish. Pour over boiling salted water, stir thoroughly and cover the dish tightly with foil and a lid. Cook the rice in the centre of a pre-heated oven at 350°F (180°C, mark 4) for 30–45 minutes, or until all the liquid is absorbed and the grains are soft.

Cooking brown rice
Brown rice can be cooked in the same way as white rice, but needs a longer time. For boiled rice allow about 25 minutes, and with the absorption method, simmer the rice for 45 minutes. Brown rice cooked in the oven needs about 1 hour.

Cooking wild rice

This can be cooked in salted boiling water for about 25–30 minutes, then drained and dried in the same way as boiled rice.

Rice mould

Cold cooked rice can be made into an attractive hot or cold main course. Heat a garlic-flavoured sauce vinaigrette and toss the rice in this – cooked peas may also be added. Pack the dressed rice and peas loosely into a ring mould and smooth the top.

If the rice is to be served warm, set the ring mould in a roasting tin of boiling water. Cover the mould with foil and simmer on top of the stove for 10–15 minutes. Place a serving dish on top of the mould and turn it upside-down. The centre of the mould can be filled with chopped chicken, flaked fish, prawns or shrimps in a creamed sauce.

If the rice is to be served cold, put the mould in the refrigerator for about 1 hour or until firm. Turn out on to a serving dish and fill the centre with seafood bound with a sharp mayonnaise.

RICE MOULD

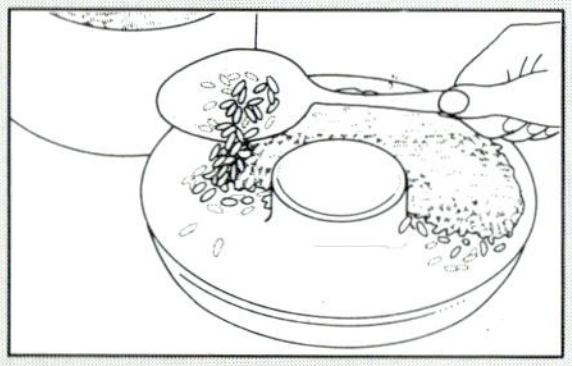

Filling the greased ring mould

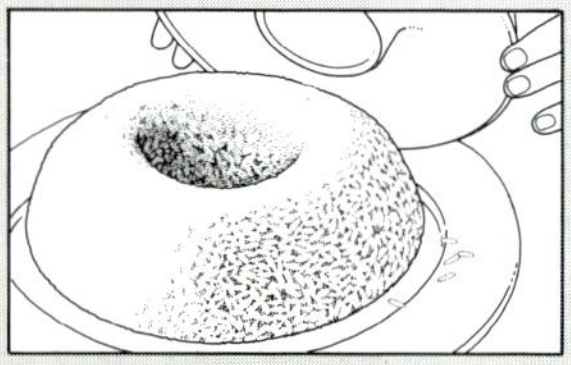

Turning out the set rice

Rice salads

Cold left-over rice makes a good basis for a variety of salads. Toss the rice in a well-flavoured sauce vinaigrette or a thinned-down mayonnaise (page 85), and serve with cold meat, fish or poultry.

For a more substantial course, mix the dressed rice with chopped ham or chicken, flaked fish and chopped pimentos, cooked peas or beans and sweet corn kernels.

COOKING AND SERVING PULSES

Soak dried peas and beans (except for lentils, which need only two hours' soaking) overnight before cooking; alternatively, bring them slowly to the boil, simmer for two minutes, then leave for an hour before cooking.

To cook, put the pulses into a saucepan and cover with fresh cold water. Add salt to taste, bring to the boil and cook gently until soft.

Average cooking times are: butter beans, chick peas, 60 min; haricot and soya beans, 45 min; split peas 30 min; lentils and dried peas 25 min. Stored beans may need more time.

Pulses, particularly butter beans and dried peas, are served as an accompanying vegetable. Haricot, chili and black-eyed beans, as well as dried whole or split peas, can be added to soups and stews.

Kidney beans are traditionally used in chili con carne, mixed with minced beef, onion and chili powder.

Lentils are cooked in soups and also in vegetable rissoles or in croquettes.

FRESH HERBS AND THEIR USE

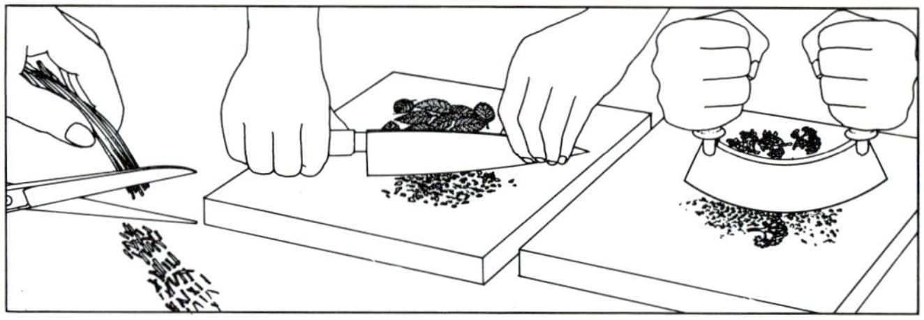

Fresh – or dried – herbs are much used in cooking to impart additional flavour to a dish. The choice of herb is entirely personal, but certain herbs go particularly well with certain foods.

Basil Use with oily fish, roast lamb, chicken, duck and goose. Also with tomato dishes.

Bay Use in bouquet garni; with oily fish, pork, veal, goose and in pâtés and terrines.

Chervil As garnish to soups, with delicate fish and shellfish. Also in salads and herb butters.

Dill Use to flavour sauces, salad dressings and mayonnaise. As garnish to fish soups, and to flavour lamb and mutton stews.

Fennel Use with roast lamb and mutton, oily fish and to flavour sauces. Fennel seeds are ideal with roast pork and chicken.

Garlic The traditional French flavouring, particularly with tomato and shellfish dishes. Much used in stews, dressings and herb butters.

Marjoram Ideal with strongly flavoured oily fish, also with roast lamb, pork and veal, chicken, duck and partridge. A favourite herb with tomato dishes. Marjoram may be used as substitute for the Italian herb oregano, although marjoram has a much less powerful flavour.

Mint Fresh mint sauce is traditional with roast lamb and mutton. Use to flavour peas, new potatoes and carrots. Fresh leaves are used as a garnish with fresh fruit salads and iced tea.

Parsley The traditional garnish with fish and many soups. Used to flavour sauces and vegetable dishes. A necessary ingredient of bouquet garni and maître-d'hôtel butter.

Rosemary A favourite herb with oily grilled fish, and much used to flavour roast lamb, pork, duck and goose. May also be added to casseroled potatoes. Rosemary leaves are long and spiky, so they should be chopped with a sharp knife before being used.

Sage Mainly used in stuffings for pork, chicken and duck. Also used to flavour oily fish, especially eel.

Savory Summer savory has a more delicate mint flavour than winter savory. Both are used to flavour salads and soups, grilled fish and egg dishes. Especially good with runner beans.

Tarragon Use to flavour white wine vinegar for pickling and in salad dressings and mayonnaise. Excellent with oily fish, in omelettes and for herb butters.

Thyme The traditional ingredient of a bouquet garni. Use to flavour oily fish, and roast pork, veal and poultry.

Fats and Oils

Fats and oils play an important part in cooking, as they contribute to or sometimes alter the flavour of food, especially when frying. The term "fat" can be taken generally to include all fatty substances, but it can also mean those which are solid at room temperature, those which are liquid being called "oils". Conveniently, this division more or less coincides with the division into saturated and unsaturated fats.

FATS

These are mainly derived from animal foods, such as meat and dairy products, but can also be produced from oily fish, nuts and vegetables.

Butter
Butter is made from the fatty substances skimmed from full cream milk. It is churned and then pressed to squeeze out water, and sometimes salt is added. It is used as the cooking medium for egg dishes and for sautéing and shallow frying over moderate heat. It is not suitable for frying at high temperatures as it burns easily, but a mixture of oil and butter will withstand quite a high heat without turning black.

Clarified butter, or ghee
This can be heated to a much higher temperature than ordinary butter without burning, and is therefore more suitable for frying and also for brushing food, for example fish, that is to be grilled. It is an expensive cooking medium, as 1 lb (450 g) of butter produces only about 10 oz (275 g) of clarified butter. To make it, melt the butter in a small pan over gentle heat and cook without stirring until the butter begins to foam. Continue to cook without letting it brown until the foaming stops. Remove the pan from the heat and let it stand until the milky deposits have sunk to the bottom, leaving a clear yellow liquid. Pour this carefully through muslin into a bowl. Clarified butter can be used in liquid or solid form and will keep well in the refrigerator.

Maître d'hôtel butter
A popular garnish for grilled meat or fish. Blend a tablespoon of finely chopped parsley with 4 oz (100 g) of softened butter and season to taste with salt, freshly ground pepper and a few drops of lemon juice. Other herbs, such as tarragon, chervil or chives, can also be used.

Dripping
This is the rendered fat from beef, mutton or poultry. A roast joint or bird will usually yield quite a lot, or it can be bought already rendered down. As it has a fairly high water content, it tends to splatter and is better used for roasting and shallow-frying than for deep-frying.

Lard
This is processed from pure pork fat and is excellent for frying. It is also used in baking some pastries and cakes.

Margarine
Made from vegetable oils blended with milk and vitamins, and sometimes with butter, margarine is interchangeable with butter for baking purposes and for sautéing. Most margarines are highly processed and therefore not acceptable to wholefood devotees. The fat content is the same as that of butter. From the point of view of low cholesterol content, soft margarines made from polyunsaturated vegetable oils are the best. Harder margarines are likely to have been processed in a way which in effect turns unsaturated fats into saturated ones.

Suet
Suet is the fat deposit from the loins and round the kidneys of beef or sheep. It is sold fresh for grating or already shredded and packed; it can be used in pastries, puddings and stuffings.

OILS

Edible oils are derived from fish, vegetables, cereals, fruit, nuts and seeds. They vary in colour and flavour, and choice is a matter of individual taste. Cold-pressed oil is the most natural (and most expensive) form, smelling and tasting strongly of its origin. Refined oil (often misleadingly called "pure") has had most of the vitamins and virtue bleached out or otherwise chemically removed, although some vitamins may be added back.

Corn oil
Fairly inexpensive and a good all-purpose oil with a mild taste.

Olive oil
Valued for its distinctive fruity taste and its affinity with certain foods. Suitable for frying and also for salad dressings: for these the best, but alas expensive, is the first pressing, also known as virgin oil.

Peanut oil
Also known as groundnut or arachide oil, this is a pleasant-tasting oil which will withstand quite high heat without burning.

Safflower oil
Expensive, but often recommended for a cholesterol-lowering diet as it is extremely high in polyunsaturated fats and in particular linoleic acid, the one essential fatty acid which cannot be manufactured by the body.

Sesame oil
Made from sesame seeds, this has a distinctive taste. It is much used in the Middle East for baking and also makes a good salad dressing.

Soya oil
A neutral-tasting oil, this is high in polyunsaturates and not too expensive.

Sunflower oil
An excellent all-round oil: can be used for frying and for salad dressings, high in polyunsaturates but cheaper than safflower oil.

Walnut oil
Very expensive; its strong nutty taste is much appreciated in salad dressings.

Home Freezing

The freezer is a time and money saver for anyone who cooks for a family. It enables a cook to plan well ahead, both in bulk-buying and in cooking. And, if the rules for the preparation, packaging and thawing of the raw materials are carefully followed, frozen food loses nothing in freshness and quality.

FREEZING PRE-COOKED FOOD

For successful freezing follow these pointers.

1. Working surroundings must be scrupulously clean, as freezing does not destroy germs in food.
2. Use top-quality ingredients and season lightly; more seasoning can always be added later.
3. Always slightly undercook dishes which are to be frozen, allowing for the time the food will be in the oven to heat up.
4. When recipes call for the addition of cream or egg yolks, omit these before freezing and add them when the dishes are being re-heated. Do not freeze dishes with custard or mayonnaise.
5. Omit garlic before freezing (it can be added later) unless the food is going to remain in the freezer for only a short time.
6. Cool all dishes thoroughly before packing and freezing.
7. Garnish re-heated food before serving, not before freezing.
8. Pack and label all pre-cooked foods carefully and note the number of portions.

FREEZING FRESH FOOD

Vegetables

Freeze only young, unblemished, freshly picked vegetables.

Most vegetables must be blanched before being frozen. Put the prepared vegetables, 1 lb (450 g) at a time, in 6 pints ($3\frac{1}{2}$ litres) of boiling water. The water should be brought back to the boil within 1 minute of adding the vegetables. Blanching time varies for different vegetables (see chart). Immediately after blanching, the vegetables should be plunged into iced water to cool and to prevent further cooking. Drain the cooled vegetables thoroughly and pack in rigid containers or polythene bags.

Vegetables will store for 1 year unless otherwise stated.

Herbs

Soft-leaved herbs, such as basil, chives, fennel, mint and parsley, freeze well. Wash the herbs, shake off the excess water and dry them. Put the herbs into sealed plastic bags, label and freeze.

A convenient way to freeze parsley for flavouring sauces and stews is to finely chop the fresh parsley and pack it into a refrigerator ice-cube tray. Fill the tray with water and freeze. Remove the cubes from the tray, put them into a sealed polythene bag and store in the freezer, where they will keep for up to six months. To use the cubes, remove from the bag and drop into the sauce or stew to dissolve two or three minutes before it is cooked.

FREEZING VEGETABLES

Vegetables	Preparation and Packaging
Artichoke, globe	Remove coarse outer leaves and stalks; trim tops and stems, removing 'chokes'. Wash in cold water, blanch in acidulated water for 7 min. Cc and drain. Pack in rigid containers
Asparagus	Remove woody parts, cut into even lengths, and wash well. Grade intc thick and thin stems. Blanch thin stems for 2 min, thick ones for 4 min Cool and drain. Pack tips to stalks in rigid containers or wrap small bundles in waxed paper or foil
Beans (French, runner, broad)	Wash well. Trim French, slice runner and shell broad beans. Blanch f 3 min, cool and pack in polythene bags
Broccoli	Trim off woody parts and outer leaves. Wash in salted water; divide into small sprigs and grade in sizes. Blanch for 3–5 min, cool and drai Pack in rigid containers, stalks to tips
Brussels sprouts	Choose small, compact sprouts. Remove outer leaves and wash thoroughly. Grade into sizes. Blanch for 3 min, cool and drain. Pack ir polythene bags
Cabbages (green and red)	Choose young crisp cabbages. Wash thoroughly, shred finely, blanch for 2 min, cool and drain. Pack in polythene bags
Carrots	Choose young carrots. Remove tops, wash and scrape, leave whole. Blanch for 5 min, cool and drain; pack in polythene bags
Cauliflower (storage time: 6 months)	Choose firm, compact, white cauliflower. Wash and break into florets. Blanch for 3 min in acidulated water, cool and drain. Pack in polythen bags
Celery	Use crisp, young stalks; remove stem bases and leaves. Cut into 1 in ($2\frac{1}{2}$ cm) lengths. Blanch for 3 min, cool and drain. Pack in polythene bags. Alternatively, pack in rigid containers and cover with some of th blanching liquid; leave $\frac{1}{2}$ in headspace
Corn on the cob	Freeze fresh, young corn only. Remove husks and threads. Blanch for 4 min, cool and dry. Pack individually in waxed paper or foil
Courgettes	Select young courgettes. Wash, trim off ends and cut into $\frac{1}{2}$ in (1 cm) slices. Blanch for 1 min, cool and drain. Alternatively, sauté in a little butter, cool quickly. Pack in rigid containers, leaving $\frac{1}{2}$ in (1 cm) headspace
Mushrooms (storage time: 3 months)	Wipe clean, but do not peel. Mushrooms more than 1 in ($2\frac{1}{2}$ cm) wide should be sliced. Sauté in butter, cool quickly and pack in rigid containers, leaving $\frac{1}{2}$ in (1 cm) headspace
Parsnips	Trim, peel and cut into quarters, or slice and dice. Blanch for 2 min, cool and drain. Pack in polythene bags or rigid containers
Peas	Shell young peas. Blanch for 1 min, shaking basket to distribute heat evenly. Cool, drain and pack in polythene bags
Potatoes	Freeze only small new potatoes whole. Blanch for 4 min, cool, drain an pack in polythene bags
Spinach	Select young leaves, trim off stalks. Wash thoroughly, drain. Blanch ir small quantities for 2 min. Cool and press out excess moisture. Pack in rigid containers, leaving $\frac{1}{2}$ in (1 cm) headspace
Tomatoes	Best frozen as purée or juice. *Purée:* skin, core and simmer in their own juice for 5 min, or until soft. Pass through a nylon sieve or liquidiser; cool and pack in rigid containers in quantities suitable for use. *Juice:* wash, quarter and core tomatoes. Simmer for 5–10 min. Press through a nylon sieve and add 1 level teaspoon salt to every 2 pints (1 litre) of juice. Cool and pack in rigid containers

oking
ok frozen in boiling salted water for 10 min until leaves are tender and easily removed
ok frozen in boiling salted water for 5–8 min
ok frozen in boiling salted water: whole ans and broad beans 7–8 min; sliced beans 5 min
ok frozen in boiling water for 5–8 min
ok frozen in boiling salted water for 8 min
ok frozen in boiling salted water for 8 min
ok frozen in boiling salted water for 8 min
ok frozen in boiling salted water for 8– min
aw at room temperature for 1 hour and add casseroles and stews. Cook in blanching uid for 10 min, to serve as accompanying getable
ok frozen corn in boiling salted water for 4– ain
ok frozen in butter
ok frozen mushrooms in butter, or add to ws and casseroles
ok frozen in boiling salted water for 5– min
ok frozen in boiling salted water for 7 min
ok frozen in boiling salted water for 15 min
ok frozen spinach in melted butter for 7 min
e frozen purée in sauces, soups and stews
aw juice in container in the refrigerator and ve chilled

Garnishes

A well-chosen garnish adds texture, colour and flavour to a dish. It should be fresh and simple rather than cluttered, and if the dish is hidden by a sauce, the garnish should give a clue to what is in the sauce. For instance, a dish served *à la véronique* – that is, with a sauce containing white grapes – is always garnished with small bunches of grapes. See also soup garnishes on page 83.

Breadcrumbs

Fried crumbs are a traditional garnish for *au gratin* dishes. Melt 1 oz (25 g) butter or margarine in a frying pan, stir in 4 oz (100 g) fresh breadcrumbs and fry over moderate heat until the crumbs are evenly browned and golden. Turn frequently.

Carrot curls

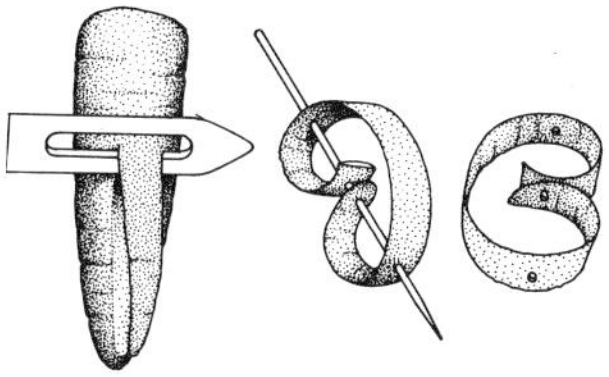

Clean the carrots and pare down the length of each carrot to remove a wafer-thin slice. Twist the slices, fasten with wooden cocktail sticks and put in iced water to curl.

Celery tassels

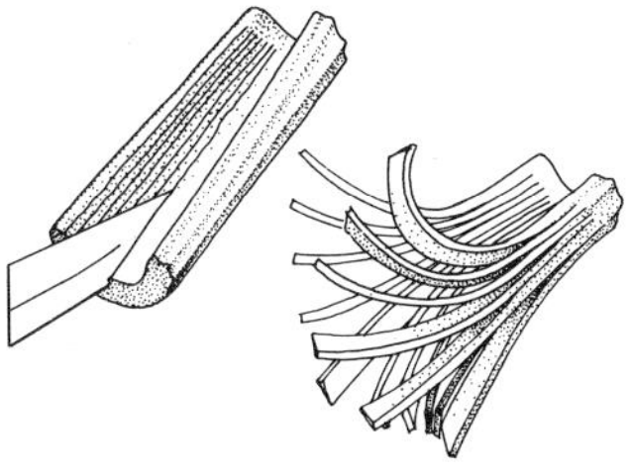

Scrub the celery stalks, cut them in 2 in (5 cm) lengths, then cut down the lengths at narrow intervals almost to the base. Leave the stalks in a bowl of water until they have curled.

Cucumber

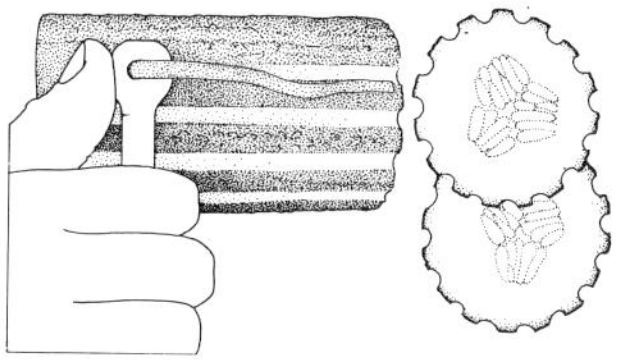

Sliced cucumber is a traditional garnish. Deckled or ridged cucumber makes a more unusual decoration: wipe but do not peel a piece of cucumber; score it along the length with a fork or canelling knife, so that it has a serrated edge (resembling a cogwheel) when cut into slices.

Radish roses

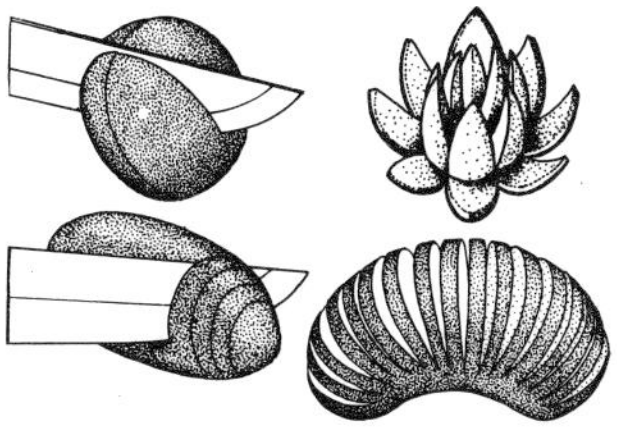

Use to garnish cold entrées, hors-d'oeuvre and salads. Make 6–8 cuts lengthways through a radish from the base towards the stalk; put the radishes in a bowl of ice water until they open like flowers. Long radishes look attractive when cut at intervals along the length to open out concertina-fashion.

Tomatoes

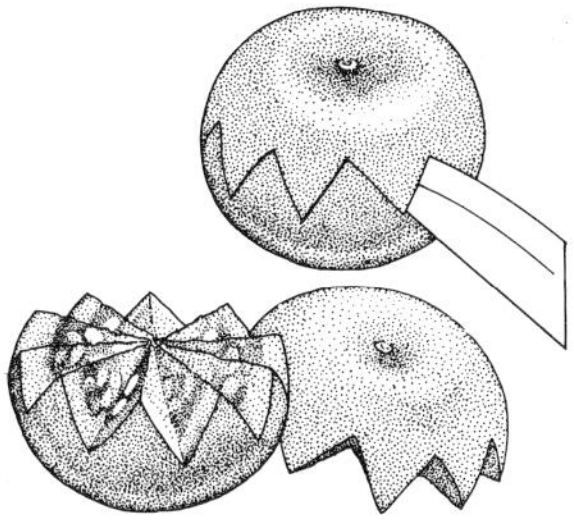

Serrated or vandyked tomatoes can be stuffed or used as tomato halves as a garnish for salads and flans. Choose firm tomatoes of even size. Using a small sharp knife, make a series of small but deep V-shaped incisions round the circumference of the tomato. Carefully pull the two tomato halves apart. Oranges, grapefruit and melons may also be separated in this way.

Twists and butterflies

Tomatoes, cucumbers, beetroot, lemons and oranges make attractive garnishes to any number of dishes, both savoury and sweet. Slice the vegetable or fruit thinly, though not wafer-thin. For twists, cut each slice through to the centre, then twist the two halves in opposite directions and place in position. For butterflies, cut two deep V-shaped incisions to meet near the centre of each round lemon slice. Remove the two wedges to leave an attractive butterfly shape.

Garnishes and Decoration

Angelica
Buy angelica in strips of a good green colour without too much sugar. Excess sugar can be removed by placing angelica for a short time in hot water; drain and dry well. Use chopped, cut into strips, diamond or leaf shapes.

Chantilly cream
Used as a piped or spooned decoration for sweets. Whisk ½ pint (300 ml) of chilled double or whipping cream in a deep cold basin, using a hand whisk. When the cream becomes opaque, add 3–4 level teaspoons caster sugar and a few drops of vanilla essence and continue to whisk slowly until the cream just holds its shape. Whipped cream thickens by the pressure needed to force it through a nozzle, so it should be light and fluffy to begin with. Pipe the cream through a fabric forcing bag and use a vegetable nozzle.

Chocolate
This takes on many forms as a decorative finish to cold desserts, classic gâteaux and simple cakes. Kept in a cool airtight tin, chocolate shapes will store for about 1 week.

Squares: break cooking chocolate into a small bowl, place over a pan of hot water and allow the chocolate to melt slowly. Line a baking tray with non-stick or waxed paper. Pour the melted chocolate in a thin stream over the paper, and with a small palette knife spread the chocolate to a thin smooth layer. Leave to cool until firm, then cut the chocolate into squares with a warm sharp knife. Peel the paper carefully away from the squares.

Leaves: melt the chocolate as for squares and meanwhile clean and dry small rose leaves. Hold the leaves with fine tweezers and dip the underside of the leaf in the melted chocolate. Leave to dry chocolate side up. When the chocolate has set, carefully ease the leaves away.

Glacé cherries
These should be washed, in warm water, to remove the sticky syrup, and dried before being used whole, halved or chopped.

Grapes and red currants
These are used frosted, either singly or in small clusters, to garnish sweet mousses, fruit soufflés and ice creams. Brush single or small clusters of black or white grapes or strips of red currants with lightly beaten egg white; dredge heavily with granulated or caster sugar. Leave on a wire rack to dry.

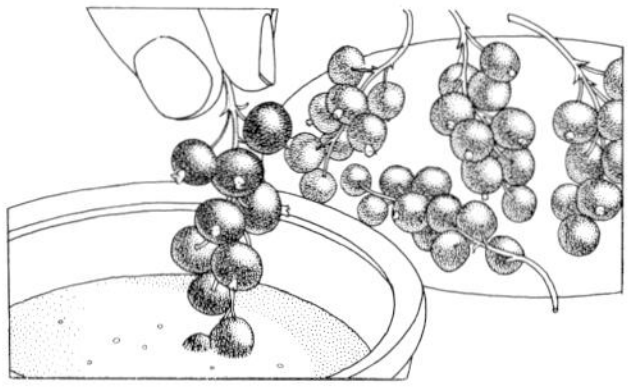

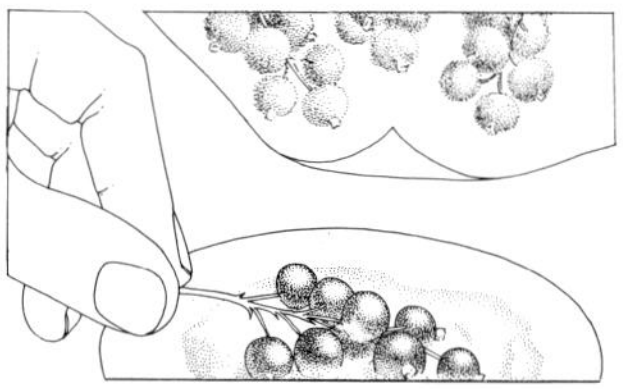

Lemon and orange spirals and twists
Used to decorate long drinks and the plain surface of desserts, such as cheese cake. Using a potato peeler, pare off lemon or orange peel, free of white pith, in a continuous spiral. For twists, cut each slice through to the centre, then twist the two halves in opposite directions.

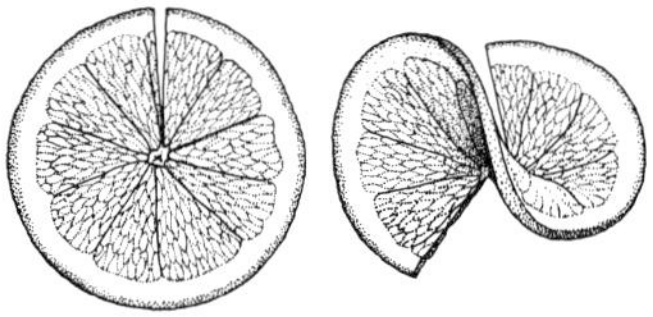

Mint leaves
Select firm small sprigs or individual leaves, brush them lightly with egg white and dredge thoroughly with caster sugar.

Nuts
Almonds are bought whole, halved or finely chopped (nibbed almonds), or flaked. Plain or roasted, all make quick finishes for trifles, gâteaux and sweet soufflés. Whole almonds, bought with or without their skins, can be used whole, split in two along their natural seam, cut into slivers or chopped. For slivered almonds blanch whole unskinned almonds in boiling water for 2–3 minutes; rub off the skins and, while still soft, cut the almonds into strips.

Pistachio nuts should always be blanched to remove the skin. Put the nuts in boiling water and soak for about 5 minutes – a pinch of bicarbonate of soda brightens the green of the nuts. Pour off the water and add some cold. Ease off the skins by pinching each nut between thumb and forefinger, and dry the nuts before using.

Hazel nuts need to be toasted before the skins can be removed. Place the shelled nuts in a single layer on a shallow pan and toast under a medium grill until the skins are dry and the nuts begin to colour. Cool slightly, then rub the nuts against each other in a bag to loosen the skins.

BLANCHING ALMONDS

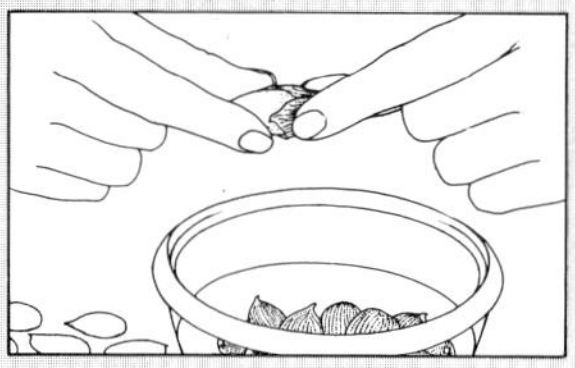

Slide off softened skins

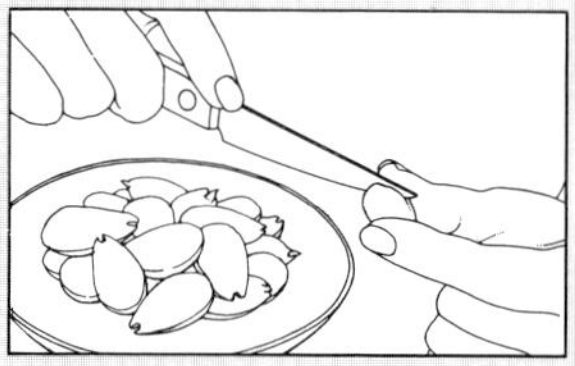

Split almonds in half

Spun sugar
Used as a decoration for Austrian *torten*. Bring 1 lb (450 g) sugar and ½ pint (300 ml) water to the boil. Boil until the syrup reaches 312°F (155°C). Remove from the heat and stir in a pinch of cream of tartar. As the syrup cools it forms fine threads when dropped from a wooden spoon. Holding an oiled spoon horizontally, pass the syrup over the handle, twirling the fine threads.

A to Z of Cookery Terms

A

acidulated water Cold water with a little lemon juice or vinegar added: this prevents discoloration of some fruits and vegetables

al dente Of pasta; cooked – but firm to the bite

allumettes Vegetable strips of matchstick length

antipasti Cold or hot Italian hors-d'oeuvre

arrowroot Starch made by grinding the root of an American plant of the same name. Used for thickening sauces

au gratin Cooked food, covered with a sauce, sprinkled with crumbs or grated cheese, dotted with butter and browned under the grill

B

bain marie 1. A large pan of hot water, or 'bath', in which a smaller pan is placed for cooking contents or to keep foods warm. 2. A double saucepan

beating Mixing food to introduce air, to make it lighter and fluffier, using a wooden spoon, hand whisk or electric mixer

binding Adding eggs, cream or fat to a dry mixture to hold it together

blanching Boiling briefly 1. To loosen the skin from nuts, fruit and vegetables. 2. To set the colour of food and to kill enzymes prior to freezing. 3. To remove strong or bitter flavours

blending Combining ingredients with a spoon, beater or liquidiser to achieve a uniform mixture

boiling Cooking in liquid at a temperature of 212°F (100°C)

bouquet garni A bunch of herbs, including parsley, thyme, marjoram, bay, etc., tied with string; or a ready-made mixture of herbs in a muslin bag

braising Browning in hot fat and then cooking slowly, in a covered pot, with a little liquid

brine Salt and water solution used for pickling and preserving

C

cannelloni Large macaroni tubes, which are stuffed with savoury fillings

capers Pickled flower buds of the Mediterranean caper bush

casserole 1. Cooking pot, complete with lid, made of ovenproof or flameproof earthenware, glass or metal. 2. Also, a slow-cooked stew of meat, fish or vegetables

champignon Mushroom; champignon de Paris, cultivated button mushroom

chilling Cooling food, without freezing it, in the refrigerator

clarified butter Butter cleared of water and impurities by slow melting and filtering

cocotte Small ovenproof, earthenware, porcelain or metal dish, used for baking individual egg dishes, mousses or soufflés

colander Perforated metal or plastic basket used for draining away liquids

concassé Roughly chopped. Applied to vegetables, such as tomatoes

corn starch Finely ground flour from maize, which is used for thickening sauces, puddings, etc.

crème fraîche Cream that has been allowed to mature but not to go sour

creole Of Caribbean cookery; prepared with pimentoes, tomatoes, okra, rice and spicy sauces

curdle 1. To cause fresh milk or a sauce to separate into solids and liquids by overheating or by adding acid. 2. To cause creamed butter and sugar in a cake recipe to separate by adding the eggs too rapidly

D

dice Cut into small cubes

dough Mixture of flour, water, milk and/or egg, sometimes enriched with fat, which is firm enough to knead, roll and shape

F

fines herbes Mixture of finely chopped fresh parsley, chervil, tarragon and chives

folding in Enveloping one ingredient or mixture in another, using a large metal spoon or spatula

freezing Solidifying or preserving food by chilling and storing it at 32°F (0°C)

G

garnishing Enhancing a dish with edible decorations

gelatine Transparent protein, made from animal bones and tissue, which melts in hot liquid and forms a jelly when cold. Used for sweet and savoury dishes

ghee Clarified butter made from the milk of the water buffalo

gill Liquid measure equal to $\frac{1}{4}$ pint or 5 fluid oz (150 ml)

gnocchi Small dumplings made from semolina or potatoes

grecque, à la 1. In the Greek style, e.g. cooked in stock with olive oil. 2. Garnished with savoury rice and dressed with oil and vinegar

H

haricot Dried seeds of the haricot bean plant

haricot vert Green bean

herbs Plants without a woody stem, used for their aromatic properties

hors-d'oeuvre Hot or cold appetisers served at the start of a meal

I

infusing Steeping herbs, tea leaves or coffee in water or other liquid to extract the flavour

J

jardinière, à la Garnish of fresh, sliced and cooked vegetables, arranged in separate groups

L

lasagne Wide ribbon noodles, sometimes coloured green

legumes Plants with seed pods, such as peas and beans

lentils Seeds of a legume, soaked and used in soups, stews and purées

M

macaroni Tubular-shaped pasta of varying lengths and shapes

macédoine Mixture of prepared fruit or vegetables

N

niçoise In the Nice style, e.g. cooked with tomatoes, onion, garlic and black olives

noodles Flat ribbon pasta made from flour, water and egg

nouilles Noodles

P

paella Dish of saffron rice, chicken and shellfish, which is named after the large shallow pan in which it is traditionally cooked

paprika Ground, sweet red pepper

par-boiling Boiling for a short time to cook food partially

pasta Paste made with flour and water, sometimes enriched with egg and oil

pastry Dough made with flour, butter and water and baked or deep-fried until crisp

pearl barley De-husked barley grains, used in soup

pease pudding Purée of cooked, dried peas which is made into puddings, boiled and served with pork

pectin Substance extracted from fruit and vegetables. Used to set jellies and jams

petits pois Tiny young green peas

pilaf, pilau Near-eastern dish of cooked rice mixed with spiced, cooked meat, chicken or fish

pimento Green or red sweet pepper

pizza Open-faced pie consisting of a yeast dough topped with tomatoes, cheese, anchovies and olives

poaching Cooking food in simmering liquid, just below boiling point

polenta Corn meal, or flour made from maize, dried and ground

pot barley Whole barley grains, containing the bran and germ

potage Thick soup

preserving Keeping food in good condition by treating with chemicals, heat, refrigeration, pickling in salt or boiling in sugar

A to Z of Cookery Terms

printanier Garnished with spring vegetables
purée 1. Sieved raw or cooked food. 2. Thick vegetable soup which is passed through a sieve or an electric liquidiser

Q

quiche Open-faced pastry case filled with a savoury mixture

R

ramekins Individual oven dishes
ratatouille Stew of aubergines, onions, peppers and tomatoes cooked in olive oil
ravioli Small savoury-filled pasta envelopes
reducing Concentrating a liquid by boiling and evaporation
rigatoni Ribbed macaroni
risotto Savoury rice, fried and then cooked in stock or tomato juice and finished with cheese

S

sauté To fry food rapidly in shallow, hot fat, tossing and turning it until evenly browned
scallion Young onion with an undeveloped bulb
seasoned flour Flour flavoured with salt and pepper
seasoning Salt, pepper, spices or herbs which are added to food to improve flavour
sifting Passing flour or sugar through a sieve to remove lumps
simmering Cooking in liquid which is heated to just below boiling point
skimming Removing cream from the surface of milk, or fat or scum from broth or jam
soufflé Baked dish consisting of a sauce or purée, which is thickened with egg yolks into which stiffly beaten egg whites are folded
soufflé dish Straight-sided circular dish used for cooking and serving soufflés
spaghetti Solid strands of pasta
starch Carbohydrate obtained from cereal and potatoes
steaming Cooking food in the steam rising from boiling water
stewing To simmer food slowly in a covered pan or casserole

T

tagliatelle Thin flat egg noodles; fettuccine are similar
terrine 1. Earthenware pot used for cooking and serving pâté. 2. Food cooked in a terrine
timbale 1. Cup-shaped earthenware or metal mould. 2. Dish prepared in such a mould
truffles Rare mushroom-like fungus, black or white in colour, with a firm texture and delicate taste. Expensive delicacies, truffles are mainly used for garnishing. White truffles, sliced paper-thin, go particularly well with pasta and plain risottos

V

velouté 1. Basic white sauce made with chicken, veal or fish stock. 2. Soup of creamy consistency
vermicelli Very fine strands of pasta
vinaigrette Mixture of oil, vinegar, salt and pepper, which is sometimes flavoured with herbs

W

whey Liquid which separates from the curd when milk curdles. Used in cheese-making
whipping Beating eggs until frothy and cream until thick
whisk Looped wire utensil used to beat air into eggs, cream or batters

Y

yeast Fungus cells used to produce alcoholic fermentation, or to cause dough to rise
yogurt Curdled milk which has been treated with harmless bacteria. In the Middle East it is served as a sauce with meat, fish and vegetables; in Europe mainly with or in desserts

Z

zest Coloured oily outer skin of citrus fruit which, when grated or peeled, is used to flavour foods and liquids
zester Small tool for scraping off zest

Index

The Good Health Cookbooks

The Publishers wish to express their gratitude for major contributions by the following people:

Editor: URSULA WHYTE
Art Director: MICHAEL McGUINNESS
Designer: SANDRA DEON-CARDYN
Diet Consultant: MIRIAM POLUNIN
Home Economist: VALERIE BARRETT
Additional Photography: PHILIP DOWELL

The Publishers also wish to acknowledge the help of the following:

Gilly Abrahams for editorial help; Fred and Kathie Gill for proof reading; Mary-Anne Joy for help with calorie counting; Terri Lamb for design assistance; Vicki Robinson for indexing; and Michelle Thompson for food preparation. Additional photographic props were supplied by Graham and Green.

The Good Health Cookbooks are based on THE COOKERY YEAR, **to which the following made major contributions:**

Editorial Adviser: ELIZABETH POMEROY
Photographer: PHILIP DOWELL
Home Economist: JOY MACHELL

Writers:

Ena Bruinsma
Margaret Coombes
Derek Cooper
Margaret Costa
Denis Curtis
Theodora FitzGibbon
Nina Froud
Jane Grigson
Nesta Hollis
Kenneth H. C. Lo
Elizabeth Pomeroy
Zena Skinner
Katie Stewart
Marika Hanbury Tenison
Silvino S. Trompetto, MBE, Maître Chef des Cuisines, Savoy Hotel
Suzanne Wakelin
Kathie Webber
Harold Wilshaw

Artists:

Colour:
Roy Coombs
Pauline Ellison
Hargrave Hands
Denys Ovenden
Charles Pickard
Josephine Ranken
Charles Raymond
Rodney Shackell
Faith Shannon, MBE
John Wilson

Black and white:
David Baird
Brian Delf
Gary Hincks
Richard Jacobs
Rodney Shackell
Michael Woods
Sidney Woods

Black and white photography:
Michael Newton

Typesetting: Tradespools Ltd, Frome **Printing:** W. S. Cowell Ltd, Ipswich **Binding:** Dorstel Press Ltd, Harlow

RGHCV–16-004